Praise for *A Mini*

"This superb collection of essays by Phil Berrigan, by turns provocative, challenging, and inspiring, marks the return of one of the greatest voices for peace, nonviolence, and reconciliation of our time." — **James Martin, SJ**, author of *Jesus: A Pilgrimage*

"*A Ministry of Risk* offers a truly profound challenge to transcend fear and take action. 'War fever betrays a monstrous contempt of humanity,' Philip Berrigan wrote. This book can help people to break the fever." — **Norman Solomon**, author of *War Made Invisible*

"*A Ministry of Risk* provides a window into the radical and deeply inspiring journey of Phil Berrigan — a journey, in Phil's own words, of 'good against evil, truth against falsehood, nonviolence against violence, conscience against State, life against death . . . the same witness is necessary today.' May it be so! This book should be required reading for all of us who are trying to be Christian." — **Marie Dennis**, Director, Pax Christi's Catholic Nonviolence Initiative, and author of *Choosing Peace: The Catholic Church Returns to Gospel Nonviolence*

"This book is a must read! Carefully compiled by Brad Wolf, it illuminates the extraordinary life of Phil Berrigan, a Prophet of Nonviolence who endured many sacrifices and long imprisonment for resisting the forces of death and empire. Wanting to be remembered as one who welcomed the cross of Jesus, Berrigan's Gospel witness is exemplary: his steadfast commitment to follow God's command to love, to resist all earthly powers that sanction oppression, injustice, and killing no matter the cost, and to be filled with the hope that Jesus has forever overcome the powers of this world. With the Doomsday Clock at 90 seconds to midnight, we need to live and proclaim, as Berrigan did, God's reign of justice, peace, and nonviolence and create the Beloved Community." — **Art Laffin**, author of *The Risk of the Cross: Living Gospel Nonviolence in the Nuclear Age* and editor of *Swords into Plowshares*

"If you've ever wondered what the Apostle Paul's life and witness to the risen Christ might look like if the New Testament were to be written in the U.S. empire during the nuclear age, this book goes a long way toward completing that picture. Assembled from Philip Berrigan's own writings, interviews, and speeches, which span nearly sixty years, Brad Wolf's chronicle captures brilliantly, and as it evolved, the voice of the most single-hearted person we knew. The unity of word and deed; the refusal to allow one's conscience to be purchased with creature comforts and social privilege; an unrelenting commitment to personal and communal disarmament, formed around the practice of smashing the murderous idols of war and white supremacy — these were the only weapons Phil wielded. This was the only armor Phil wore as he strolled repeatedly in and out of our nation's carceral and military hellholes, telling the truth with his own body, always bathed in the same indestructible, ridiculously joyful hope. Having once shared a cell block with him for the better part of a year, I find it impossible today to overestimate the liberative value of the mentoring that these words offer, during such a delusional time as the twenty-first century." — **Mark Colville**, Amistad Catholic Worker and Plowshares activist

"I knew Phil from the civil rights days in Baltimore, before we poured blood on draft files in 1967. Phil reminds me of the poetic line from Spender: 'I think continually of those who are truly great.' Or Rilke at the end of 'Archaic Torso of Apollo' when he wrote: 'You must change your life.' This line especially applied to Phil and to me and to so many of his followers." — **David Eberhardt**, member of The Baltimore Four

"Reading Brad Wolf's *A Ministry of Risk* is a journey into the life and times of Philip Berrigan, a complex, courageous, and brilliant Catholic priest, and a man who devoted his life to nonviolent resistance to war, for which the United States government sent him to prison time and again. Phil was a prophet, trying to warn the world to beat its weapons into plowshares. In this new book, we get to know Phil as a priest, husband, father, and radical who inspired millions of people to question the madness of preparing to destroy the world in the name of peace." — **Fred A. Wilcox**, author of *Fighting the Lamb's War: Skirmishes with the American Empire*

"Are you willing—truly willing—to take up the cross? To be not just a follower of Christ but to bear witness? Philip Berrigan was. Read his words. Reflect deeply on them. And act." — **Retired Lt Col (USAF) William Astore**, author, antiwar activist, and retired professor of history

"Brad Wolf skillfully presents Phil Berrigan's prophetic messages about militarism and racism. Young generations facing ecological collapse, 'forever wars,' and nuclear proliferation have much to learn from Berrigan's courageous resistance to military might." — **Kathy Kelly**, author, pacifist, and peace activist

"What comes through in these writings are the journeys that Phil traveled. From a loyal, passionate soldier in the middle of war, to a passionate nonviolent resister of war. From a dedicated priest of the Catholic Church to a married father of three children. From a law-abiding citizen to a peace felon who served many years in prison. And then, also, the journey from a young man to a wise elder. All are a journey of faith, of becoming human. And as we read this collection of Phil's writings, we will find ourselves on a journey with Phil. We will see ourselves growing with him in humanity and love and resistance. Brad Wolf has done an amazing job of compiling the writings that we need to read to follow Phil's journeys and make them our own." — **Susan Crane**, member of the Jonah House Community in Baltimore with Phil Berrigan and a Plowshares participant

A MINISTRY OF RISK

A Ministry of Risk

WRITINGS ON PEACE AND NONVIOLENCE

Philip Berrigan

EDITED AND WITH AN INTRODUCTION
BY BRAD WOLF

FOREWORD BY BILL WYLIE-KELLERMANN
PREFACE BY FRIDA BERRIGAN
AFTERWORD BY JOHN DEAR

FORDHAM UNIVERSITY PRESS   NEW YORK 2024

Visit us online at www.fordhampress.com.

Library of Congress Cataloging-in-Publication Data available online at https://catalog.loc.gov.

Printed in the United States of America

26 25 24   5 4 3 2 1

First edition

For Lisa, Dylan, and Emma

A ministry of risk goes unerringly to the side of the victims, to those threatened or destroyed by greed, prejudice, and war. From the side of those victims, it teaches two simple, indispensable lessons: (1) that we all belong in the ditch, or in the breach, with the victims; and (2) that until we go to the ditch or into the breach, victimizing will not cease.

— PHILIP BERRIGAN

Contents

Sources with Abbreviations

CU   Cornell University Library, Division of Rare and Manuscript Collections, Archives, The Daniel and Philip Berrigan Collection.
DD   *Disciples and Dissidents*. Athol, Mass.: Haley's Publishing, 2001.
DP   DePaul University, Special Collections and Archives.
FTLW   *Fighting the Lamb's War*. iUniverse, 2011; Wipf and Stock Publishers, 1996.
NMS   *No More Strangers*. New York: Macmillan, 1965.
OBBI   *Of Beasts and Beastly Images*. Portland, Ore.: Sunburst Press, 1978.
PJPR   *Prison Journals of a Priest Revolutionary*. New York: Ballantine Books, 1971.
TTD   *The Time's Discipline*. Baltimore: Fortkamp Publishing, 1989.
WTPG   *Widen the Prison Gates*. New York: Simon & Schuster, 1973.

Supplemental Texts

At Play in The Lion's Den. Orbis, 2017.
Daniel Berrigan: Essential Writings. Orbis, 2009, 2016.
Disarmed and Dangerous: The Radical Lives and Times of Daniel and Philip Berrigan. HarperCollins, 1997.
Swords into Plowshares. Wipf and Stock, 2003.
The Berrigan Letters. Orbis, 2016.
The Catonsville Nine. Oxford University Press, 2012.
The Harrisburg 7 and the New Catholic Left. University of Notre Dame Press, 1972, 2012.
The Trial of the Catonsville Nine. Fordham University Press, 2004.
Uncommon Martyrs. iUniverse Press, 1991, 2011.

So if you find the following negative, caustic, angry—remember that they come from one who has questioned domestic racism and modern war for ten years; who has resisted militarism and war-making repeatedly; who has experienced not only prison but solitary confinement and long fasts; who has endured the charade of three political trials and who faces a fourth; and who probably will be in and out of prison for the remainder of his life. In sum, my experience has been out of the ordinary, and it comes purely from attempts to answer the question "What does Christ ask of me?"

— PHILIP BERRIGAN, SPRINGFIELD FEDERAL PRISON, MISSOURI, 1971

Children, let us love not just in word or speech but in deed and truth.

— JOHN 3:18

Once the unrest of Christ has been let into a person's heart, they become incomprehensible and a cause of scandal.

— ROMANO GUARDINI

Foreword: Witness and Wisdom

Bill Wylie-Kellermann

In researching and selecting the writings of Philip Berrigan for A *Ministry of Risk*, Brad Wolf has undertaken a great gift of service to movements for justice and peace. Veterans and elders of social struggle may find they have been yearning unbeknownst for such a volume, but it also seems written as a prayer for the young people of those stunning new movements arising among us. It is witness and wisdom from kindred history to a fiercely urgent new moment. Thanks be.

I was myself a young person when I first met Philip (with hundreds of others) in December 1972. I had followed his brother Daniel, my seminary "professor," up to Danbury, Connecticut, for Phil's release from federal prison. There followed nearby a eucharistic celebration with movement hymnology by Pete Seeger and blessings by Rabbi Abraham Heschel. The next summer I sat with Phil on the steps of the U.S. Capitol, while fasting and vigiling with a mock "tiger cage" prison cell like those used to torture Vietnamese political prisoners. We discussed what resistance community might look like back in my home state of Michigan.

Another year hence I would be handcuffed to Phil through the handles of a Pentagon door, locking out with our bodies its deadly business. And I remember exactly where I was in September 1980 when I heard news of his part, with seven others, in the first Plowshares action at General Electric in King of Prussia, Pennsylvania: I was watching it on TV in the Richmond City Jail, on a thirty-day bit for another Pentagon action organized simultaneously by Jonah House.

Wolf has chosen these excerpts impeccably well, beginning with the auto-biographical Prologue about Phil's time with the Army infantry at the German front in World War II. He was, by his own account, all in, convinced that the more death he faced, the better off the world would be. "I was Philip the Bold, son of Thomas the Brave, toughest Irish kid on the block." It is the perfect point of departure for tracing his conversion to gospel nonviolence. Moreover, it's striking that in his conversion he retains so much of himself in character. Disabused of bravado and naiveté, he remains nonetheless, perhaps even more so, bold. There is no lack of audacious nerve in the pages of Berrigan's life and witness. Now, however, his boldness is transfigured in the service of gospel and peace.

Because these pieces are structured chronologically—by the date of the writing or sequence of events—they allow broad recognition of the development in Berrigan's thinking and theology, not to mention his way of life. Woven through like a thread are excerpts of his autobiography, *Fighting the Lamb's War*, filling in details from a later, more mature perch.

In this regard, special attention is due the opening section, largely concerned with his spiritual-political formation in the Freedom Struggle. Phil had been disgusted by the racism he witnessed during Army basic training in the South. His call to priesthood was inexorably woven with that experience as he chose the Order of St. Joseph precisely for its commitment to the African American community. Almost immediately, however, he became critical of the structural segregation so readily accepted by the Order. He saw it up close in his assignment to a New Orleans church. In consequence, Philip became repeatedly and perpetually troublesome to his superiors, moved constantly by the Order from one parish to another.

Wolf includes an autobiographical excerpt on the "Freedom Rides" of 1961, organized by the Congress of Racial Equality (CORE), with interracial groups traveling into the South by bus, publicly testing segregation laws enroute. The first two interstate actions were met by mobs, burning one of the buses and beating the passengers bloody. When the call came for clergy to join the actions, Phil responded immediately and (as was to become a pattern) talked his brother into it as well, though Daniel's superiors denied permission.

Phil went ahead, preparing not only for civil disobedience (in effect, to be the first Catholic priest in U.S. history to be so arrested) but also readying himself for injury and even death. As he recounts, however, his plan was scuttled when news reached the bishop in Mississippi, who threatened Phil's Order if he were not called back. He was. For both brothers, this experience of church authority would rankle their consciences going forward.

The brothers did go on to walk together in the March on Washington in 1963, and wrote thereafter a joint editorial in the Syracuse newspaper. They walked again side by side across the Edmund Pettis Bridge after Bloody Sunday in 1964 and proposed writing a book together. Once again: permission denied. So they wrote separately. Phil's first book, *No More Strangers*, was endorsed on the cover by Stokely Carmichael, who said Phil was "the only white man who knows where it's at."

Between D.C. and Selma, Phil participated in the retreat Thomas Merton convened at Gethsemani Abbey on "the spiritual roots of protest." For all who attended it was formative, and indeed from it flowed not only the emergence of the Catholic left but, one could say specifically, the draft board actions in Baltimore and Catonsville. Yet Phil seems not to have written about the retreat, even in his autobiography. Hence, in these entries, Merton peeks out here and there, but there is no naming for him of that pivotal moment. The closest Phil comes is in his testimony during the Catonsville trial. In answer to a question about how they conceived the action, he replies that they tried to come from "the Christian roots of protest." Perhaps enough said.

Among the gifts of this anthology is that it helps to disentangle Philip's theological and literary legacy from Daniel's—to bring him out from under the poet's shadow. One example illustrates the problem. When it came time to write the action statement for their burning of draft files at Catonsville, Maryland, in 1968, it seemed proper for Dan to stand back as he had only belatedly joined the community at Phil's cajoling. Realizing they were all Catholics, the eight others set about writing a critique of Church complicity in the Vietnam War coupled with an analysis of the policies and weaponry involved, their cost in human suffering. Phil's voice was primary and strong in the lead. Meanwhile, Daniel undertook his own mediations, crafting a piece that has become a touchstone of movement literature—whose lines are recited by heart among activists. "Our apologies, good friends, for the fracture of good order, the burning of paper instead of children, the angering of the orderlies in the front parlor of the charnel house. We could not, so help us God, do otherwise." To this point neither previous scholarship, nor Wolf's own diligent search of the archives, has turned up the alternative original text.

That the chosen draft board in Catonsville was hosted in a Knights of Columbus Hall was specifically pointed at the Catholic Church. Later, when the Berrigan brothers' iconic images in Roman collars appeared on the cover of *Time* magazine in 1971, it further implicated and challenged their church. Grounding himself, Phil wrote, "I will take my stand with the Christ of the Gospels and of history . . . I must believe that the encyclicals and the pronouncements of the Council are enough to build a society of justice and peace." He commends Catholic Church social teaching to students in a baccalaureate address and argues again for these teachings at length in an open letter to the Catholic Bishops Synod in Rome.

Some in the Church pointedly blamed Vatican II for the Catonsville Nine action. They were not really mistaken. Protestant theologian and friend of the Berrigan family William Stringfellow identified this connection:

> [T]he Berrigan brothers and others of the defendants had been involved over a long time, particularly since the extraordinary papacy of John XXIII, in the renewal of the sacramental witness in the liturgical life of Christians. They had become alert to the social and political implications of the Mass. . . . [It was] a liturgy transposed from altar or kitchen table to a sidewalk outside a Selective Service Board office, a fusion of the sacramental and the ethical standing within the characteristic biblical witness.

It is worth tracing the sacramental elements at work in this book. As Phil writes, "If the priest is to be the man of reconciliation at the altar and in the pulpit, his action there demands a consistency of life in what he does and what he says. Otherwise, the Eucharist becomes less than a new relationship to all people, and the word of God less than light to all."

One sacramental act bears particular mention—the marriage of Liz and Phil, for which they truly suffered, though hardly in equal measure to their joy. For good reason, the story is told and retold in these pages. They married on April 7, 1969, in a private ceremony with only themselves present, in Saint George's Episcopal Church in the Bronx. It's noteworthy that for Roman Catholics marriage is the only sacrament undertaken by lay people (except for baptism in extreme conditions). Each, as a minister of Christ's grace, confers the sacrament on the other. A priest, ordinarily present, is there only to witness on behalf of the church.

This is to say that Phil and Liz married not in the authority of their orders, priestly or religious, but in the authority of their baptisms. They had certainly foreseen that it would mean the sacrifice of their orders to this new vocation, and perhaps even excommunication, which it did indeed. But even more, they would endure (with dignity) the malicious humiliation and ridicule recounted in these pages. Still, they regarded their marriage as the religious and political act it was and offered it as a present contribution to peace.

After the Harrisburg acquittal, there was a large public celebration of their marriage at St. John the Divine Cathedral in New York City. Dan preached, noting, "In the last bloody decade, every time we have had a wedding it is because we have been facing a new crisis. And the converse is true: Every time we were facing a new crisis, in God's Providence, we had a wedding."

I commend the marriage story told herein, because this sacramental and vocational act issued in life beyond measure. For four decades, that marriage (and family) was the anchor of the Jonah House Community. Many others came, would stay a year or two, contribute much, build deep, but then move on to other places and roots. Some have called Jonah House "a school" for this very reason, mentoring resisters and scattering them like seeds. A banner hung in the stairwell proclaiming, "The greatest apostolic duty is to keep one another's courage up." This was marriage as apostolic vocation.

Jonah House practiced a rigorous discipline in 1972. The community would be gathered on the weekend for study (Bible and current analysis), prayer, and contemplation, then Monday morning a number would disperse up and down the East Coast. John Bach, a draft resister imprisoned with Phil, and a community co-founder, would hitch-hike the New Jersey Turnpike to New York City, there to meet with a little group of us at Union Seminary, then with others in the East Village and in Jersey City. End of the week, home for refueling in the common life. The same books and texts were being studied up and down the coast.

Among the books we sat with were William Stringfellow's *An Ethic for Christians and Other Aliens in a Strange Land* and Jim Douglass's *Contemplation and Resistance*. Eventually, nonviolent actions would break out simultaneously. An East Coast conspiracy to save lives.

There is also a sacramental issue hidden in the title of this anthology: *A Ministry of Risk*. It stems from an ordination homily Phil preached. Sacred vows embracing sacred risk. He connected it to his own vocation, remembering the homilist at his "First Mass" in 1955. The preacher, an ex–Air Force chaplain, told him bluntly from the pulpit:

> "If you're not prepared to suffer, you will become a poorly disguised hypocrite. If you don't like egg on your face—and worse—you have no business with Christ." I took him with some seriousness—he was myopic politically, but a Christian of generosity and integrity. And he was right.

Which is to say, finally, these pages reflect Phil as Theologian of the Cross. Not Cross as cheap atonement or cheaper grace, but in the sense of discipleship, akin to Dietrich Bonhoeffer's costly grace: "When Christ calls someone, they are bid to come and die." The ethics of the Cross are entwined throughout this collection. Recall Phil's implicit readiness in the Freedom Rides. Or: "It strikes me once again . . . that obeying God's word is very likely to get one killed." He reflects on the self-immolations of the Vietnamese and of Norman Morrison at the Pentagon and implies he had considered it himself, choosing instead the alternative of long imprisonment.

A dozen times the ministry of risk is coded biblically by "Calvary" as in "following the Man of Calvary was more than we bargained for . . . vain and pompous unless it invited ridicule, risk, prison, death itself." All versions and shadows of the same thing.

Still and yet. William Stringfellow was once asked what he meant by "resurrection," and he replied reflexively, "Phil Berrigan in jail." Cryptic at the time, he later reflected:

> I have visited a good many prisoners . . . [including] many whom I esteem as witnesses to the resurrection. . . . I remember particularly many visits that I've had the occasion to make to Danbury Prison where some of the war resisters were confined there, and it was remarkable. . . . They were certainly inconvenienced and otherwise burdened by being confined but were not, however, conformed as human beings by the mere fact of their imprisonment. They were still free men. . . . The captives were more free, as human beings, than their captors.

So be it. In these pages you will indeed find articulated a nonviolent ethic of the Cross but even more so uncover the freedom, the ethics, the witness of resurrection. Amen (and alleluia!).

Preface

Frida Berrigan

At home, in the basement at 1933 Park Avenue, my father wrote at a big desk. The desk was made of an old door, balanced on two filing cabinets. The shelves were fashioned of cinderblocks and planks and crowded with theology books, Bibles, and biographies. Little treasures like a turtle shell full of coins and little boxes full of foreign stamps peeked out of the cinder block holes. There was a postal scale, pictures of his parents and brothers, holy cards, an ashtray, Wite-Out bottles and a collection of pens in a mug with a broken handle.

The paperwork for the Jonah House house-painting business was here—estimates and receipts and contacts. And stacks of manuscripts written by friends looking for Dad's seal of approval or keen editor's eye. A calendar, an address book, and stacks and stacks of letters, waiting to be answered.

Just over his left elbow sat a bookcase full of his brother's books. The complete works of Daniel Berrigan were always within arm's reach. It was not a vanity case; there was no dust on these books. Their spines were creased, their pages thumbed with use.

The desk was not comfortable or fancy. It was a place to work—utilitarian and simple. When he wrote there, my father sat on a piano bench, with just a thin pillow cushioning him from the hard, flat surface. Here, like everywhere, he disciplined himself. Willing his long torso straight, he sat without any chair back or support, adding a core workout to the mental work and love of correspondence.

Mostly, my father wrote letters longhand, on legal pads or scraps of paper. Letter after letter after letter: focused and methodical, warm and folksy, full of news or full of advice or full of questions. He preferred No. 10 envelopes and always delighted in re-using stamps that had somehow missed the postman's cancel mark.

So much of what is in this book was written at that desk, after a day standing on a forty-foot ladder, or sitting in meetings planning actions, or holding a placard at the Pentagon or at the White House. He also wrote a lot in prisons, and that would have been even more uncomfortable. There he would have sat on the edge of his bunk, hunched over, writing on a pad propped on his knees, struggling to concentrate amid the noise and the bad light. In later years, as rules in jails and prisons got tighter, he would have had to make do with a Golf pencil for a writing implement.

Back at home, if it was necessary, he'd pull forward a dark blue electric typewriter and peck out his letters with clumsy precision. His big working-man hands dwarfed the keys. It was never a good idea to interrupt him when he was typing; his concentration was fierce as he fumbled with technology.

The desk was at the bottom of the basement stairs, where our family lived in two rooms. The floors were covered in carpet samples and all the furniture was found or made. For years, my brother, sister, and I shared one room, and Mom and Dad shared the other, their few clothes and possessions arranged amid the ladders and tools for the house-painting business.

When he had finished with his letters for the night—a stack of five or six if he was "going easy" or ten or twelve if he had "cut the mustard"—he'd move over to a rocking chair next to the bed. There he'd read, first, a serious book: Ched Myers, Jose Miranda, Sister Rosalie Bertel, Leonardo Boff. And then, after an hour or so, he'd move on to a mystery novel—Dick Francis, John MacDonald, or P. D. James.

There are pictures of him as a stern and handsome priest. But that is not the man I knew. My dad was not a vain or flashy man. He wore a belt and suspenders. He cut his own hair. Long years of teaching had left him with varicose veins, and he wore black support hose. In the summertime, he wore knee-high tube socks over the support hose and then long shorts, so that a few inches of his legs actually saw the sun. He stayed tidy, trim, and presentable, but he looked every inch the working man. That is who he was. For a very long time, he wore an old green army coat and an Irish cap or stocking cap, depending on how cold it was. When we worked outside for the Jonah House paint crew, he wore a ball cap to protect his large forehead and nose from the sun.

The long distance between the handsome young priest and the grizzled older laborer came into high relief at my sister Kate's graduation from high school. Dad was in prison at the time, so my brother and I stood with our mom as we waited for the outdoor ceremony to start. A school administrator, the assistant principal, as I recall, came up to my mom. She was a well-dressed, youthfully middle-aged African American woman, and she wanted to shake my mother's hand. We thought she was congratulating Liz because Kate was an amazing student and a lovely human being or because Liz is a woman of substance and courage and moral leadership in Greater Baltimore.

But, we were wrong.

The woman wanted to shake Mom's hand because she had taken catechism from Phil Berrigan when she was a girl. She told mom that he was so good-looking that she and the other girls called him "Father What-a-Waste" behind his back. "Congratulations, Mrs. Berrigan," she said, mis-naming my mother, who kept McAlister at a time when doing that was very rare, "we all wanted to marry your man. The girls from Saint Peter Claver are all so jealous of you!" My mother, who had no idea how to respond to this cheeky introduction, laughed with discomfort and shuffled toward the ceremony with the rest of the crowd.

Phil Berrigan was not nostalgic. He never bemoaned his age or shed that "Father What-a-Waste" mystique. He was practical, spare, and intense. He had a whole series of daily habits that seemed comical and old-fashioned to me as a high school student. He did calisthenics, breathing exercises, and headstands. He knelt in prayer and read the Bible aloud in a low voice. He did eye exercises and neck rolls and sliced raw garlic on top of his cereal the way another person might sprinkle raisins or dates or bits of banana.

Now that I am almost fifty, I see the wisdom in these daily habits meant to keep the body, mind, and spirit supple, strong, and ready. But there are some things about my father that I will never understand. He seemed to have no real taste buds. He mixed different kinds of cans of soup together when he made lunch at home. He'd grab a can of minestrone, a can of cream of mushroom, and a can of chicken noodle more or less at random and mix them all together in the soup pot. He'd cut up all kinds of fruit—and I mean all kinds of fruit—for Sunday morning pancakes. Grapes, grapefruit, oranges, peaches, apples, they'd all go in together with raisins and peanuts and whatever else we had on hand. When he made our school lunches, he'd spread margarine and peanut butter on one piece of bread and mustard and cheese on the other piece and smoosh them together. The only way to eat one of his sandwiches was to peel it apart and eat it as though it were two separate sandwiches. Our sister avoided this unpleasantness by getting up ten minutes earlier and making her own lunch, but I endured these periodic brown bag surprises well into high school.

Was it the Great Depression and his early experiences of deprivation? His experience in World War II and then many years later in prison, where you ate what you could get quickly and without complaint? Was it a long-embedded

reaction against the clerical comfort he'd rejected as a young priest who said
No to being assigned a Black housekeeper or cook? Was it moral asceticism?
Was it a physical ailment as a result of his long years as a pack-a-day smoker?
Did that kill his taste buds so he really didn't taste the difference between clam
chowder and split pea soup? I won't ever know for sure, but I think it was a
combination of all of this and an athlete's understanding that food is fuel for
the work to come.

After my dad died, my mother quipped that he had experienced all seven
sacraments. I had no idea what the seven sacraments were. We were raised in
a pre-Constantine "small-c" church of bread and wine perched on (another)
piano bench, consecrated by lay people and passed around the circle of Catholics, atheists, Jews, and refugees from all sorts of faiths, seeking something
homemade and human.

The sitting and standing and kneeling, the rote recitation and forced so-
lemnity of Roman Catholicism came to me second-hand and in bits and
pieces as an adult. So I had to ask: What are the seven sacraments, and why
would it be rare to experience all seven? Baptism, first communion, confirmation, confession, Holy Orders, marriage, and last rites. Most cradle Catholics
get six topics, because you either become a priest or a husband, not both. But
Dad had all seven, and when she dies, I guess my mom will be in that small
club as well.

My dad was often surprised by what I did not know about Catholicism, the
Bible, and the history of the Church. He sought to teach my brother and sister
and me all he thought we needed to know. Over a number of years of weekly
Bible study in our parents' basement bedroom/house-painting business stor-
age area, he basically led us through the same kind of Bible study that was
happening in Christian base communities in Central America. Put yourself in
the Bible story and ask: Who is in power, who is in pain, who is Jesus helping
to heal? Only with the benefit of hindsight can I see that Phil Berrigan had a
pastoral relationship with me and my brother and sister. He learned how to be
a father by being a Father, and we were a much smaller but more infuriating
flock for him to educate than the girls at Saint Peter Claver. He was attentive,
loving. and stern in equal measure.

This fatherly care mostly happened while we were doing something else. I
was often called to be his extra set of hands on a whole series of terrible Saturday morning chores that included picking up trash around the neighborhood,
changing the oil in our car, and plucking flowers from our neighbors' yards for
the bouquet of flowers for the altar at Sunday liturgy.

"Go on in and grab us a few posies," he'd suggest in a soft voice, as we ca-
sually loitered outside a local church's front garden. He'd hand me his pocket

knife to cut the roses and a handkerchief to protect my hands, and then he'd start whistling to make this minor burglary seem fun and relaxed. We'd repeat this at a few other stops around the neighborhood and amble home with a beautiful bouquet, much to the local homeowners' and beautifiers' dismay.

Once or twice a year, we'd soak rags in tar and then shove them into rusted-out holes in the wheel wells and undercarriage of the car. We'd sand down the rusted edges and then cover the whole mess with fiberglass. A day or two later, he'd call me back and we'd sand down the glassy patches and paint them over with a color that was in the same quarter of the color wheel as the main body of the car. I can still smell the tar and the fiberglass, still feel the warmth of the car and the curb we knelt on to get the right angle. I still marvel at the hardness of the fiberglass, feeling the glassy fibers under my fingernails.

Patch, repair, care. He did that to our bruises and scratches and ripped pants legs, too. Patch, repair, care. Is that what he did to our faith, our community, our national heart too, as he called us to peacemaking, nonviolence, beating swords into plowshares? Patch, repair, care. I think so.

In one letter to me, long ago, from that door-sized desk, my dad wrote to me, responding to my sadness about being away from a boyfriend while at college.

"Do you know that Liz and I have been married twenty-five years this year? And of those twenty-five years, we've been separated from one another for nearly eleven years? The separation is always agonizing—you never get used to it. But you handle it—the very integrity of your life is at stake. You know the alternatives are deadly—the numbing mediocrity of most Americans, living as parasites off people in the Third and Fourth worlds.

"What do I hope for you and Jerry and Katy? Not that you follow in the footsteps of Liz and mine . . . but that you understand the need for justice as the basis for peace. And without justice, there's no peace. So the world, and this country, needs peace like nothing else. And the central characteristic of the Gospel is peacemaking. The two above come together for Liz and me—two imperatives that are one. So, if the three of you choose this 'way,' it shouldn't be on our authority, but on the authority of the Gospel and the authority of human need."

That, along with a little news from home and a gentle admonishment that my handwriting was terrible, was a typical letter from my dad.

"Anyway, my dear, I've preached long enough. . . . Much love to you, many hugs, a hundred and one kisses. Peace of Christ—Phil."

Introduction
Brad Wolf

In December 1970, while serving a six-year federal prison sentence for non-violent resistance to the Vietnam War, Father Philip Berrigan reflected on his expectations when first joining the seminary and the subsequent path he and his brother Daniel had taken together as Roman Catholic priests. Informed by hard-won wisdom and a far deeper understanding of his faith, he was unrepentant, clear-eyed, certain of purpose. With characteristic understatement, Phil wrote in his journal, "No need to retread the ground walked on since. We have learned that following the Man of Calvary was more than we bargained for."

Phil's connection with the Man of Calvary was intensely personal, vivid, prophetic. "The sinless one continues to haunt me," he wrote. Once the "unrest of Christ" had entered Phil's heart, he did indeed become a scandal, as Romano Guardini warned. Incomprehensible to some. The word *scandal* is from the Greek *skandalon* and refers to a stumbling block, something that gets in the way. Phil was certainly that. And more.

Soldier, priest, servant, and scholar. Activist and author. Felon, fugitive, prison witness, and revolutionary. He would add to that list husband and father, family man, communal man. Phil could not be contained, categorized, or silenced. He was a strategist, a tactician, and to a large degree a hopeful realist. "True hope," he wrote, "is both a grasp of reality and a nonviolent plan to communicate it." He was strong-willed and assertive, yet he also bore a dry humor, such as when after refusing to appear for prison and becoming a fugitive from justice he said simply, "We have trouble with surrender."

Phil was a man on the move. Physically, intellectually, spiritually. He journeyed from resistance to revolution to liberation as he grasped the intrinsic violence and deceit of his country, its militarism, materialism, and racism.

He saw the dreadful toll it took on the poor and defenseless of the world. Phil knew that the political and economic system supporting "the American way of life" had to not only be resisted but also eradicated. Reform could not cure the sickness. The entire structure had to be replaced. Only a shared, communal understanding of this fact, believed and lived each day, would lead to liberation.

On January 25, 1971, Phil and Dan landed on the cover of *Time* magazine under the heading "Rebel Priests: The Curious Case of the Berrigans." Both were still serving federal prison sentences for destroying government draft files, failing to appear for incarceration, and eluding arrest. New federal charges had just been filed alleging they had conspired to blow up government buildings and kidnap President Richard Nixon's national security advisor, Henry Kissinger. Though these new charges were spurious, the full force of the government was being brought down on the Berrigans. To many Americans at that time, the case of the Berrigans was more than curious. It highlighted something far deeper. The country was splitting at its political, social, and spiritual seams.

Phil had once written that "Becoming a man is becoming what Christ was." Imprisoned, denounced by his Church, hounded by the authorities, and jeered at by the public, Phil was learning just how difficult such a process could be. Later he wrote, "Following Christ becomes the fundamental problem. He leads, and we so often renege. We are slow to follow Jesus in living the Gospel and building community, slow to follow, resisting as He resisted illegitimate power, slow to follow into jail as He was jailed. Slow and then a halt." Imprisoned though he was, Phil was not about to "renege." The military and the seminary were good preparation for prison, providing a taste of the rigors, rules, and sacrifices he had to endure. Phil was right where his faith intended him to be.

Philip Francis Berrigan was born on October 5, 1923, in Two Harbors, Minnesota, the youngest of six boys, to a poor Irish Catholic family eking out an existence on the frozen frontier of Lake Superior and later on a hardscrabble farm in Syracuse, New York. His father, Thomas, was a tough and tumultuous socialist who became an avid reader of Dorothy Day's *The Catholic Worker*, imparting his strong political views to his boys. Phil's mother, Freda, provided the loving warmth in the family, as well as bringing home an endless supply of library books that Phil and his brother Daniel quickly devoured. Despite the family's poverty, they regularly shared meals with the poor who came knocking on their kitchen door, Freda dividing the meager portions again and again so all would have something to eat.

As a boy, Phil was athletic, bright, and fierce. He grew to be Hollywood-handsome, sometimes bearing a smile, sometimes a snarl, often a mischievous and knowing Irish grin. Charismatic, brave, and scholarly, Phil was as well read as he was impatient. He embodied the idea that the cup of salvation is caffeinated. That impatience would be on full display years later when Phil repeatedly argued that one must act quickly if the government is threatening to incinerate the world or committing brutalities upon the poor. But confronting the U.S. government came at a cost, and Phil would be in and out of prison for much of his adult life, paroled for the last time in 2002, just months before he died from cancer at the age of seventy-nine.

When Phil returned home from the Army after three years of combat service in Europe during World War II, he was adrift, trying to make sense of his life, thinking about what he had seen and done as a soldier. His brother Dan had joined the Jesuits, a rigorous Catholic order, and Phil was impressed with the man Dan had become. During his military training in the Deep South, Phil saw the brutality and ugliness of America's racism, and so after a period of discernment, Phil joined the Josephites, a Catholic order dedicated to serving African Americans. The religion and politics he had learned from his family and from the pages of *The Catholic Worker* were bearing fruit.

In 1955, Phil received his first assignment as a priest, working with the impoverished African American community of Washington, D.C. The conditions there appalled him. He spoke out, criticizing the white community, specifically the white Catholic community, for allowing such injustices to occur. This gained him both recognition and condemnation. To silence him, he was transferred to an African American Josephite high school in New Orleans, where he taught English and religion. Spirited and hardworking, willing to help at any time day or night, he was respected and well liked by his colleagues and students.

By 1957, Phil was challenging segregation laws in New Orleans, forming solidarity groups, and speaking out for the poor. He marched in rallies, recruited, and organized. He challenged state and federal laws he saw as immoral, inhumane, and un-Christian. Phil's convictions led him to confrontation. His diocesan superiors were not pleased.

In October 1962, the Cuban Missile Crisis struck Phil with a sobering blow. A handful of people in power were deciding the fate of the world, playing a game of "nuclear chicken" with all of humanity at risk. He felt betrayed, angry, and compelled to do something. If the current system conferred this degree of deadly power on a few men, the system must be challenged, its people shaken from slumber.

Phil's evolving beliefs got him transferred again, first to New York City where he quickly riled the Josephites there, then to Newburgh, New York, where his superiors hoped to silence him in that remote, economically depressed town. He gained friends in Newburgh among the poor and African Americans by organizing relief centers to disburse food and clothing, and by speaking out against the injustices he witnessed. He also gained enemies, especially when he began to criticize America's growing involvement in Vietnam. A Catholic priest voicing an opinion on a subject like Vietnam was too bold and controversial to permit. He was transferred to Baltimore, warned again to remain silent on matters of race, politics, and war.

By 1965 Phil had published his first book, *No More Strangers*, about race in America; penned numerous articles on segregation and war; given hundreds of speeches; and gained a reputation as a man of intellect and conviction. He also infuriated conservative Catholics, exasperated his Josephite superiors, and came under the watchful eye of federal authorities. In 1965, neither Phil nor Dan could possibly have imagined the lengths they would go to in order to stop the war in Vietnam, or the lengths to which the U.S. government would go to wage this war and silence their rebellious, prophetic voices.

Phil's frustration at the somnambulance of the American public regarding the atrocities in Vietnam was intensifying. He had already been detained by authorities while protesting at Fort Myer, Virginia, but the action didn't lead to his arrest or a much-desired public debate. Innocents were dying in Vietnam while young American men were being drafted and ordered to kill in a foreign country most couldn't find on a map. Something dramatic was needed.

During the Vietnam War, the U.S. Selective Service system was responsible for registering men for the military and administering the draft. The system epitomized to many the evils of an imperialist country that conscripted its young into wars waged to expand American control of lands and markets across the globe. The Selective Service system created paper draft files for all American males between the ages of eighteen and twenty-six. Those who did not receive exemptions were called for military service. To Phil, those draft files were villainous, morally and spiritually illicit, "human hunting licenses" for the men drafted and for the men, women, and children those draftees would kill.

On October 27, 1967, after much discussion and planning, Phil, James Mengel, David Eberhardt, and Tom Lewis entered the U.S. Customs House in Baltimore, which held draft files for the Selective Service system. The group had notified the press in advance, seeking maximum publicity to highlight their objections to the war and stir public debate. Once inside, the men moved quickly to the file cabinets behind the clerk's desk. As government employees stared in shock, the group withdrew handfuls of draft files and poured blood on them, destroying the files and symbolically reenacting the spilt blood of Americans and Vietnamese. The police arrived quickly, followed by the FBI. The four were arrested and jailed. Public scrutiny followed. They soon became known as the Baltimore Four.

Undeterred and free on bail pending his trial, Phil quickly began organizing another action, against a different Selective Service office. Time was short, both for himself because his trial was likely to result in a lengthy prison sentence, and for the people of Vietnam who continued to die in extraordinarily high numbers. He knew that his next action would need to be bigger, more controversial, able to spark more national debate and soul-searching. He also knew it would result in a heavy prison sentence, coming as it did on the heels of his Baltimore action.

Dan Berrigan, already outspoken against the war, had traveled to North Vietnam to free American POWs but had not yet participated in these types of direct actions against the government. Dan was ambivalent about Phil's plan, but after lengthy discussions Phil convinced him that given the war's immense devastation, destroying draft records was morally and spiritually a justifiable means to save lives.

This larger action would occur at Catonsville, Maryland, and the number of people involved would more than double. All were Catholic, clean-cut, respectable. Two were Roman Catholic priests in the middle years of their lives. The group was well educated and articulate. Some were missionaries and published authors. They could not be easily dismissed as "hippies." Their actions, combined with their backgrounds, were bound to strike a nerve in the American conscience. The Catonsville Nine would embrace acts of faith and resistance as old as the Bible and apply them in the age of napalm.

On May 17, 1968, after meticulous planning, Phil, Dan, David Darst, Mary Moylan, John Hogan, Marjorie Melville, Tom Melville, George Mische, and Tom Lewis drove to the Catonsville Selective Service office and assumed their posts. They diverted the office clerks and quickly removed draft records from the file cabinets, loaded them into wire baskets they had brought with them, then exited the building, where the press was waiting in the parking lot. Using homemade napalm to reinforce the message, the nine set fire to more than 400 draft records as TV cameras rolled. They calmly recited the Lord's Prayer while the files burned. Police sped to the scene. They had no intention of fleeing since apprehension and arrest were an integral part of their prophetic action.

It was difficult for many Americans then and still difficult for some today to accept destruction of government property as an appropriate act of nonviolence, even if that property is only paper. Yet over the ensuing decades Phil would repeatedly assert that some property is so malevolent it does not have the right to exist, whether it be "human hunting licenses" or nuclear weapons.

The trial of the Catonsville Nine began in October 1968 and became a focal point of the anti-war movement. Hundreds of police in riot gear surrounded the courthouse as thousands of demonstrators gathered outside demanding that the nine be freed. Each day speeches were given by the likes of Dorothy Day, Noam Chomsky, I. F. Stone, and Robert Bly, decrying the war in Vietnam and the government's repression and persecution of objectors at home. Media from across the globe converged on the Baltimore courthouse.

The trial itself lasted less than a week. All nine were found guilty. Phil received a sentence of three years, to run concurrently with his six-year Baltimore sentence. He was eventually released on bail pending appeal until his case could be heard by the appellate court. In April 1970 his appeal and those of his co-defendants were denied. The Catonsville Nine were ordered to turn themselves in and begin serving their prison sentences.

Rather than submit to prison, Phil and Dan and three others made a bold decision to continue their resistance by refusing to surrender, going underground and becoming fugitives. They did not fear prison since they knew they would eventually be captured and incur additional penalties. Instead, they believed they could support the anti-war movement more by risking even greater prison terms to demonstrate the sacrifices needed to end a war that was consuming Southeast Asia and fracturing America.

Among the many shocking events of the 1960s, two Catholic priests on the run from the FBI was certainly one of the more bizarre. How had it come to this?

In a 1958 speech given at a retreat for a Catholic youth group, Phil asked his young listeners, "What's it going to be with you? Are you going to recognize God's goodness in your behalf and submit to His desires for your salvation? Or are you going to go through life playing both ends against the middle, playing cozy, not committing yourself, sitting on the fence?" At the time, he was likely asking himself the same probing question. By 1968, his answer was clear.

Phil's time underground lasted ten days. He was apprehended by FBI agents in St. Gregory's Church in Manhattan. Dan's run from the authorities lasted longer, gathering enormous media coverage as he led police on a somewhat comical chase for four months, suddenly appearing at demonstrations and pulpits speaking against the war, then quickly being whisked away before federal agents could close in. At Cornell University, Dan spoke to a large anti-war audience with FBI agents hoping to arrest him in attendance. Knowing the agents were there, Dan issued a powerful indictment of the war, then joined others onstage wearing giant puppet costumes posing as Christ's

Disciples. He was quickly whisked away to a safe house before agents could apprehend him. The FBI director, J. Edgar Hoover, was furious at having his agency publicly humiliated. The Berrigan brothers became his personal enemies for the remainder of his life.

The draft board raids at Baltimore and Catonsville generated a new type of resistance in the anti-war movement. Once it became known that the government kept no copies of these paper draft files, others began destroying the files at Selective Service offices across the country. The raids were literally stopping young men from being conscripted to kill. Draft file actions occurred in Milwaukee, Camden, Indianapolis, Chicago, St. Paul, Boston, Philadelphia, Rochester, Los Angeles, and Pasadena. The list of draft raids grew by the month while the number of draft files destroyed escalated to the thousands. The "human hunting licenses" were being systematically revoked.

On January 12, 1971, while housed in federal prison, Phil was indicted yet again and charged with conspiracy to kidnap government officials and sabotage government buildings. The allegations were explosive, just as J. Edgar Hoover intended them to be. The FBI director had met in secret session with a handful of U.S. senators and, with little to no evidence, told them of a plot his agents had uncovered to blow up government tunnels in Washington, D.C., and kidnap President Nixon's national security advisor, Henry Kissinger. The men behind it, according to Hoover, were Philip and Daniel Berrigan. Hoover was determined to put the brothers away for life.

While in Lewisburg Federal Penitentiary in central Pennsylvania, Phil had continued to correspond with those in the anti-war movement, discussing, debating, and then often dismissing a variety of actions they could take to stop the war. He had enlisted the help of a fellow inmate to surreptitiously deliver the letters back and forth to elude review by prison authorities. The inmate, Boyd Douglas, was one of many inmates permitted to leave prison for study at nearby Bucknell University. He was also an FBI informant, planted and paid to find damning information on the Berrigans. Douglas photocopied the letters and delivered them to federal agents.

Among the ideas discussed in the letters were plans to tamper with steampipes beneath government buildings to disrupt the business inside, as well as the idea of holding a mock war crimes tribunal with a top government official as a witness. The suggested witness was Henry Kissinger, who might have needed to attend against his will. All these plans were discarded as unsuitable, but nonetheless they were in writing for J. Edgar Hoover and the U.S. Justice Department to use in creating a case against Phil and his colleagues.

Also among the letters were personal ones between Phil and Sister Elizabeth (Liz) McAlister, a member of the Catholic order called the Religious of the Sacred Heart of Mary. Phil and Liz had met a few years earlier at various social justice gatherings. Their friendship had grown into a romance, and their affectionate letters became a prize for the leering eyes of Hoover. He would not only try to jail Phil but would also attempt to publicly humiliate him.

A grand jury was convened in Harrisburg, Pennsylvania, the most conservative town the Justice Department could find in central Pennsylvania. They wanted a strongly pro-war jury. Phil and several others, including Sister Elizabeth McAlister, were indicted on a variety of charges based on the ideas discussed in the letters. If convicted of all charges, Phil could face life imprisonment. Boyd Douglas, the letters, and Phil's relationship with Liz became the central focus of the trial.

Phil wrote publicly and privately about his relationship with Liz, having to defend their love against degrading attacks from the government, the Church, and the public. The two had exchanged vows in a church in 1969, officiated only by each other. Later, they did so publicly and officially. Throughout it all, Phil would repeatedly state that he would gladly place the integrity and honor of his relationship with Liz against the honor and integrity of the Catholic Church and the American government's support of war. Nonetheless, the reading of their personal letters during the Harrisburg trial and the criticism that followed were bitter pills to swallow.

"I'm Philip Berrigan, a Roman Catholic priest, a member of the Society of Saint Joseph, seventeen years ordained, in prison twenty-nine months of a six-year sentence for draft file destruction." So began Phil's proposed opening statement at the Harrisburg trial. "I committed civil disobedience and waited for arrest twice in Baltimore and at Catonsville. I waited for arrest twice because I was ashamed of young men taking the heat for me. I waited for arrest twice because a person must live what he believes and take the consequences. In Christ our Lord, word and deed were one—one life. He never said anything that He didn't do; He never believed anything that He didn't live."

Word and deed. Making them one was the work of a Christian, a kind of work Phil constantly measured himself against, living his life as a liturgy. "Every advance in liberation presupposes submission to the spirit—to the desert as the soul's climate, to crucifixion of pride and fear, to leaps of faith into risk, into financial and physical helplessness, into imprisonment, and possibly into death," he wrote. At tremendous cost to himself and those he loved, Phil sought to follow the Man of Calvary.

The trial of the Harrisburg Seven generated headlines and drew thousands of anti-war supporters to the courthouse during the early months of 1972. The trial did not go as planned for J. Edgar Hoover. The government's case was weak, built on the hope that explosive allegations would convince a conservative jury to throw the book at the defendants regardless of the meager evidence provided.

After weeks of testimony, the jury deliberated at length, then finally informed the court they were deadlocked. No verdict could be reached. (Phil and Liz were found guilty of the minor charge of smuggling letters in prison.) A mistrial was declared, and the government later quietly withdrew the charges against the defendants. It was a stunning defeat for Hoover, one from which he never fully recovered. The FBI director passed away a short time later. Phil completed his earlier sentence and was finally paroled from prison on December 20, 1972.

After his release Phil wrote, "I regret nothing that I have done, nor do I resent anything done to me. Government is what it is (we understood it well); government people are what they are (we knew many, and the stripes are similar); both had to do what they did to me, to Dan, and to other resisters. But the fact of *that* and our recognition does not remove the conflict; nor does it pacify or domesticate us. Our dialogue will continue—from without and within jail." The anti-war movement was winding down, and the tumultuous 1960s were over. Phil and Liz would enter a new phase of resistance—living in faith, family, community, and voluntary poverty.

In 1973, Phil and Liz created Jonah House in a blighted, high-crime area of Baltimore. The house was an intentional community of political resistance and spiritual discernment. With at least a dozen others living there, Jonah House became a robust and active home offering communal care, faith, and planning in nonviolent resistance. In 1974, Phil and Liz welcomed their first child, Frida, followed by Jerry in 1975 and Kate in 1981. Births and birthdays, school and manual labor, food gathering and sharing, plans for nonviolent actions and imprisonment, anniversaries and deaths would all occur at Jonah House. The FBI was often an uninvited guest, routinely surveilling the building.

Building peace was always hard work, but in the apathetic, materialistic aftermath of the 1960s, it was especially so. Nuclear weapons—the creation of them, their possible use, their tactic as deterrence, the mere fact humankind possessed them—weighed heavily on Phil. Those weapons were "the scourge of mankind," but they also revealed a deeper evil destroying the human soul. Phil believed that we built our intentions into those weapons, our intentions not just to use them but also our disturbing intentions about fellowship, about love of each other as Christ loved us, about our passive disposition toward mass murder. Those weapons were killing us, physically and spiritually. Their mere existence was evil, sinful.

Phil eschewed partisan politics, knowing full well that both of America's major political parties were guilty on the issues of militarism, racism, and marketing consumerism as a necessity of life. He was, however, a political man. "Religion is the interior of politics, politics the exterior of religion, with an interdependence at once reinforcing. A truly political person is one who loves the victims sufficiently to resist their victimizers, to resist the powermongers of state." And so, through the Johnson, Nixon, Carter, Reagan, Bush, and Clinton years, Phil would write, speak, and act against the American government and their costly war-making policies. The audiences may be smaller, but the issues no less pressing.

During the 1970s, Phil and Liz participated in various nonviolent actions that landed them in prison. They tried to stagger their actions and prison terms so that one of them was always home with the children. In 1980, Phil carried out an action along with seven others in King of Prussia, Pennsylvania, to expose the dangers of the General Electric nuclear missile facility. They illegally entered the plant, where they poured blood on documents and hammered the nose cones of nuclear weapons, beating "swords into plowshares" as the prophet Isaiah foretold. They were charged with more than ten different felony and misdemeanor counts. The Plowshares movement was born, starting a new and ongoing series of similar actions carried out by activists across the globe, actions continuing to this very day.

Phil and Liz would separately join in new Plowshares actions, serve their sentences, return to their children, family, and friends at Jonah House where they would try to live as normal a life as possible for a community committed to living the literal Word of Christ. They continued to write, speak, hold retreats, travel, protest, and march. In total, they would spend eleven years apart because of imprisonment. Phil's last Plowshares action would occur in 1999, when he was seventy-six years old, leading to a prison sentence that would have him released in 2002. Terminally ill with cancer, he dictated his last statement against war shortly before his death at Jonah House on December 6, 2002.

Phil's life and writings are so intertwined that they speak as a public testimony of spirit and reality. Autobiographical, political, historical, and theological, his writings can be blunt as a polemic and insightful as a prophecy. When read in chronological order, Phil's writings tell the story of a man evolving, of a Catholic trying to be a Christian, while at the same time telling of a country devolving into a savage war abroad and violence and repression at home. The contrasting paths are striking. Phil's voice is that of a sentry, the sentry of Ezekiel warning people of the coming sword, calling out to save not only his own soul but that of the world around him, while his government beats the relentless drums of war and seduces its citizenry into a culture of fear and death.

Phil's witness for life over mass death summons us today as we watch dueling empires issue nuclear threats, as climate catastrophe closes in, as drone wars and proxy wars kill with unrelenting pace, as the "military-industrial-congressional-media complex" grows to gargantuan proportions. Though not all are called to spend years in prison, each is called to act, to form a ministry of risk and walk the path toward unwavering love and defense of humankind. By offering the most important things he could—a life of faith and resistance, revolutionary fellowship with victims in the breach, and a bruising yet beautiful journey toward liberation—Philip Berrigan did his best to answer the haunting question "What does Christ ask of me?"

Prologue: Worlds on Fire

Philip Berrigan

Written in 1996 for his autobiography, Fighting the Lamb's War, *this essay has Phil reflecting on his military service as a combat soldier during World War II.*

Before I left for basic training, my brother invited me to visit the Jesuit Novitiate at Poughkeepsie. Daniel wanted me to think a little harder about going to war, and he arranged for me to take a four-day retreat at Saint Andrews. The rector provided me with the exercises of Saint Ignatius, and I walked alone, praying for guidance, trying to decide what to do. Should I ask for a deferment of military service? Should I agree to enter the seminary and begin to study for the priesthood? What did God have in mind for me? I didn't really want to be a priest, and I longed to join my older brothers at the battlefront. I wanted to join the hunt for Adolf Hitler, to hack him into pieces, and to count the demons as they flew out of his wounds. I wanted to charge pillboxes, blow up machine gun nests, and fight hand to hand with my country's enemies. I was nineteen years old. Willing, and most able, to be a warrior.

I hugged Dan goodbye, thanked the Jesuit fathers for their kindness, and saw my parents one more time before boarding a train for Camp Gordon. There were no bands or cheering crowds. No rousing speeches or rhetorical binges. Our parting was quiet, loving, gracious, and altogether devoid of drama. As young men had been doing for centuries, I rode off to slay the enemy. A tough and rather cocky kid, striding toward the valley of death. Never imagining, for one moment, that I might come home like the soldier in Dalton Trumbo's novel *Johnny Got His Gun*. A limbless torso. Blind, unable to speak, yet fully alive. Capable of feeling love and loneliness and despair.

Abandoned to a miserable hospital bed, knowing that the nurses and doctors considered me little more than a cooked carrot.

War is a necessary *rite of passage* for turning boys into warriors. Someday, if we listened closely, trained hard, and got real smart, we too might become real men. Before that happened, we could play at being soldiers, killing the enemy during war games. I became an expert marksman with a .37-millimeter anti-tank gun, an obsolete weapon but the best we had for our training. We fired at our targets from a 300- or 400-yards range, and I was very good, knocking enemy tanks off like clay pigeons, parboiling Nazi soldiers inside their steel ovens. I received a promotion to corporal for being the best at headquarters battery with this weapon.

I went to infantry OCS—Officer Candidate School—at Fontainebleau. Then I was assigned to the 8th Infantry Division, a hardcore combat unit that had already fought its way across northern France and on into Germany, stopping close to the Danish border.

When I graduated from OCS, I was a skilled killer, trained in the use of all small arms, clever with a bayonet, good with a submachine gun and the Browning automatic rifle. That is exactly what I was: a highly skilled young killer.

I saw the results of blanket bombing in Munster, a German city completely leveled, utterly destroyed, by Allied planes. Our bulldozers scraped roads through the ruins, shoving rubble and rotting civilians into great, putrid-smelling heaps. Miraculously, a Catholic hospital was still standing, and one afternoon I happened to be talking to an officer who claimed that something strange was going on in the cellar of the building. He said that the place was stacked floor to ceiling with bodies and, even stranger, that German doctors were conducting experiments on these corpses.

So down we went into this frightful charnel house where forty or fifty civilians were bobbing up and down in huge vats of formaldehyde. Some were decapitated. Others appeared to be untouched. A teenage boy floated in one vat. His head was missing, but the rest of his body was perfect. Not a mark on that poor boy. The captain had been right. In the middle of all that carnage, those doctors were conducting research, trying to learn better ways to save the lives of people who were ripped to pieces in bombing raids or blown apart in artillery strikes. Preparing for the next war, even though this one was still a long way from being over.

I was blasé and cynical about the dead. The Germans had been terrorizing Europe for years, and now it was payback time. I didn't really regard the civilians in those vats as innocent bystanders. They were the enemy. Just part of the rubble of the Third Reich. I felt neither pride in what we had done nor remorse for the victims of our bombing. I did what soldiers must do in order to justify their actions. I demonized the German people.

In Catholic Church and parochial schools, I had learned that God created human beings in His own image and that all human beings carry the divine within us. In order to kill other men and women, I needed to make them less human. I needed to become anesthetized; more, I had to believe that I would never become one of those mutilated things. I'm not like them, God was on my side. Unlike them, I was blessed, surrounded with the armor of pure goodness.

My brother Tom was a first lieutenant in the 29th infantry, and he began noticing our unit's trucks, so he ordered his driver to catch up with one, found out where we were located, and drove into our camp one day. I hadn't seen him in two-and-a-half years, but I knew he had been through hell, fighting all the way from the beaches of Normandy into Belgium. We shook hands and hugged, nearly in tears, trying to catch up on all the news, knowing that this might be the last time we would see one another alive.

I went with him to the front, where American troops were dug in on a very wide arc, fully expecting to be overrun because they didn't have enough men. Two regiments were spread over a twenty-mile front; they were very sparse. It wouldn't have taken much for the Germans to break through those lines and then come for us. Our unit had been under mortar fire. We lived through bombing attacks and were pounded by the Germans' terrifying .88-millimeter anti-tank gun, an excellent, highly accurate weapon. We took some casualties, but I was still a reckless kid who thought he could stroll, unscathed, through the Valley of Death. I had come to Europe to do a job that, I thought, would involve great danger. The more death I faced, the better off the world would be. I needed to keep proving that I wasn't just an ordinary soldier. I was Philip the Bold, son of Thomas the Brave, toughest Irish American kid on the block. More ignorant, I know now, than brave.

I helped free the world from Hitler's reign of terror. I served my country in war time because I thought that's what patriots do. God may tell us not to kill, but when the state calls, we must obey. We must become skilled, remorseless killers, willing to use any means to defeat the enemy.

Years after my return from the killing fields, I looked into the mirror of my own violence. What I saw there forced me to rethink and redefine the meaning of sanity. I realized that while I considered Adolf Eichmann a war criminal and despised him for participating in the Holocaust, we actually had a few things in common. Like him, I had only been following orders. Like him, I was sane enough to do my duty, and do it well. Like him, I believed that wars are fought for noble reasons. We were both true believers—one a mass murderer, the other a killer on a smaller scale.

When I first started to think about these things, my heart turned to stone, my head swam with clouds of confusion. Examining my own responsibility for the death of 70 million people in World War II, it occurred to me that the U.S. government, and I as a soldier, had adopted some of the worst aspects of Nazism. The Luftwaffe bombed London, so we had the right to firebomb Dresden. The Germans murdered civilians *en masse*, so we were entitled to slaughter their women and children. Our actions were not crimes against humanity, they were retaliation for *their* crimes. Their actions were barbaric, our reactions were just. I vacillated between feeling betrayed, in the sense that I was betraying some sacred trust, some sacrosanct ideal.

My world began to shift, rather slowly at first, more dramatically as I read and thought and prayed, seeking answers in a nation that condemned its warriors to the silence of agreement. Seventy million dead. Hundreds of billions of dollars in damage. Physical and psychological and spiritual wounds that would never heal. And after the war, my country helping high-ranking Nazis find safe haven from justice, protecting the very people against whom I and my brothers had fought.

No, such things were not compatible with reason or sanity.

Then what, I wondered, did it all mean? Eventually, but not until the early '60s, I would conclude that war is the big lie, subordinated to, and entrenched by, lots of little lies.

For many years I clung to my own set of lies, hiding within the shell of collective agreement. In time, that shell began to crack. Light streamed in, forcing me to re-examine killing, making me take a hard, nonrhetorical look at war. I saw a boy standing on the field of battle, bristling with weapons, preparing to shed his blood, and spill the blood of his enemies, for *his* king, *his* emperor, *his* state, some grand, everlasting ideal. An ancient figure, stooped with the knowledge that the killing had gone on for centuries and could well continue until the end of time.

The boy took off his helmet, and I could see the pain in his eyes, see that he wanted to lay down his sword and shield, but that he feared the consequences. It was one thing to die on the field of battle, quite another to be banished to the realm of cowards. I reached out to him, and found myself. We walked together, this ancient young warrior and I, knowing that the road we were taking would be lonely, even more dangerous than the battlefield had been. No one would recognize us when we returned home. There would be no welcome for traitors who break their swords into pieces, leaving their armor and their weapons "down by the riverside."

FTLW

A MINISTRY OF RISK

PART I

A Catholic Trying to Be a Christian

1957–67

Peace is the issue and duty of our times, and the words but faintly convey the reality of need or task.

— PHILIP BERRIGAN

Christ in Our Midst

One of the earliest published writings of Phil, this essay already reflects his wide range of reading and theological influences.

What does the world need? The Church will tell you: Christ, and nothing more. Within her fold, how often we hear this statement or variations of it. I remember an old Monsignor in the Bayou country of Louisiana, a man ill and thin with cancer, and his calm remark, "We must do our work, Father, until God calls us." Or the work of Benedict XV during the first great war. Or Saint Pius and his desire "to restore all things in Christ." Or Charles de Foucauld [soldier, priest, author] and his vocation of service in North Africa. Or the Little Sisters of the Poor. Or Saint Paul's immortal "But I know only Christ, and him crucified."

Undoubtedly the most remarkable example of the teaching office of the Church is to make practical and palatable to human activity the Christian message. In this consists her universality, as Yves de Montcheuil [priest and author] said. It is her genius, the breath of the Holy Spirit, and by it she will always remain in, of and true to her age.

Nor need the Christian look far for what Christ was or what He taught: The evangelists did their work too well for that. Whether it be at Bethlehem, or among the noisy crowds, or wrung by the excess of Calvary, the God-Man is too clearly drawn to be obscured by two thousand years or marred by merely human appraisal.

His role was one of savior, not of judge, as He himself told Nicodemus—a role dramatized by the slavery so vividly described by Saint Paul. He was in our midst as one who serves. And only at the twilight of His life, on the night before He would so supremely serve us on the Cross, did He ask for imitation. "If you love me, keep my commandments. By this will all men know that you are my disciples, that you love one another. A new commandment I give you, that you love one another as I have loved you."

Christianity is more than a body of doctrine or moral code. It is more than a way of life. It is Christ living in us and gaining entrance to others only through our instrumentality. And once He begins to live in a person, even some of the most ignorant and obscure, His plan achieves reality in one and promise in many. "He who believes in me, the works that I do he shall also do, and greater than these shall he do . . . ."

Saint Pius, you inspired this work. Give it increase.

October 1957, *Worship* magazine

What's It Going to Be with You?

On Sunday, July 27, 1958, Phil spoke at Father Higgin's Youth Club Retreat, providing remarks and posing questions to his audience of adolescents.

Before beginning the first talk, I would like to make a few preliminary remarks. Whether you know it or not, this is one of the most important days of your life, and the effects of this day are going to live with you for the rest of your life and perhaps even save your soul.

We have been told by Christ that we know not the day nor the hour when He will call us. We live in a world on the verge of war, and in our own communities all of us are familiar with violence and sudden death. This may be the last opportunity we have to strengthen ourselves against the day of death and trial and therefore, it is most necessary that we take full advantage of it.

You'll notice that the first prayer of the retreat was said to the Holy Spirit. This has a reason. He has full charge of us, we are in His keeping, and He desires nothing more than our salvation. Yet with all His power He can do nothing with us unless we let Him. He cannot work against our free will of choice. If you young gentlemen insist on thinking about last night's date or some pretty young filly or the movie at the local theater or what you could be doing besides being here, you'll get nothing from this retreat. If the young ladies desire to think about clothes or the good-looking boy with a cowlick over his right eye next door or getting married early or how nasty your parents were in sending you here, you'll get nothing from this retreat.

The Holy Spirit needs perhaps three things from you. First, a good deal of silence on your part, for how can He teach you within your soul if you're constantly yapping with your neighbor. Second, He needs your effort, for He's not going to do it all. He needs a few thoughts of yours, a few ideas that you have in your head or get from me during this retreat, ideas and thoughts that He can help you think over, deepen and make your own. Third, He must have from you a desire for improvement. If you're satisfied with yourself, if you think you are the best and that "Mrs. Jones's" youngest son is as good as he can be, then you had better leave now. You're wasting your time, my time, and you're throwing a magnificent opportunity back in God's face.

Now let me tell you a few things about my part in all of this. I don't have a very big part, actually. I'll just give you a few general ideas which you think over and make your own. You'll take what God allows me to say and then ask yourselves, "What does this have to do with me?" You apply what I have to say to yourselves. After the conferences, get by yourself, preferably before our Lord in the Blessed Sacrament, and discuss things with Him. If you're going to do any talking, do it with Him, and He'll have plenty to say to you in return through His spirit, Who is living within you.

"What shall a man give in return for his soul? What shall a man gain if he owns the whole world and loses his soul?"

We cling to life with all our strength, we love it and it is precious to us because of some inner reason within us. Because we're meant for God. Because He made us and loves us and wants us with him. Because He sacrificed everything for us, even His own Son, because He paid a great price for us, His Son's blood, and He's not going to let us go easily. So, that is why you are here.

Our Lord tells of the beggar who lived off the crumbs of a rich man's table and he was disease-ridden so that the dogs used to come and lick his wounds. But he was a success and the rich man who used to give him the scraps from his table so grudgingly was buried in Hell. There was the failure, there was the loss, there was the fool. Prominence in this world, for the most part, means nothing, and God judges success differently than do people.

Everything you do in life, the simplest and tiniest conscious acts, have something to do with whether you save your soul or not.

What's it going to be with you?

Are you going to recognize God's goodness in your behalf and submit to His desires for your salvation? Or are you going to go through life playing both ends against the middle, playing cozy, not committing yourself, sitting on the fence?

These are the questions you should be asking yourself today.

July 27, 1958, CU

The Freedom Rides

Written by Phil for his 1996 autobiography, Fighting the Lamb's War, *this passage refers to his experience attempting to integrate the segregated airport in Jackson, Mississippi, shortly after the Freedom Rides had garnered international news. Ordered home by his diocesan superior general, Phil grudgingly left before he could complete the action. It would be one of the rare times he would follow such orders from his superiors.*

On May 4, 1961, a group of Freedom Riders boarded a bus in Washington, D.C. They planned to travel through Virginia, North Carolina, and South Carolina, arriving in New Orleans on May 17, the anniversary of the 1954 Supreme Court decision in *Brown v. Board of Education*. The Freedom Riders had been warned that racists were prepared to attack, and to kill them, in order to keep interstate buses segregated. At Anniston, Alabama, 200 angry segregationists stoned one of the Greyhound buses carrying Freedom Riders. A firebomb tossed through the rear door of the bus exploded shortly after the Riders jumped to safety. In Birmingham, a mob attacked the Trailways bus carrying more Freedom Riders, beating William Barbee so badly he would be paralyzed for life. An informant had warned the FBI that the Freedom Riders would be attacked in Birmingham, but the Bureau's agents failed to appear. Bull Connor's [the infamous Birmingham police chief whose vicious tactics against civil rights demonstrators gained international attention] police also stayed away from the bus station, leaving the mob to attack the Freedom Riders.

    After the furor over the Freedom Riders had died down a bit, James Farmer, director of the Congress of Racial Equality (CORE), put a call out for priests, ministers, and rabbis to fly into Jackson, Mississippi, in order to integrate facilities at the airport. I heard about this, responded immediately, and got permission from my superior in Baltimore to go. Dan [Phil's brother] heard the call as well, but his provincial in Buffalo refused to grant him permission to travel to Jackson. We met with James Farmer in New York City, and he went over the action very carefully, telling us that we might well be beaten, or even killed, in the Jackson airport. Officials in Jackson, Mississippi, and at the airport would be alerted that we were coming. Members of CORE would be on hand to help us. Farmer assured us that there would be no leaks to the press. So the world would not be watching until after we had been beaten, and possibly jailed, in Jackson.

We boarded a plane early in the morning, landing in Atlanta where we were to pick up a flight to Jackson, Mississippi. I had barely disembarked from the plane when airport officials surrounded me, insisting that I accompany them to answer "an urgent phone call." The receiver thrust into my hand, I heard my superior general say that Bishop [Richard Oliver] Gerow of Jackson, Mississippi, was extremely upset over the pending action. Bishop Gerow wanted to know why these Josephites were coming into his diocese, said he wasn't going to tolerate having us there, and demanded that my superior withdraw permission for our visit. We were ordered to drop our plans, and hop the first flight back to Baltimore, which we did.

FTLW

JFK and the Cuban Missile Crisis

Written for Phil's 1996 autobiography, this passage recounts his experience during the 1962 Cuban Missile Crisis.

John F. Kennedy was Irish Catholic, two big strikes against him when he ran for president. He was handsome and tough, liked a good joke, and wouldn't turn down a drink. All of which endeared him to millions of Irish Americans like my own family. After the election, my brother Dan even sent President and Mrs. Kennedy copies of his books, with a lovely inscription that read: "They go to you with the prayer that your courage, cheerfulness, and moral and cultural leadership continue to hearten our country and our world." We believed in Kennedy's Peace Corps, supported the Alliance for Progress, and when the president was assassinated, I broke down and cried. I had no idea that he had sent CIA assassins to kill Fidel Castro, that he was escalating the arms race, that his macho posing brought us to the brink of nuclear war, or that he was sinking the nation, inextricably, into the Vietnam quagmire. I just bought the image instead of looking at the man and what he was really doing here and abroad. The media wove the wool tight over my eyes, though soon enough the veil would lift, never to fall again.

I was living in New Orleans in 1962 when President Kennedy took the country to the edge of the nuclear abyss. Terrified people fled north, hoping to survive World War III. The roads and highways leading out of Louisiana and Mississippi were lined with tarpaper shacks, and the Black families living in those hovels could not escape. If atomic warfare broke out, the grandsons and granddaughters of slaves would be the first to die. The Russians blinked,

JFK proved his manhood, the Cuban Missile Crisis ended, and I commenced a lifelong study of the connections between militarism, racism, and poverty.

My research led to one conclusion: Congress was giving the Pentagon vast sums of taxpayers' dollars to manufacture, test, and deploy weapons of mass destruction. The government was building thousands of nuclear weapons in order to protect the American people from communism. Blacks had to live in shacks, and their children had to die from hunger and disease, so that the military could build bombs.

It wasn't difficult to make the connections between racism, poverty, and militarism. I concluded that war is the overarching evil in this country. Every other social lession is related to our willingness to blow up the planet. We're willing to do that; otherwise, we wouldn't have these weapons. We built them with a very definite intention, which is that under certain circumstances we will use them. Racism, discrimination against women, poverty, domestic violence, all are connected to this intention.

FTLW

The Nature of Christian Witness

This writing highlights Phil's consistent belief that the Gospel is to be taken and lived personally with an emphasis on the Christian's duty to perform the works of mercy, despite the potential risk and suffering.

It is quite impossible to expect the growth of a person to truly human stature without reference to our Lord. For the Christian, humanity must mean Christ, both in growth and in the realization of adulthood. In the Redemption, Christ took our life to Himself, and the single task of life is a responsive and loving reaction to that act. A person must now put on Christ.

Honesty requires one to underscore that the object of witness is humanity, people, each and every person. Without people and their fallen-state, there would be no reason for God's present order of things, for the Incarnation, or for Christ's redemptive plan. In spite of our theoretical acceptance of this truth, we subscribe to a persistent and paradoxical Christian heresy which takes as the point of departure a witness to God without witness to people, which attempts to live Christian truth without communicating it, which claims love of God but fears love of the person. It is a heresy which has long cloaked itself as a religious and moral system, but it is a selfish and pragmatic ethic. Its emphasis upon worship at the expense of the works of mercy is evidence that we unconsciously seek in religion a divine sanction for personal pride, a climate suitable for sentiment, a philosophy that will pad and cushion one from the demands of life or allow us to deal with only its most palatable forms, justifying a contact with life that is peculiarly detached and contemptuous.

By way of contrast, the Christian witness will not seek for themself the dangerous luxury of any appraisal of Christ that Christ Himself has not taught.

The Gospels and the Church speak too strongly to him or her for that. Nor should their worship detract from service of neighbor; it rather prepares them for such service. They see Christian institutions as helpful and effective as long as they are well used, but they are not wedded to them as absolutes which are above evaluation and in some cases above replacement. The law they view as a thing of mighty importance, as indeed Christ viewed it, yet the Christian knows that unless legality has a base in love and is interpreted by love it can become a weapon to club and cripple people, instead of encouraging them and supplying guidelines for conscience.

The world may challenge their values, indict their life, cause them suffering, demand from them unceasingly their time, effort, and money, but they still love the world as the matrix of their humanity, the preserve of their church, the home where they are born into life and into God. So, they will take from the world with gratitude and give to it with largesse of spirit, knowing that even as they nourish their being on its elements, they must renew it by the gift of their spirit.

Generally, it can be said that the difference between the ordinary Christian and the Christian witness is a different relationship to reality and a different capability of grasping it. For the first, the objective world is seen in a glass darkly, moral insight is rare, egoism is impulsive, effort is displayed, suffering is feared. On the other hand, the Christian witness begins by assenting to reality and has a wholesome uneasiness over the insufficiency of their grasp of that. But they affirm its presence and accept their responsibility of seeing it more clearly, knowing that public change will depend largely on what they are and become.

1965, NMS

Segregation and the Nuclear Arms Race

I would like to consider two questions which seem to me particularly indicative of our malady and illustrative of the direction that our action must take. I refer to national segregation and the international arms race.

It may become clear in the course of reflection that these two are related problems and that segregation is psychologically creating a climate in which our massive reliance on nuclear weapons may flourish. It may become obvious that we as a people are losing more and more command of our own morality, and that it is being more and more dictated to us through our refusal to accept others. It may become obvious that the tyranny we impose upon our own citizens, one-tenth of our population, has now threatened to take an international form in the larger neighborhood of the world. It may become obvious that human injustice is no longer content to take specialized forms, or to exist under local restrictions, but as a hydra contrives a new face for every area of the world. It may become obvious that the commonly dispassionate decision of the American people to relegate the African Americans to the cellars and slums of American life makes it not only easy but also logical to enlarge our oppressions in the form of international nuclear threats.

I submit that the two phenomena, segregation and the arms race, are very much connected and that vicious seeds of one help to promote the other and that, conversely, if we solve our national segregation problem, we will gain strength to pursue avenues of action on the international scene that will further our Christian integrity and ensure the peace.

This connection of segregation with a world arms race is by no means an imaginative one. To the ordinary White American, the African American is an unknown quantity, who inexplicably has taken upon himself a course of action which threatens to expose White supremacy, its myths and virulence, in the full light of day. The communist threat is still a relatively new phenomenon to us and, therefore, still laden with anxiety, still unpredictable in its course. But it is essentially of the same nature as the African American "threat." Both African Americans and communists directly and aggressively challenge our assumed identity, what we believe ourselves to be, what we wishfully think of ourselves.

On the one hand, we have nativist supremacy associated with the white skin to inflate our ego; on the other, the engrafted supremacy springing from a superior ethos, a superior way of life, superior wealth, and so on. And consequent to this pride, an international transference of policy and attitude occurs, a policy with the same psychosis as the one employed so widely and effectively at home. Very shortly, we have internationalized our attitudes of injustice and exclusivism, our determination to preserve our status quo of privilege and possession. And this to such an extent that we are still creeping toward that apex of irresponsibility in which nuclear war appears more and more logical as the bold sanction of our national integrity.

The ordinary Christian life is not presently oriented to the crucial concerns of human experience — the winning and preservation of peace, the elimination of racial and religious discrimination, the proposed assault upon poverty, the appraisal of the nation-state concept. We must remove whatever it is that insulates us from contact with these problems, since the future of humankind will depend upon the course that they take.

The Christian, therefore, must open themself to an education by these profound and momentous movements, for they can express a ministry of experience, even as they look to them for a ministry of direction. In this way, the dialectic between theology and life is maintained, a reciprocal influence is established — the Christian returns to their theology to speak to it of life and returns to life to speak to it of theology.

NMS

Questioning the Christian "Credo"

In the unspoken presumption of Christians today that they are not of the world, nor responsible to the world, we see the common development of values that are extremely worldly, in the pejorative sense. According to this mentality, the world is understood as a place to live in, to enjoy, to use, and even to exploit; but not to direct, to endow with the stamp of one's spirit and hands, to work and suffer for. There is little sympathy for a love of the world as God loved it; little thought of redemption, as Christ redeemed it; or reconciliation, as the Spirit reconciles.

It is a fact for chagrin that Christians are commonly satisfied with a religion centered about the negative, about prohibitions that clearly define unlawful action, while stating very little what one must do as Christian duty. Community attitudes, in such a climate, come off second-best; the task of creating more habitable living conditions, of strengthening institutional life or creating ad hoc institutions, of improving human relationships through economic opportunity and better law—such imperatives are often left to the politicians.

The Decalogue can say, "Do not steal, and you are obligated to respect the property of others," but such a precept leaves many a loophole for avoiding the positive duty of using wealth to eliminate poverty by a better distribution of goods, by creating decent jobs and the training to hold them, by regarding automation as a community concern, by guaranteeing the rights of the poor through social and legal institutions. Since we do not work to eliminate conditions which degrade human dignity, thereby making human fulfillment and salvation next to impossible, we become partners to the crime, and the human misery that we allow to descend upon others punishes us in a strict spiritual counterpart.

If our Christian "credo" possesses the worth that we claim for it, it is worth questioning and, in its present state, it is worth reform. It is worth questioning in its absolute, as being liable to further development and more clarified expression. It is worth questioning in its relative forms, as to whether they best elucidate immutable and transcendental truth. And the instruments of tests are the Gospel, the living tradition of the Church, the Holy Spirit, and the needs of all people. The Church endows us with all her resources purely for engagement with life, which in the Christian sense means other people.

NMS

I Will Take My Stand, Come What May

As for me, I will take my stand, come what may. I will take my stand with the Christ of the Gospels and of history, and though that picture of our Lord be a limited one, it is the best that I presently have. I will take my stand with Him who met the violence of ignorance with the truth of His Word and Person; Who cared for bodies that He might heal souls; Who faced the violence of Jewish hypocrisy with truth, works and infinite compassion; Who bowed to the violence of our sins in the Passion; Who prayed for His murderers on the Cross.

As I read Him, the only violence He allowed was that endured by the Kingdom of Heaven; or the violence arising from the conflict between truth and error, love and hate; or the violence which must often be accepted in fidelity to His Name. I will take my stand with Him who said, "Love your enemies, do good to them that hate you." Who told Peter to forgive his brother seven times seventy times. Who again told the same man to put up his sword, "For all that take the sword shall perish by the sword." Who gave a new commandment before He died and told us to love one another with His love. Impractical? Yes, but impractical only because our faith is so pitifully meager and our love so pitifully thin.

I will take my stand, however feebly and faintly, with the martyrs and confessors of twenty centuries of Christianity, with Paul and Ignatius of Antioch, with Thomas More and Franz Jägerstätter, with all those who would rather die than remain silent before the arrogance of power and oppression. I take my stand with Gandhi, who taught and lived that "nonviolence is the law of our species as violence is the law of the brute"; with Pius XII, who said, "If ever a generation ought to hear the cry 'war on war' rise from the depths of its conscience, it is certainly the present"; with Pope John XXIII who said, "War can never be an instrument of justice in a nuclear era"; with Pope Paul VI, who called peace a "duty," and who said that peace is possible only "if we accept Christ, if His word becomes the charter of civilization and life."

I will take my stand also, though trembling and unworthy, with the millions of peacemakers across the land and in the world, men and women of every race, creed, and ideology, who through the preference of the Spirit and the Providence of experience have come to see the image of God in the individual, and who intend to protect that image, to purify it and elevate it to full promise.

I for one do not have to allow violence, terror, or murder in any form; I for one do not have to stand by mutely helpless and sick with cowardice while racists and warhawks sell out our heritage and pawn our civilization, as though these things could be sanctions of their paganism and sick compulsions. But I must believe that Christ, His Word, and Sacramental Flesh are enough to heal and unify all people; I must believe that the encyclicals and the pronouncements of the Council are enough to build a society of justice and peace.

I will therefore protest the lunacy of modern war in South Vietnam or elsewhere; I will protest the progression of air strikes, which makes absurd the offer of unconditional negotiation; I will protest the solidification of the communist world that our savagery and stupidity is causing; I will protest the control of mentality, government, and wealth by Secretary of War Robert McNamara and [National Security Advisor] McGeorge Bundy, whose power grows in proportion as they are proven wrong. I will protest idolatry and default within the Church, which today blesses the Pentagon as it blessed the *Wehrmacht* [the armed forces of Nazi Germany] two decades ago. I will protest these things and act against them. So help me Christ!

April 1965, CU

Peace Is the Duty of Our Time

On May 29, 1965, Phil spoke to graduates on Baccalaureate Day at Marymount Manhattan College.

"Brethren, let him who boasts, boast about the Lord. For it is not he who commends himself that is approved, but the one whom the Lord commends" (I Cor. 10).

You may have heard it said—I know that I have—that there are certain predictable factors in a graduation talk or sermon. Speakers will invariably present their version of the world's reality, attempt to demonstrate that this or that grim condition exists, and then suggest that the graduates step into the breach, apply the medicine, and look about determinedly for other problems to remedy. This is a certain mixed blessing, as you would suspect, for a great deal depends upon the presentation of reality, its validation and pertinence; and a great deal depends upon the capability of the student to receive and to implement what is said. I will certainly presuppose your quality of receptivity. It remains to be seen whether what I say is valid, relevant, or both.

Nor is our relationship here this evening purely a question of you being told by me as sort of a finale to an educational history of being told. Before I came here to tell you, you have told me by your witness and work in Harlem; you have told me by what Marymount students are prepared to do in Baltimore this summer. In fact, the student community of this country, of which you have been a part, has been telling me and the older generation for years what ought to be done, what Christianity and democracy are all about, from the time of the first sit-ins and Freedom Rides in the South to the present teach-ins over Vietnam. Those manifestations of nonviolence in Greenwood, Nashville, Jackson were sponsored and initiated by students, and from them has come a whole philosophy of disarming an unjust community, reducing the violence of unjust law and custom.

If we commit any crime against the students of this country or the world, it is perhaps this—the agencies and structures that will engage their imagination and use their talents for the good of humankind are fearfully lacking. And so it is that student potential, in view of massive and diverse need, is but partly realized—the attrition connected with fighting to be of use drains off both numbers and reservoirs of willingness and talent. Realistically, this situation before and after graduation becomes a student problem, and it must be engaged by students. What this means is open to considerable interpretation, but obviously, the Peace Corps is not possible to all. But the poor are everywhere. Civil rights activity is literally everywhere, and because we can no longer avoid it, the issue of peace and war is everywhere.

Peace is the issue and duty of our times, and the words but faintly convey the reality of need or task. There are no alternatives to peace today that can be rationally considered, simply because alternatives are a confrontation with a hellish nightmare but faintly described in Dante's *Inferno*—hundreds of millions of dead, the living worse off than the dead; atmosphere, water, soil, animal and vegetable life corrupted and destroyed, genetics attacked; vast areas of the Earth reduced to the semblance of a huge cinder, through which wander the stricken remnants of a decimated race. Unimaginable, that is true—but real, and very, very possible.

The president, certain Pentagon officials, all have mentioned the possible use of nuclear weapons in South Vietnam. It is presently saved to conjecture that were the Chinese to make an aggressive move against us in Vietnam, they would quickly receive nuclear retaliation. Even as the American mentality was "hardened" some years ago for an overkill capacity which now takes 10 percent of our tax dollars to maintain, a capacity which could reduce over one hundred Soviet cities to indescribable rubbish, so are we all being "hardened" today to the first tentative use of these obscene engines of destruction in Vietnam.

There are no rational, or human, or Christian arguments that can be mustered to support such a stand. We are not allowed by God or person or human right to risk or to become destroyers of our planet, advocates of mass murder, enemies of human society or civilization. Yet the inhuman and mad arguments continue to come from those who have blessed such monstrous policy: "You are selling your country out" or "I'd rather be dead than Red" or "What practical alternatives do you have?" The fact of the matter is that those who work for peace are saving their country, since America cannot exist apart from a world that is at peace. The Gospel offers us many alternatives; that a nation which is the most powerful in world civilization can organize and mobilize for peace, just as we have done for war.

Violence breeds violence, violence escalates violence, violence narrows the scope of human choice, violence reduces a human situation to the level of barbarism, an animality. And yet, in a particularly insane and reckless way, we cling to it as a solution to international problems, as, indeed, nearly the only solution.

It may become obvious that at this point in international relations, or in fact, in race relations at home, we are obsessed with ideologies rather than with persons. Abroad, these ideologies take the form of democracy versus communism, or Christianity versus Marxism; at home, it is White supremacy versus Black inferiority. The consequences of this are a frightful dilemma, wherein we are squeezed between two oblivions, so to speak—namely, the means decided upon to further democracy versus communism will destroy both; or the means decided upon to continue White supremacy will cause a mild or a serious form of domestic war at home.

On the other pole, the oblivion which ideology will not let us accept is political and economic competition with the communist world, or full acceptance of the African American within our midst. At home and abroad, therefore, we are faced with ideological war, and it is a historical fact that wars of this type have been the bloodiest in history. It is indeed a supremely ironic situation, insofar as our religion tells us that humankind is one, that people are essentially the same everywhere, and that the Gospel allows no violence against others. It merely commands love.

The Church has been particularly impotent in the face of war, whether of the conventional type or of the present nuclear impasse, because it has always been against war in general but never in particular. We now know that the Catholics of Germany supported and blessed the war experiment of Hitler, just as the American Church remained totally silent before American saturation bombing and our use of nuclear weapons in Hiroshima and Nagasaki. And we are well on the way to pursuing the same course today, since Pope Paul VI has called for a negotiated peace in Vietnam five times, to be greeted with utter silence by the American Church.

At the present time, the United Nations, or NATO [the North Atlantic Treaty Organization], or OAS [Organization of American States], or SEATO [Southeast Asia Treaty Organization] are incapable of resolving international questions. They are, rather, organs of regional interest or sounding boards for nationalism. What is needed is a world body of government, with supreme executive, legislative and judicial functions, promoted and supported by all nations, with power of law and sanction.

The groundwork for this crucial and desperately needed reality will be laid, please God, by many of you. This will necessarily mean that we must exploit the similarities between the communist countries and ourselves, rather than make the present mistake of stressing differences. Both our societies are future-oriented, both are secularized, both are optimistic, both seek in ideology and practice the betterment of humankind's relation to its environment. In addition, there are growing segments of communist intellectuals and bureaucrats who feel that Marxism cannot afford to maintain its present bankruptcy of spirit. They feel that it must seek out a spiritual and moral dimension or die.

The future of human beings, as well as the foundation of world government, is more assured by any act which brings people together to make them more aware of common humanity than of mutual difference or antagonisms. The type of Christianity which would prompt such action is necessarily a nonviolent one, in which Christians are particularly adroit at analyzing the seat of violence, assuaging it through truth and creative service, even bearing its brunt with their own persons, there to terminate it, to kill it, as it were.

The story is told of an Italian peasant who was discovered by an American correspondent accompanying our army as it swept north to Rome in the latter part of 1944. The tides of war had rolled over him, his family, his village several times in those bitter years. His wife, children and relatives had been either killed or deported. He was found alone amid the ruins of the only life he knew. The correspondent spoke with him through an interpreter and was able to notice the man's despair, his shock, but above all his fierce, consuming hatred. He told the story of this man and sent it back to the States, and in it, there was this tremendously significant sentence: "Here was a man," he wrote, "that was now totally convinced that the only profitable course was violence." In other words, the peasant's story was by no means ended. The violence that had robbed him of everything would be paid back with interest.

The greatest thing that any of you can do is to be conscious agents of reconciliation, emissaries of the Lord who came to break down our enmity at the price of His Blood. "Blessed are the peacemakers," He told us, "for they shall be called the children of God." "For it is not he who commends himself that is approved but the one whom the Lord commends."

1965, CU

Faithful Enough to Suffer, Daring Enough to Serve

It is somewhat of a limited view, in my opinion, for anyone to decide that the Church has a role in the promotion of world peace. The term "role" suggests something not quite essential or permanent; and in this case, it may imply that the Church, at one time or another, depending on the demands of history, could discharge itself of the responsibility of peacemaking. And so, it may be better to say that peace is both the life and business of the Church, since the Church is essentially the peacemaking community; it is the organic community; it is God's reconciliation in the world. Within this view, it is still possible to grant infidelity and failure, still possible to tolerate a misplaced trust in an institution, denomination, religious lobby, or pietistic coterie, as long as the Church agrees upon itself for what it is. In other words, if a passionate desire for peace and the works of peace are not present, if the formation of community is not paramount—we do not have the Church, but something unworthy of the name.

To be a world force in peace, however, and not merely an inconsequential remnant, the Church must constantly re-learn itself as it is—a poor, evangelical and universalist community which is confidently striving for the delicate balance between the Word of God and its service among humanity. We do not presently have this grasp. More than that, our theology is muddled as to be very much at the root of our impotence, attempting, as it often does, to make grace a quid pro quo, to worship God and not love people, to create institutions and ignore community, to place ideology before reconciliation. In some contrast, Bishop Robinson [Anglican Bishop John A. T. Robinson, author of *Honest to God*] offers a considered point when he says that theology is now anthropology. It is not precisely that, but theology should explore the divine intervention in humanity, it should offer divine dimensions to human life, it should make possible human relationships which hitherto had been impossible.

Yet it seems very clear that neglect of the individual is a pervasive and embarrassing weakness in our theology that often fails quite utterly to understand human condition, aspiration, and potential. Theological renewal is now apparent, and it carries with it the hopes of humanity; yet the trivial and irrelevant character of renewal is often fully apparent as the weakness which sponsors it, as though some sort of groundless hope were operating that we can renew our theology and the Church without casting off the heavy baggage of centuries—national alignments, protective custody by the state, institutional wealth and security.

A case in point is the nationalism of the Church and the ready use of it made by the state. The old virtue of patriotism, which makes allegiance to the nation far more important than allegiance to humanity, has been studiously embedded and cultivated by the Church, and it still is. World realities, however, can no longer tolerate that distortion—what was once named a virtue is now an open vice.

In addition, our celebrated separation of church and state becomes, in this context, not separation but alliance, with Caesar being served in the name of God, and with the state receiving both blessing and support for nationalistic policy and program. The evidence is dramatically and tragically present in tacit or open support of arms and arms budgets; by large consensus to the aggression in Vietnam; by indifference to the UN; by silence in face of discriminatory immigration; by the feeble favor we give foreign aid and auxiliary programs. It may be no exaggeration to say that when it comes to the foreign scene, the Church subscribes far more often to nationalism than to the Gospels. For we have decided, without admitting it, that we are immeasurably more interested in the privileges of state allegiance than in the risk of dedication to international justice.

Nationalism, by way of clarifying its dynamism, has an inherent tendency to arm itself. As an ideology, it possesses built-in violence—moral, political, and economic—and consequently, it is profoundly insecure. Any attempt to defend itself on conceptual or practical levels would be quite foolhardy, leaving it little alternative but to rely on the protection of arms. Nationalism, therefore, has its arms budget, its military-industrial complex, nuclear weapons, huge armies, and propaganda machines. Very simply, it is a philosophy of weapons that grips humanity in terror, that exploits the riches of humankind in creation, that ignores the despair of the poor, that hurries us onto an Armageddon which few want and fewer want to avoid.

The Church, as one of the patrons of nationalism, must logically consent to the Cold War, an arms race, American intervention in the Dominican Republic and Vietnam. Tragically enough, neither active favor nor discreet silence is asked for by the state, yet they are invariably given. Meanwhile, Pope Paul VI pleads for peace on every occasion, and the World Council of Churches has expressed its mind with no less urgency. Nonetheless, our collaboration with war stands, proving as it does the adage "The Church is always against war, but never against this war."

According to the mind of Christ, the Church is what He is—truthful, loving, nonviolent, compassionate, forming what He is, the new creation, the new person, the new covenant, the new kingdom. As such, therefore, there is required of it perpetual acts of faith and obedience—not because these acts are necessarily effective to an end, or politically expedient, but because they are asked by the Lord. In this age, faith and obedience may mean breaking our idols—whether these be wealth, institutions, political privilege, ideology, or any form of doublethink which masks itself as theology. Faith and obedience may mean nonviolence in a violent world, poverty in a poor world, heroism in a fearful world, compassion in an inhumane world. The Church must be what it is—leaven in the mass, light of the world, catalyst within human chemistry— a community faithful enough to suffer and daring enough to serve.

The Church is the custodian of life; let us all now have more reverence for what we guard. "Happy are those who make peace, for they will be known as sons and daughters of God!" (Mt. 5: 9).

October 3, 1965, Central Nassau, CU

The Priest and Society

If the priest is to be the man of reconciliation at the altar and in the pulpit, his action there demands a consistency of life in what he does and what he says. Otherwise, the Eucharist becomes less than a new relationship to all people, and the Word of God less than light to all people. Growth in Christian life is impossible without the experience of living Christianity in the main lesions of society, both for priest and laymen. The priest is charged with the formation of laypeople; this would mean his partnership in the lay witness, in all of its aspects.

Should he organize boycotts, lead picket lines, attack governments when they are abusing power or doing nothing? Yes, if necessary. History proves quite conclusively that the Christian Church has been in trouble with the Gospel only when it has made its fiat to government. Generally, it can be claimed that the American power structure (and the Church shares complicity in this) is nationalistic, White supremacist and bourgeois. Its mystique and composition are self-sustaining and self-perpetuating. It cannot of itself change to accommodate justice or international and domestic levels; it must be, rather, purified by a counterforce of risk, truth, and love.

Pope John XXIII is responsible for an adage that might be useful here: "Unity in essential things, freedom in non-essentials, love in all things." When a conflict arises between clerical conscience and official decision, fraternity between priest and superior is first threatened. Therefore, the lines of communication must remain open. Within differences, the priest must remember that his mission is both the renewal of the Church and society. One must not be attempted at the expense of the other.

Moreover, in the practical order, the priest is often in a better position to influence renewal of the Church structure than his superior, presupposing he commits himself to the arduous task of real communication. He must, there-fore, sometimes request hearings, must question decisions, must offer defense and even protest. What his response to silencing would be depends on an immense number of factors—temperament, maturity, the best interests of all involved, fidelity to the Holy Spirit. As to the issues of race and peace today, submissive acceptance to silencing might be more damaging to the Church and to the human community than a protest against it.

January 8, 1966, *Ave Maria: National Catholic Weekly*, CU

Liberation from the Pathology of War

War fever betrays a monstrous contempt of humanity. It hides behind a bewildering variety of biblical trappings, pretending virtuously to be concerned about human rights and values, while in reality it pays for itself through misery of the poor and the colonialism of people of color, trusting only in the power of dogma and weapon. It is unconscious of its own tragedy and the tragedy it breeds. It feels little compassion for those fighting its battles and for those who are its victims. It is a pure product of our national pathology, and it is as explicit as the Gospel in saying that those who are not for it are against it—those who do not gather with it will scatter.

What is one's life to be in the face of a war which destroys values as fast as it destroys people, which sucks us all into its tangled skein of ambiguity and viciousness?

One must dissociate from it and oppose it, that much is clear. One must embark upon an exhaustive analysis of The American Way of Life, laying it bare for diagnosis, surgery, choice, and rejection. One must be familiar with what there is in our hearts and our society which makes Vietnam, and armed containment and overkill capacity and new imperialism, not only possible, but inevitable. Only then can a person react against manipulation by government, by bourgeois interests, by public indifference and cowardice, by ideologies like nationalism and racism. Only then can a person be liberated and made capable of liberation.

Gettysburg, Pennsylvania, July 25, 1966,
The Gazette and Daily Newspaper, CU

Pacifist or Peacemaker

For one, I would rather leave the term "pacifist" than take it. Semantics is part of the problem, I suppose. When one learns that another is a pacifist, not a great deal more is known about their convictions. Does their pacifism have its source in religion, humanitarianism, or neutrality? Is nonviolence a way of life or not? Is the other opposed to the war in Vietnam or to all war? Are they advocating bilateral or unilateral nuclear disarmament? Will they refuse combat military service or all military service? Indeed, the definitions of pacifists are limited only by those who advocate pacifism.

In any objective sense, the biblical conception of peacemaker offers far more insight and precision. The Christian incorporates their Lord, who is both peace and peacemaker (Eph. 2:14). Sonship to the Father demands the role of peacemaking (Matt. 5:9). Christ is the embodiment of God's love for the world (John 3:16), and the peace He gave us was the communication of Himself (John 14:27). Peace is the fruit of love, and love of neighbor is the Christian charge and debt (Rom. 13:8), the summation of all law and commandment (Rom. 13:10). Matthew makes it clear that love is untested unless an enemy is loved (Matt. 5:44). God's approval of us will depend largely upon our service of those who, in the loose sense, are enemies — service by the "haves" to the "have-nots," food from the well fed to the hungry, hospitality by the housed to the stranger (Matt. 25:35). Finally, Luke's view of the neighbor in his parable of the Good Samaritan is quite inclusive (Luke 10:33).

War is obsolete, or humanity is. And the time for choices is running out. Indeed, hope for peace and civilization depends largely upon a Christian decision that is Christian, a decision neither remote nor immediate. We *must* become convinced that nothing we do makes any sense unless it is connected with the making of a just and lasting peace.

The Sign, August 1966, CU

The Gospel Means Peacemaking

The following theme of Christian Witness was addressed in an earlier writing by Phil entitled "The Nature of Christian Witness" in No More Strangers *but was revised substantially below.*

I think all of us can very quickly remember the Lord's last admonition, which was also a prediction: "And you will be witnesses to me in Jerusalem, and in Judea and in Samaria, and even to the uttermost parts of the world" (Acts 1:8). To reduce the word "witness" to meaning is to describe someone who has seen something, or to describe someone who tells what he has seen. I happen to keep the two possibilities separate here because the problem of being a witness of value is twofold: first of perceiving what is seen and, second, telling it as it is.

Those two, however, are practical problems, and they in turn rest upon the problem of what one is—in other words, reality is filtered through personality, is preserved, distorted, or destroyed by it. And reality is communicated to others as one is—intact, distorted or destroyed. Both in reception, therefore, and in projection, the problem of witnessing is the problem of truth. Is the influx of reality truly as it is, or is it somewhat or greatly distorted by the apparatus that is me (or you)? Consequent to that, do we tell it as it is, or do we tell it as we would like to have it?

An example immediately comes to mind—when Norman Morrison [a Baltimore Quaker who protested the Vietnam War by setting himself afire as Buddhist monks had done in Vietnam] immolated himself before the Pentagon, perhaps a dozen people witnessed the whole scene. Now granted that is a bitter thing to see a person die this way, but nonetheless, nearly a dozen differing testimonies were offered, some points being in obvious contradiction. About the only fact agreed upon was that a person was burned to death, and that he used a flammable liquid to make this happen. Other than that, people saw largely what they needed to see.

This is sort of a long way around to the point, which is: The view one has of the Lord's Redemption, His Death and Resurrection. And how one announces it by keeping it. Now keeping it, I would suggest, or living it, is quite dependent upon knowing what it is, then and now. A fact essentially the same, then and now, and therefore timeless, but manifesting itself first in the God-Man, and after in His Body which is humankind.

What then of Calvary and the Tomb? It would seem to me that Christ became fully human only when He became fully us — in our weakness, bewilderment, and death. Until then, there was a certain detachment, a certain removal from our condition — the Holy One of God identified Himself with the masses, taught them, healed them, served them as servant, but there was no final and irrevocable act of becoming us. During the Passion, however, the tortuous process began, and slowly and inexorably He became not just the nature taken in Incarnation, He became every person burdened with humanity, He became us. His death was not only caused by what might be called His assimilation of humanity, it was defined by this happening. "When I am lifted up," He said, "I will draw all things to myself." Us, first of all, and then all things through us.

His agony came from struggle with the powers of darkness which held us in captivity, with accepting us as we were, poor, confused pawns — fearful, hateful, anti-social. To draw us into the confidence, love, and integrity that was Himself was a cataclysmic act causing in Him alternates of forgiveness and despair, abandonment and trust. He had in the past received the offscourings of society with perfect composure and joy — people diseased, possessed, foul with their residue of lust, greed, and hate. But this fully becoming human was another matter, this "putting on" of human beings at war with themselves, anti-God, anti-self, anti-human. He broke down the partitions and barriers within His one humanity, which was one because of the one living God which He was also. Peter says that He bore our offenses and carried our sorrows, but Paul was closer to the mystery in saying He became sin for our sake. And in doing so, He became fully human, while at the same time becoming fully God. For what He did for us could only be an act of God.

In this consideration, therefore, God proved Himself fully and finally in His Son, whom He exposed to the horror of becoming all of us. Whom indeed, He caused to be all of us. At no time else was His power so shown, His love so concluded, His compassion so displayed for our wonder. And when the Resurrection happened, it was no more than a seal on what had been accomplished—one creation died, and another emerged, the old person died, a new one emerged. From the hopelessness of a hopeless situation, victory came forth—the person was now Jesus Christ, who was also God's Son.

From that point on, no one need be what he or she is or seems to be. Their definition comes not from their condition, breadth, or narrowness of mind, real or distorted view of life, courage, or cowardice, but what they are in Jesus Christ. And this is the very basis of hope, that one need not be what he or she is, one need not remain where he or she is.

What does such a process mean now? Simply this—even as Christ became fully human through the Cross, so we are becoming fully human (more aptly, Christ) through the same instrument. History is no more than a record of the pain and joy of this process—it's two steps forward and one in retreat. But in all confidence, indeed in all reality, we ought to know its final outcome, because the outcome has irrevocably been decided. And though in terms of our age, we might expect as a possibility the death of civilization, even that eventuality will not interfere with what God has done to us in His Son. That ought to be to us not only belief, but a central fact, a fact through which all others must gain their own truth.

I would suggest in all groping and hesitancy, that the nature of Christian witness is the same operation that Christ endured in becoming us—one cannot become human until one becomes all people. Since we are Christ, His word is ours, His spirit our spirit, His desire to die to accomplish us, ours. In a word, everything that can be said of Him can be said of us, even the parallel risks between us in running the course. No one can honestly say that He did not possess our fears, our reluctance, our horror in dirtying himself with the soil of apathetic or frightened or vicious human beings. Yet conviction in love forced Him into the darkness of risk where nothing is predictable, nothing safe or sure, nothing to hold onto but one's faith. One acts and takes the plunge, it would seem, because it is immeasurably more terrible not to do so, and because one believes.

Being human today undoubtedly means the work of peace—it is responding to the most profound need and yearning in the world today. In our time, we see the most startling convergence of the Gospel and human need. The main characteristic of the Gospel has always been peacemaking, while peace is not just a need, it is a necessity. What a boon it would be if we could muster our Christianity sufficiently to consider the Gospel imperative of peacemaking in the same light as the necessity of peace, indeed as the same thing? For we believe that the Gospel is light and life, while light and love are impossible to humanity without peace.

Being human involves taking on the human condition, which in turn means confronting the wars under which we live. I don't mean the arms under which we live—I mean the salient aspects of violence or injustice under which we live.

February 28, 1967, CU

PART II
Resisting the Vietnam War
_1967–73_

Resistance will outrage the high and mighty, who tolerate such convictions neither from Christ nor from any of us.

— PHILIP BERRIGAN

Diary from the Baltimore City Jail

On October 27, 1967, Philip Berrigan, Tom Lewis, James Mengel, and David Eberhardt entered the U.S. Selective Service office in Baltimore, Maryland, which held the files used to draft young men into military service in Vietnam. The four removed files from the cabinets in front of stunned employees and poured blood on the draft files, symbolizing the blood spilt in Vietnam. A high-profile trial ensued. Phil and his colleagues became known as "The Baltimore Four." This action laid the groundwork for future anti-war demonstrations that would occur across the country in the coming years.

Tom and I have just finished offering the Eucharist with Father Francis Tobey, the prison chaplain. He used one of the many canons—the words of consecration were these: "This my Body which is broken for you" and "This is my Blood which is shed for you." I reflected that Christians cannot very well deny that His Body was broken for us, and His Blood shed for us. What they will deny, in their fear and ignorance, is both Incarnation and Redemption as timeless facts—the Lord's Body is broken and his Blood shed in the victims and offscourings of world society—those who have no chance to know God's justice or experience it.

And so, Christians will acknowledge the words and deny the reality—more than that, they will refuse complicity in breaking the bodies of men and shedding their blood through the engines of war, or by more discreet forms like starvation, imposed ignorance, economic and political oppression. By a most profound paradox, those who receive the Body of Christ often break the Body of Christ with It—they conscript the Eucharist as a weapon of war against humanity.

Jim Mengel, who chose to remain out of jail with his family, and yet matches us in our fast, came in last night to see us. He reported talking with his local superior in the United Church of Christ, whose conversation with many people included a "negative" reaction. Jim felt somewhat taken aback by it all. Tom and I took pains to assure him that otherwise would be surprising. This war, or war in general, will not come to an end except through a reversal of the acts of war—there will be no magic in outlawing war, any more than there is magic in beginning it, supporting it or marshaling it for the ultimate rationality of The Big Bang, which nationally we draw ever closer to every day. I remember Carl Oglesby telling me in Ann Arbor of part of a conversation he'd had with an old Chinese scholar in Hong Kong: "Your country must suffer—it has never suffered, but it will."

The old man had a point. The only national trauma we have had in our history was the Civil War, and that is now too far from memory. Every major nation in the world that questions our Vietnam intervention has had suffering that dwarfs our own. China, crushed by Europe and America during the Open Door Policy, humiliated by the Japanese and educated by the indescribable suffering of its revolution. Russia, its pride destroyed by World War I, torn by the horrors of its revolution, the victims of 20 million casualties in World War II. Japan, reduced to impotence by us in World War II, made into a nuclear test tube by our experiments at Hiroshima and Nagasaki. England and France, both crippled in solvency and manpower by two world wars. No, we have not suffered, and our pride matches the absence of that experience.

But we will suffer as a people, and that suffering will take one of several courses. We will continue our obstinate and heavy-handed idiocy up to and through World War III and burn as the world burns with us. Or we will keep our counsel while America is torn by bloody revolution (for which there is ample precedent) until domestic chaos makes impossible the false unity needed to fight war. Our decent Americans will learn, as they do not now understand, that proportionate power is no longer in their hands—that power rests today with the economic conglomeration and their political representatives in Washington, and that regaining power must mean introducing nonviolent revolution. Otherwise, power will be taken from its inhuman masters by inhuman means, foreshadowing its inhuman use by new masters.

After release from jail for participating in a protest in Washington last Friday, Dan referred newsmen at a press conference to the substance of Pope Paul VI's encyclical "The Development of Peoples." Dan wanted it made very clear that our defacement of draft files illustrated a concrete application of the encyclical. A limited interpretation then—rich nations defend national property as rich people defend their property. Rich nations employ conscripted armies and nuclear arsenals as insurance for wealth, even as rich people employ guards, legal counsel, votes. Draft files as government property are not only symbolic of private property, they are the first cog in a mechanism of defense. To attack draft files, therefore, is to attack both militarism and war as an unjust preoccupation with private property. When human greed reaches such a monumental apex, then property can indicate death in its owners, even as it sponsors death to maintain its own unholy mastery.

In Scripture, blood signifies life, depending on how it is shed. To loose the blood of another unjustly is to choose death — to shed one's blood for a brother is to choose life, and to possess life more abundantly, thus Christ's Resurrection was humanly (and divinely) consequent upon His Blood shed for us. By His Death our Lord was illustrating a law implanted in humanity by His own Incarnation and Redemption: "A person who loses his life (blood) for my sake will find it." Those files to us are death or, more precisely, the mechanism of death. Our blood upon them is a tribute to life and a covenant with it. Our way of saying: No more war, war never again.

Wednesday, November 1, 1967, CU

Christianity and Revolution
Are Synonymous

Written by Phil in 1996 for his autobiography, this passage refers to the trial of The Baltimore Four, which took place in April 1968. While released on bail for his Baltimore action, Phil and eight others (Dan Berrigan, David Darst, Mary Moylan, John Hogan, Marjorie Melville, Tom Melville, George Mische, Tom Lewis) had acted again in Catonsville, Maryland, removing large numbers of draft files from the Selective Service office and burning them in the parking lot with homemade napalm. Phil references the Catonsville action in this passage.

Judge Northrop [presiding judge for the Baltimore Four trial] cocks his head to one side, as though he is listening to celestial music. He shuffles his notes, sighs heavily, and pounds his gavel.

"Six years," he announces.

Two thousand days away from friends and family. Two thousand nights in a steel cage. Time enough to break even the most recalcitrant spirit with the wheel of solitude, rotten food, and permanent disgrace. Sooner or later, I will be forced to accept a life of quiet desperation. I will agree to shuffle silent, obedient, head bowed to the imperial state. Time enough to shut this crazy priest down, for good.

I listen to the judge with an intense lack of interest, his words falling like dead leaves. I am neither depressed nor frightened. Judge Northrop's sentence hardly matters. I feel exalted.

No hiding the facts. Our act was premeditated, and our intent was absolutely clear. On October 27, 1967, Tom Lewis, David Eberhardt, Jim Mengel, and I did walk into the Baltimore Customs House. We did attempt to destroy draft records, pouring our own blood over licenses to kill human beings. Our first trial ended in conviction and we were released on bail pending sentencing. Vietnam was burning. Watts, Newark, Detroit were burning.

On May 17, 1968, eight friends and I struck again, this time at a draft board in Catonsville, Maryland, where we carried hundreds of draft records out to the parking lot and doused them with homemade napalm—soap chips and gasoline from a recipe we found in a Green Beret handbook.

Were we sorry? No, we most certainly were not. Would we do it again? Yes, we surely would. We understood that when the prosecutor got through denouncing us and the judge instructed the jurors, federal marshals would wrap chains around our wrists, manacle our wrists to chains, shackle our ankles. The 3-H treatment: Hobble. Humiliate. Hurt. Our guards would order us to strip naked, force us to squat over mirrors, to bend forward and spread our cheeks. When this ordeal ended, doors would crash shut, squeezing us into a few square feet of concrete and metal.

We just wanted the judge and jury to see that our government was dousing Vietnamese children with the same terrible stuff we poured over those draft files. Our government was blasting plastic pellets (because X-rays could detect metal, but not plastic) into children's flesh. We were cooking Vietnamese in white phosphorus, poisoning their food and water with herbicides, burning down their homes, violating international treaties, showing contempt for God's law. Compared with the suffering of the Vietnamese, a few years in prison seemed a very small price to pay.

I was shocked by the misery and the ugliness of life in jail, but I felt a great satisfaction being there. Jail just made the most sense to me, and it still does, because that is where one identifies with the poor, and where one becomes a spokesperson for their dignity and their rights.

The prisoners in Baltimore City Jail needed us very badly. They needed someone to talk to, someone who would listen to their anguish, someone they could trust, and who would counsel them. Tom Lewis and I helped them write letters to their judges and we tried to contact their families. The remarkable thing, to us, was that most of these men were in jail for nonviolent crimes, yet they were being treated like assassins.

So, there we were, stuffed into the rabbit hutch, and I had no regrets at all. None whatsoever. We had gone to Baltimore to destroy draft files in order to save lives. I knew, and I accepted, the consequences of my actions. The state might make the laws, but it did not have a license to kill in Southeast Asia, or anywhere else.

Dan and I went to prison [for the Catonsville action] because we believe

that Christianity and revolution are synonymous. Jesus Christ was a nonviolent revolutionary; therefore, Christians have a duty to subvert society in order
to create a world where justice prevails, particularly for the poor, who must be
treated with fairness and love.

FTLW

Trying to Serve Love

Phil wrote the following while incarcerated in the spring of 1968.

I'm not at all clear about what to call this; in fact, I have no definite idea of the form my writing in jail will take. It will not be a diary, nor will I be writing what should rightly be called meditations or reflections. Simply an unconventional look at the world through the mirror of prison life. Hopefully, a Christian look.

A title is unimportant and can be left to others. What is important is why I am in prison, what prison life signifies for a Christian, and what a prison sentence may indicate for the future.

Jail for me was an entirely voluntary affair, one of the predictable consequences connected with serious political dissent. This is not to say that I chose jail, or preferred it, but only that I felt civil disobedience was a Christian duty and accepted jail as a consequence.

In any event, there will be others like me, and as a priest perhaps I can offer other clerics a service comparable to that offered our young men by the David Millers and the Tom Cornells [anti-war activists imprisoned for burning their draft cards] and other young Americans jailed because of their opposition to war.

But why should I expect Catholic priests to be leaders in this form of witness? It seems at least that some elusive and mysterious influences are converging in this direction. Certainly, Vatican II is "at fault," with its emphasis on freedom of conscience; so is the civil rights movement and its nonviolent philosophy. Always in the background has been the long preparation of the ground by the Catholic Worker movement and its undeviating concern for the poor, for African Americans, and its "yes" to the world of justice, freedom, and peace. There is also the challenge provided by American young people and their insistence on values the Church should champion, but seldom does. Finally, we should also take note of the two-edged absolutism of Catholic discipline: It produces, admittedly, many human casualties, but can it not also provide the training ground for saints and heroes?

Most Christians and most Americans have great difficulty in seeing the I (the self) as being the we (humanity). Consequently, we cannot feel the effects of our actions as other people feel them; we cannot see ourselves as others see us. And so, by and large, we think we can have peace by fighting wars, we think we can rape a people and have them love us, we think, by way of practical norm, that we can have everything that wealth and arms can force from others.

People have, I would say, two problems when they try to serve love. The first is to know themselves; the second is to know what they must be. As to the first, we are, in effect, a violent people, and none of the mythological pabulum fed us at Mother's knee, in the classroom, or at Fourth of July celebrations can refute the charge. The evidence is too crushing, whether it be Hiroshima, or nuclear equivalents of seven tons of TNT for every person on this planet, or scorched earth in the Iron Triangle, or Green Berets in Guatemala, or sub-human housing in the ghettos of America. A substantial share of our trouble comes from what we own, and how we regard what we own. President [Lyndon B.] Johnson told our troops: "They [the rest of the world] want what we have and we're not going to give it to them." To prevent them, one thing needs to be done: Bring home the coonskin and hang it on the wall.

Scripture tells us that one must choose God or riches. This nation has overwhelmingly made its choices, and it is riches. Our shrinking world being what it is, we are now in the process of assuring the same status quo abroad as at home, and that means keeping the "haves" on top and the "have-nots" on the bottom. Foreign policy is increasingly becoming indistinguishable from domestic policy. The curtain is no longer iron or bamboo or cotton, it is mostly dollar and to a lesser extent ruble, franc, and pound. The only present freedom we're fighting for is our own, and that is of questionable value, since ultimately it means the right to stay on top of the anthill and fight off those crawling up the slopes.

When a people arbitrarily decide that this planet and its riches are to be divided unequally among equals, and that the only criterion for the division is the amount of naked power at their disposal, diplomacy essentially tends to be a military, truth tends to be a fiction, and the world tends to become a zoo without benefit of cages. And war tends to be the ultimate rationality because reason has been bankrupted of human alternatives.

What I'm trying to say is this: Our lives, to be agencies of peace, must stand the scrutiny of both God and man, and by man I mean not our peers but the billions of people suffering from war, tyranny, starvation, disease, and the burden of color prejudice. In our better moments we may pity them, but sentiment has yet to stop bombing or feed starving children. They will hold us to our acts, and if these acts will not bear human analysis, we will be judged and condemned and withstood in the same coin.

PJPR

Times for Confronting Injustice

On May 24, 1968, Phil issued the following statement for his sentencing hearing after all members of The Baltimore Four were found guilty of their actions. He again references the recent Catonsville action.

I am grateful to the judge and to this court for the opportunity to speak. Mr. Lewis [Tom Lewis, member of The Baltimore Four and the Catonsville Nine] and I, while under conviction and awaiting sentence, have acted once more against the apparatus of war. And for that, many people have judged us "irresponsible" or "untrustworthy." One prominent and respected friend called us a "danger to the community." A remark we accept with equanimity, if not pain, since we feel our friend has the equipment to understand better.

One acts as we did because of a certain view of humanity, and of the human's world. We claim to be Christian, but that is a claim never really verified or completed. It is, rather, a process of becoming, since man is by definition one who becomes himself—a painful but glorious process, as history tells us. In the same context, we believe that God's Son became man so that man might become himself—which is to say, a Son of the Father, a brother to the Son, a temple of God's Spirit, a brother to all brothers. Becoming human, we feel, is becoming what Christ was. And this is what we have tried to do.

When one deals with humanity, therefore, one deals with the Body of the Savior, a Body for which God died, and in which He still suffers. One does not deal with it lightly or irresponsibly—it is a sacred thing illumined by truth, nourished and built up by love, served by justice, and it must be protected against injustice. These are not times for building justice; these are times for confronting injustice. This, we feel, is the number one item of national business—to confront the entrenched, massive, and complex injustice of our country. And to confront it justly, nonviolently, and with maximum exposure of oneself and one's future.

As a democratic person, I must cling to a tradition of protest going back to our birth as a nation, traditions which brightened our finest hours as people. As a Christian, I must love and respect all people—loving the good they love, hating the evil they hate. If I know what I am about, the brutalization, squalor, and despair of other people demean me and threaten me if I do not act against their sources. This is perhaps why Tom Lewis and I acted again with our friends. The point at issue with us was not leniency or punishment, not courage or arrogance, not being a danger to the community or a benefit to it—but what it means to be a democratic person and a Christian person. And if we provide the slightest light upon those two momentous questions, it is enough for us.

America can at this point treat us as it wills. If it can find justice for us and for the growing millions of citizens who refuse complicity in its crimes, then it will display a stamina of reform in full accordance with its national creed. If it cannot find justice for us, then its cup of violence will fill up and up, finally to brim over. And at that mysterious point, we defendants will have been proven right in choosing revolution over reform.

Personally, I have little doubt as to the decision this court will take in the name of our country. But whatever the outcome today, I stand where I must—for my country and for my family, here and abroad.

PJPR

All of Us Are Prisoners

The following excerpts are from Phil's prison journal of 1968, published in the book Prison Journals of a Priest Revolutionary.

Although it would be wrong to describe the United States as a police state, it is safe to say that political writing is a dangerous adventure in federal prison. Second only to escape. Obviously, my presence here indicates the threat I constitute outside, a threat both vocal and physical, flowing directly from my convictions. My "rehabilitation" would mean a reformation. And the way to promote this, apparently, is by a heavy prison sentence plus suppression of free expression. In a word, I no longer possess the rights accorded "free" citizens. A strenuous form of censorship, to be sure, but to a priest who has struggled through the doldrums of Church censorship merely a restriction of degree and a challenge to conviction and ingenuity.

The official Church has lost its fight to maintain control of thought; it must now rely on the indirect repression employed by other bureaucracies that control their subjects by institutionalizing self-interest. In a capitalist society, whose very survival depends on its proving that self-interest can be profitable and socially manageable, human freedom undergoes a redefinition, becoming subject to the profit motive which informs society. In this context, freedom is tolerated, encouraged, even made marketable—except when it interferes with production and sales.

One looks in vain for a minimally enlightened self-interest on the part of Church and government. The mark of a mature society is the concern it manifests for people, but when Church and government achieve a détente by playing only a slight variation of theme on the old saw of power, one becomes a spectator of social dissolution. The cry of "revolution" begins to be heard more frequently and more urgently.

July 12, 1968

Several months of jail have stimulated reflection on the quality of rehabilitation offered by the prison system. Rehabilitation is a large question and, the more one considers it, a despairing one. What, one might ask, is the inmate being rehabilitated for? Is it for middle-class solvency and therefore for taxpaying to finance abominable welfare systems and massive war expenditures? Is it for a solid and righteous stance supporting national racism? Is it for residence in a cultural desert whose values are as violent as they are sterile? Is it for church membership when the Church is little more than an ethical patron of the champions of raw power? Sincere prison officials apparently conceive of rehabilitation as realizing all these goals. Paradoxically, however, rehabilitation is not being realized—even for these targets.

Ours is a waste society. As long as human and material waste are kept within tolerable bounds, that will remain so. We begin by exploiting the riches of nature for profit and end by exploiting people for the same reason. Our nearly uninhabitable cities, our commercialized and ravaged country sites, our polluted water and dirty air only parallel human casualties—all of us are prisoners, even if only a tiny fraction of us are behind bars. Indeed, environmental and human waste is so profound that we cannot duck the overarching questions: Can mere rules-keeping preserve a viable society? If so, what percentage of its citizens must keep the rules to preserve its viability, and does the waste present even in the lives of the rules-keepers suggest the need for measures more strenuous than reform?

July 26, 1968

It may seem surprising to some that my freedom here is more full and satisfying than any previously experienced. But freedom depends on the degree to which one is possessed by the truth. Confronting truth is the state of being under siege and submitting to conquest as gracefully as possible. Such is the price of freedom—"The truth will set you free." Christ clarified and expanded upon this point in the hushed atmosphere of the Last Supper—the disciples would receive truth in accepting Him, not only the Father's image but the real image of humankind. When one accepts Christ humbly and without qualifications, one stands against the personal and social lie—the "world's truth"—both in oneself and in society.

July 28, 1968

I am neither a sensitive nor a sentimental man. My background, experience, and discipline, the service that must be always available for others, have forced me to keep a tight rein on sentiment, to learn to master fear, and to adopt an attitude toward life which many would even consider reckless.

A compromise with truths fills me with loathing, and an inability to conceal my position has sometimes made my reality painful to those I most love. But my family has smoothed the rough edges of arrogance, and their love leaves me a failure in love, and a debtor to it. Slowly, I am learning, and will continue to learn, that without love a passion for justice can fashion a demagogue and a brute. "Love takes no pleasure in others' sins, but delights in the truth; it is always ready to excuse, to trust, to hope, and to endure whatever comes" (1 Corinthians 13:6).

August 9, 1968

"Revolution" is today the most feared, and consequently the least understood, word in our vocabulary—for most of us, apparently, it connotes all kinds of dark and devious assaults on privilege and power. Even Christians add their own anxieties and confusions to a concept which should give insight to their understanding of and dedication to the Gospel. In fact, "revolution" is an eminently Christian word which should guide all Christian response to human process. Revolution may be un-Christian in certain instances, but a person cannot be a Christian without being a revolutionary.

Christian revolution means conversion to a crucified and risen Lord, and witness to this conversion. The Christian in the world faces in himself and around him the identical forces that make most institutional power a friend of few and the enemy of most. The "world," as the Gospel sees it, is a malicious force, both personal and social, an individual and collective psychosis that alienates the self and exploits the brother. In this view, war, racism, and poverty can be traced to our desire to avoid the Cross that is part of life, thereby "preserving one's soul by losing it."

The "new man," who emerges slowly through conversion to the Christ of Calvary, rejects his own alienation by confronting the injustices of organized alienation, the institutions of power. For his effort, he is duly hated: "The world will hate you, because it knows neither the Father nor me"—and his lot becomes as bad as or worse than that of the victims he defends.

It is at this critical point when a person experiences their Calvary in the form of ostracism, betrayal, jail, or a bullet that he gives up his soul, to have it restored to him reborn. At this point the Death and Resurrection of Christ become a living experience. In the process, although without knowing it, society gains a reprieve of punishment and a new opportunity for a life that is human.

September 9, 1968

More than any others I know, the nine people who burned draft files at Catonsville can claim to be right in what they did and dare to publicize their rightness. Of course, many will find this smug and arrogant, but I am not saying it because they were with me or I with them. Their choice was as mysterious as their right to speak is certain; their claim is that of justice because their vision dramatized the crisis of injustice besetting America.

They saw their country maintaining its colossal affluence at the expense of other men, leaving war-making as its largest industry and racism as its chief social attitude. Propaganda had replaced truth, and Hiroshima and nuclear brinksmanship seemed to be its testament to humankind. Our country's violence has a determinist momentum that creates obstacles without an erosion within.

There is more to commend these nine—their vision had consistency, suggesting a way of life uniting personal relations and public responsibility. I have every confidence that their witness will remain steadfast and their example will provide an ennobling resource to others.

History reveals us as a greedy and belligerent people, a fact that a horrified minority of intellectuals and students is learning only today. But dissent from government encroachment or tyrannical policy has never been a primary national value. Prosperity, not justice, is considered the basic function of government. Americans want help from their government in their intoxicating pursuit of wealth; and to further this goal, they are often prepared to brutalize the poor and to plunge vigorously into an unnecessary and unjust war. Sometimes we suspect that our wealth necessitates both poverty and war, but it would be unhealthy to develop scruples. When technology is joined exclusively to commercialism and war, the tendency to indict the dissenters is heightened.

People still need to learn that excessive wealth, racism, and war mean the impossibility of a human, indeed a viable, society. Peace will remain an illusion until the atrocities of war and exploitation are eliminated. People have always valued their poor, valued them enough to ensure that they will be numerous. And people have always punished their prophets. That is because the poor and the prophet force others to look at themselves in different mirrors, the former showing men as they are, the latter as they can be. Since both reflections are painful, both are hated, along with those who show them. When people no longer use their poor to exalt their own egos, when they no longer destroy their prophets, then justice will have come to the poor, and prophecy will be as treasured as power is now. Having banished the ancient call to strife and blood, a person can begin to compete in love and service. Then we will begin to live.

September 19, 1968

When it comes to defending political dissenters like ourselves, lawyers become accomplices in the game against us—if, that is, they play by its rules. They unite with the criminality of the bench in what is called a Court of Justice—a monstrous euphemism indeed. Belief in the law is no adequate excuse for this. We, too, believe in the law, but we do not believe in those who manipulate it to favor war-making, white skin, wealth, and privilege against the poor.

This is not to say that we expect lawyers to quit or to join us. But we do expect them to realize that as long as law sacrifices justice, it will never be an instrument of order. We also expect them to realize that such a sacrifice of justice is precisely what makes power illegitimate. We expect them to abandon their naïve conviction that illegitimate power can reform itself through a combination of internal goodwill and legal dissent, whether domestic or foreign.

Illegitimate power subtly or crudely corrupts the most honest of people, if only for the simple reason that it doesn't allow public honesty. Illegitimate power simply grows defensively paranoid at legal dissent, as Chicago [the 1968 street protests which were met with extreme police violence] has most recently proved. What our lawyers, along with other liberals, must learn is that illegitimate power can protract the Vietnam War indefinitely, despite majority opposition, can escalate the Cold War as it chooses, and can crush any ghetto uprising with impunity. To keep dissent within legal bounds is actually to join the insane rush of illegitimate power toward mass destruction. These are harsh lessons for lawyers, but they are beginning to seep in.

In our first trial, both judge and prosecutor—they operate as a unit against political defendants—charged us with arrogant contempt of the law. We felt, as they said, above the law. Their language was the language of guilty and frightened men, but it was also the language of bureaucratic sycophants who had digested thoroughly their lessons from the powers at the top. They knew the law's metabolism and loved its favors—so well, in fact, that they could treat its critics like personal enemies.

We are their enemies, but not in the sense that they imagined. In reality, we are their best friends. If they want to consider themselves guardians of the law, let them learn that the law responds to principle before power, to human need before vested interest, to morality before pragmatism. Let them understand that the law they represent has fallen into disrepute, not because people are especially irresponsible and lawless but because the law has become a field manual for naked power and a club against the poor.

If they would be lawyers, we would also want them to be human. There is no good reason why lawyers cannot attempt in political cases what nonviolent revolutionaries are accomplishing in the streets—namely, the embarrassment and exposure of illegitimate power. There is no good reason why lawyers defending an anti-war case can't realize that a guilty verdict has been passed before the trial begins and that they are morally obligated to dramatize such a colossal effrontery to justice. There is no good reason why there should not be as many lawyers in jail for contempt of court as there are young men imprisoned for draft resistance. The expression of such a conviction seems to me the only way to restore honor to a profession which today is nearly as dishonored as the priesthood.

If events are any index, wealth and power, as they are now conceived and administered, are obsolete. So is the law. For me there is no serious alternative to confronting their injustice, inviting their repression, and accepting jail as the first of their major defeats. Spiritually, this means to dare human renewal; socially and politically, it means to feed a revolution. Like other Americans, our own lawyers will receive invitations to the banquet. It will be to their credit to accept them and to be the first of their profession to put on a wedding garment.

PJPR

We Claim a Higher Law

On October 7, 1968, the trial of The Catonsville Nine began.

Nine people go to trial today—my brother Dan Berrigan, Tom Lewis, John Hogan, Mary Moylan, Tom and Marjorie Melville, George Mische, David Darst, and I. All Catholics. We make the point of being Catholic because our Church has given us Christianity and because we hope to make it Christian. If that possibility lies within us.

This trial is another phase of resistance—as difficult in its own way as the napalming at Catonsville or as prison itself. In court one puts values against legality according to legal rules and with slight chance of legal success. One does not look for justice; one hopes for a forum from which to communicate ideals, conviction, and anguish.

Our object is a short trial—intense, forthright, and dramatic. The government will prove what we already admit—destruction of draft files—while simultaneously excluding the "why" of burning them. It will charge that breaking the law is a crime; we will maintain that breaking the law in the case at hand is no crime but rather a moral and political duty.

The government will assert that our motive and our intent are one; we will reply that our motive was to destroy those files, and our intent was to illustrate the genocide in Vietnam and the corruption of our country. The government will make its laws an absolute; we will claim a higher law. The government prosecutes us as it would, if logically consistent, prosecute a person for destruction of property because they broke down a door to save children in a burning building. We say that such a person deserves a medal.

The prosecution hardly needs a strategy—it is that simple. It needs merely to establish beyond a reasonable doubt what we admit and, indeed, boast about. "People just can't take the law into their own hands!" The court is so blind as to exclude testimony about America's national and international illegalities—about ghetto despair, starving children, Vietnam, Guatemala. Apparently, power *can* take the law into its own hands, a fact which the court refuses to admit. For if it did, what would happen to power stripped of the protection of law?

The determination of the prosecution, therefore, is to keep the law in the law's hands for the benefit of power, a determination that puts us under the law's power, and makes us subject to its equivocal blessings.

Two huge American flags flank the judge's bench, their staffs adorned by brass eagles. Portraits of eminent jurists gaze down from the back wall with well-bred resolve, champions of the public interest. The wood paneling, lofty ceilings, and substantial furniture of the courtroom seem tasteless and affected, stamped with the pompous assumptions of an affluent society. Here privilege emphasizes its prerogatives and shields its interests. Noblesse oblige, I mutter cynically.

The long years of my devotion to the flag, to an unreflecting justification of the law and order, are before me, and I think back to the time when the exorcism of my soul began. When I began to be less of a nationalist and more of a human being. It was like undergoing prolonged surgery, and just as painful.

Our lawyers sit a few feet in front—Bill Kunstler, famed for his defense of controversial figures like H. Rap Brown and the Black Panthers; Harrop Freeman from Cornell Law School; Harold Buchman, our local attorney; and Bill Cunningham, a Jesuit priest and law professor from Chicago. They are a brilliant and devoted group, capable of making us as secure as any lawyers can.

Freeman and Cunningham have just arrived and must be sworn in to the case. The court clerk charges them with conduct "consistent with truth and honor." Good enough—that shouldn't be difficult; they have come forward simply to defend people of truth and honor. Any attempt, however, to apply "truth and honor" more widely leads to semantic problems. What of the court's truth and honor to the defense of its government and its government's wars? What is the future of this court because it chooses to make a farce of truth and honor? What adage best applies to it? "A house divided against itself will fall" or "A house undivided by justice will fall."

PJPR

The Christian Roots of Protest

Part of Phil's testimony during the Catonsville Nine trial on October 9, 1968.

Question: Did there come a time when you started thinking in terms of civil disobedience?

Answer: Yes. I came to the conclusion that I was in very, very good standing by way of American and democratic tradition in choosing civil disobedience in a serious fashion. There have been times in our history where in order to get redress or in order to get a voice, *vox populi*, arising from grass roots and from the people, people have had to indulge in civil disobedience. From the Boston Tea Party on, through the abolitionist and anarchist movements, and through World War I where we had sizable numbers of conscientious objectors, through World War II, and right on through the civil rights movement, we have, perhaps, the most rich tradition in this country of civil disobedience.

Question: Did this lead to your involvement in the blood-pouring incident at the Baltimore Customs House for which you have been convicted and are now serving a sentence?

Answer: Well, we were prepared for the blood-pouring by the fact that we had practiced civil disobedience down in Virginia; and because my brother and myself, for example, have been practicing civil disobedience for years by signing complicity statements, supporting draft resisters.

Question: In what way did this [the blood-pouring incident] express itself as an act of civil disobedience on your part, or as you conceived it?

Answer: Well, it goes without saying that we tried to come from the Christian roots of protest—the civil disobedience movement which for the most part comes from Gospel—in order to illustrate to the country the horror that we felt over blood being shed in Vietnam, the useless shedding of blood which we deem to be slaughter and pretty close to genocide, if not actual genocide.

So we took our own blood and when our equipment broke down we added animal blood to it, and we attempted, as Reverend Mengel said, to anoint these files with the Christian symbol of life and purification, which is blood. Blood and fire, of course, are the Christian symbols.

So we did this in order to illustrate to the country what we thought was happening, in a religious, in a deeply religious and moral, sense, to this country, and what we knew was happening to the Vietnamese people. This, of course, was the crime for which we were judged in April or May and finally sentenced. Mr. Lewis and I received a six-year sentence.

Question: Will you explain why, with a sentence staring you in the face, you felt—or what was your state of mind that compelled you to become involved in Catonsville?

Answer: Once again, I saw no point to my life if it continued in a rather normal fashion in this society. I thought that the issue was not my life or my future. The issue was the deepening involvement of America around the world, not only in Vietnam but in Latin America. The issue was the nature of this society. The issue was the most powerful empire the world had ever seen and the most powerful military power that the world had ever seen, and what this had done to us as a people.

My life I judged to be slightly irrelevant in terms of those overriding and overarching considerations. So, my future, in terms of a more serious sentence for the Baltimore incident, I tried not to make that a consideration.

Question: What were your theological reasons for your state of mind in the Catonsville incident?

Answer: By and large, they arise from the Christian view of God. He has a unity, the unity of the Redemption in Christ. That is, all people are redeemed in Christ, because He took upon himself their nature and became human. The Son of God became human and, of course, inserted an entirely new meaning in history, a meaning which we are still in the process of discovering.

But this means a common fellowship under the Fatherhood of God. It means that a Christian, by definition, has to accept all people as brothers and sisters and has to go through this painful and sometimes tortuous work of working out fellowship with them. I think that my philosophy of nonviolence stems rather logically from these presuppositions. I do not know that I could explain it any more clearly.

FTLW, CU

After the Trial, Hope

Philip Berrigan and the other defendants of The Catonsville Nine were found guilty on October 10, 1968, by a U.S. District Court jury for burning draft records at Catonsville. Philip had yet to be sentenced. The following was written from prison on October 30, 1968.

What did our trial mean to me? Hard to say—perhaps a lot of things that I haven't grasped quite yet. You know, many experiences in life have to be caught up with later. They often catch one unprepared, or come to one too fast, or too complicated to be absorbed.

Yet I can say this—that trial meant hope to me. Because none of us were prey to any illusions about the verdict. We understood that we would be convicted and we understood why. And that's a great freedom! Odd indeed that the court, supposedly a refuge for free men, should be an accomplice in bureaucratic injustice and should pollute the Christian springs of law, while we congratulated one another for conviction, prayed the Our Father [the Lord's Prayer], and thanked the court for its courtesy.

Joan Baez says that freedom is a state of mind. And a friend of mine from Allenwood remarks from time to time, usually to newly arrived draft resisters: "They can pen up your body, but they can't have your mind. Unless you give it to them!" An extraordinary man, he is a political prisoner like them, and knows whereof he speaks.

Additionally, that trial meant hope because of people. Now, it's very unChristian to lose hope in people—indeed, it's as bad as losing hope in God. But the fact is since October of last year and the blood-pouring we were strongly tempted to lose hope in people. With literally no help from the movement, with general contempt from the press, with only a tiny circle of friends and relatives around us, we were as lonely as Roland against the Saracens.

But people must have time. And I, for one, tended to forget that. Americans have been brutalized by affluence, by racism and war, and by the devious machinations of empire. But they are, nonetheless, a great people. Other men seem to understand this. As one quick African said recently, "You make us want to vomit more often than not. But we're stuck with you. Humankind will live or cease to live, depending on the choices that you Americans make."

Over two years ago, an official of the Arms Control and Disarmament Agency told me that the chances of avoiding nuclear war were less than half, and plummeting. They are still plummeting. Our Congress has just rejected the Non-Proliferation Treaty, which was, in effect, an agreement by eighty non-nuclear nations to cede responsibility for doomsday weapons to those powers irresponsible enough to build them and to use them. Like the United States. But the treaty was still rejected. It is that bad.

But it is that good also because people are coming onboard. Our young people, the most superb breed this country has yet produced, are coming onboard. And they are saying to the barons of industry and to the chiefs of government and military, "You don't respect us, because your values are not our values. You're ruining our country by abusing innocent people everywhere, and by threatening the world's peace. You must stop what you are doing, or you must go."

Yes, that trial meant hope—more hope than we need and more than we can use. Mary Moylan said on the stand that she went to Catonsville to celebrate life. And John Hogan said that he went to illustrate that people have a right to be left alone. Both these great people were really talking about truth and love and justice. That is to say, about life. See you at the sentencing.

October 30, 1968, *National Catholic Reporter*

Truth Creates Its Own Room

An open letter from the Baltimore County Jail to his brother Dan, published on December 6, 1968. Phil had recently read Soul on Ice, *the autobiography of Eldridge Cleaver, a political activist, revolutionary, and early leader of the Black Panther Party.*

Dear Dan:

I've just read Eldridge Cleaver's *Soul on Ice*, which an unusually honest dustjacket blurb calls "one of the discoveries of the 1960s." Providentially, Cleaver's book reached me during a period of jailhouse doldrums, when existence passed for living, and living was as appetizing as unseasonal oatmeal. Oddly enough, neither depression nor self-pity was the trouble. Rather, the trouble was a kind of moral exhaustion which reduced reality to an obscure and vapid common denominator. The world, people, and jail no longer stimulated me, and I seemed powerless to turn them on. For a time, at least, dullness and lethargy had their day.

Yet Cleaver snapped me out of it with his lucidity and outrage. Lucidity and outrage—a rare package, deplorably lacking in what masquerades as social criticism today. It was Simone Weil, I think, who observed that truth creates its own room, as though to take possession of a person. Cleaver performed such a service, dispelling the vacuum within me. As fundamentalist Christians would put it, "He performed a ministry for me."

Many things about this book move me. Generally, it is a raw and slashing attack upon American life, while preserving a delicate balance of humanity and humanness. Cleaver never insists that Whites become more than he has become, or that humanity is less possible to a White racist than to a Black man. No one can discount the obstacles he faced and overcame—poverty, Blackness, and a brilliance whose misguidance in early life made him a racist and a brute. "If I had not been apprehended," he wrote, "I would have slit some White throats."

Once back in prison, he began writing to capture an identity which he'd never really had. Writing forced him to read, and reading and writing both imparted the conclusion that life meant more than what he knew of himself, and of White America. From that turning point, he began to build an authentic humanity, as *Soul on Ice* testifies.

Cleaver's book and other similar studies are beginning to make a point with many Americans—that there is but one policy governing America's national and international life, a policy precisely tailored for expansionist capitalism. Which is to say, it is tailored to enrich further a predatory wealthy elite and to entrench further a somnolent middle class that serves to insulate the wealthy from change.

Nevertheless, the impression that lingered was nothing specific, just the intense drama of a man liberated by the honesty of his suffering. Saint Paul has a famous line telling how Christ learned obedience through his suffering. Some might think that referring this to Cleaver is odd, yet he strikes me as a man profoundly obedient to a truly human order—a man of acceptance as well as of determination. One does not develop such virtues except through suffering.

Malcolm X influenced him tremendously—today's Black Panthers are several logical steps beyond Malcolm's stillborn Organization of Afro-American Unity. When America grows up, it will treasure both men—both of whom won their humanity in jail; both of whom combined the visionary and activist roles; both passionate lovers of truth and justice; the one murdered, the other still precariously alive, destined for the leadership of his people, or for a racist bullet.

But I was telling about Cleaver's ministry to me. Despite freedom from uncommon problems in jail, I am susceptible to a common one—tedium. Now, tedium tends to feed upon drabness, routine, overcrowding; upon steel bars and body counts; isolation from community; issues and struggle. In effect, tedium tempts one to quit; to submit gracelessly and imperceptibly to cop-out; to relish appearances rather than reality; to think less, feel less and love less; to suspend life, growth, and Christianity for the duration.

Like most temptations that demean, tedium fits what seems, rather than what is, inviting one to stress the unnaturalness of confinement, bureaucratic rulebooks and rigidity, inmate hangups and custodial impersonality, moral and political uselessness, the total climate of futility and waste. No wonder that prisoners chalk off that portion of their lives, believing it barren of anything constructive. Extreme cases tend to despair—a lad killed himself at Lewisburg Penitentiary since I've been there. A long sentence and a burdensome confinement made him despondent—and powerless to cope with news of a younger brother's death in Vietnam.

Personally, tedium terrifies me as a kind of deadly abrasive which works on a person's spirit like wind and water on loose soil. The erosion that results becomes commonplace, and very nearly inevitable. To see people of intelligence (not uncommon in federal prisons) and far more innocent of crime than many of our public pillars (not uncommon either) lick their wounds and fan their resentments like punished children, mark time and feast upon distractions, longing uncritically for a society which has misused them—a society which they intend neither to hold accountable nor reform is a sense of depressing waste. I find myself vainly trying to discover in them a spark of constructive anger, but they appear to desire nothing so much as anonymity and normalcy after release.

The brush tars wide and indiscriminately, and I find myself often marked by it. Somebody said once that life consists of catching up with what one has done or going beyond it. I feel that the first case applies to me, requiring a sustained pondering of what I have done, and a present consistent with it. Otherwise, life might become a sterile compromise, setting at work a series of mysterious injuries among people depending on me. I have seen such compromises, and their effects, by men who acted well and courageously against injustice, never to recover from the consequences.

Life is more precious than liberty, one must admit, and the donation of life more difficult than the donation of liberty. But my conscience did not allow immolation, so I gave what was possible. Since resistance required trading liberty for imprisonment, imprisonment should be another way of extending resistance, and even of adding to it. It should give one the vantage point of being at the heart of moral conflict yet physically detached from it; of being at grips with what Saint John calls "the world" (the institutions of domination) yet removed from public struggle with them.

To appraise my situation from a merely political view is to go a long way toward destroying it. Friends commiserate with me and watch the political horizons anxiously, looking for a change of weather that would give strength to legal appeal or a better chance for executive clemency. They are clearly sympathetic, but not particularly perceptive. If I were the lowliest of draft resisters, buried anonymously in some federal prison, forgotten by everyone but parents and one or two friends, I would be contributing more to the peace than the most spectacular "dove" who makes headlines and rallies supporters, and whose exhortations are heard with apprehension even in the halls of government. "But God has chosen the foolish things of the world to shame the wise, and God has chosen the weak things of the world to shame the things that are strong" 1 Cor. 1, 27 seq.).

So, Cleaver has done me a service by giving me of his strength. His fight for manhood gives energy to my own, since in every case, that fight is an unfinished business. But one can face it better, knowing of another who had less to work with and becoming, in spite of that, a better person than I.

December 6, 1968, *Commonweal*

Liberation from Fear

As for myself, I fail to see how a society can be thrown into revolution except through massive civil disobedience, which in the case of America means that domestic and foreign business is rendered unprofitable, and hence inoperable. And I fail to see how extensive civil disobedience can be an effective factor unless the movement is built of people who are less concerned about power and more about justice; who are fearless but not rash; who are disciplined but not bureaucratic; who are patient but not dilatory; who are moral but not moralistic — in private and in public.

But above all, a movement must be built of those who would risk the jaws of the Beast, not in the prospect of being torn alive but rather in trust of their own weapons — truth, justice, freedom, love. Revolution is a time of personal and public purification if it is truly revolution, and the liberation principally sought after is a liberation from fear. Doesn't Scripture say something about perfect love casting out fear? Which may suggest that the chief obstacle to revolution is fear, or the fear to love. And revolution without vast resources of love will be a bloodbath and, at best, a mere shift in power.

1969, *New Politics*

Acts of Faith

Typed notes from January 1969 entitled "Statement."

To me, these acts [Baltimore and Catonsville] were ones of faith—another way of saying that they were acts of truth. I have always been fascinated by Christ's emphasis on truth, and by Gandhi's love of the truth that is God. Gandhi even subjected love to truth—God was truth to him before He was love. Or to put it another way, Gandhi believed that if a person was truthful, they were loving.

I suppose our acts attempted to say that people are really brothers and sisters, that they are accountable for other brothers and sisters, and that they must therefore resist evil in those holding power. It would seem to me that the first process in building a new society must be an attack upon those institutions of power that are obsolescent. To me, wealth as an institution is obsolescent; so are those institutions which legislate and protect wealth—the nation-state, industrial conglomerate, the middle-class church or synagogue, either capitalist or socialist economics, the military establishment. I maintain that the crisis has not made them obsolescent, that humanity has, and always has.

CU

Our Responsibility to Each Other

A liturgy written by Phil for May 4, 1969.

Opening Prayer

How many and how enormous are the tasks that you lay upon us, O Lord!

For if we were to stop genocide in one country while allowing people to kill one another in other countries, it would not be sufficient.

If we were to disarm nations but not to end the brutality with which the police attack Black people in some countries, brown people in others, Muslims in some countries, Hindus in others, believers in some countries, fascists in others, it would not be sufficient.

If we were to end police brutality, but not prevent the rich from wallowing in luxury while others starve, it would not be sufficient.

If we were to train people to understand the prophets while forbidding them to explore their consciences and ecstasies, it would not be sufficient.

How much, then, are we duty-bound to struggle, work, share, give, think, plan, feel, organize, resist, speak out, and hope on behalf of humankind.

Prayer of the Faithful

That we may bring to our world the light of Christ's liberation of man, and give glory to our Father, let us pray to the Lord.

That our work in our world may strengthen the spirit of man, let us pray to the Lord.

That the spirit of God will work through us, that we may take up our Cross and fulfill the world, let us pray to the Lord.

That the mission given us by Christ will not scare us away by its harsh demands of gentleness, let us pray to the Lord.

That mankind may receive its prophets with open receptivity and love, let us pray to the Lord.

That the people of God may recognize its responsibility to the people of Latin America, Asia, Africa, and our cities to preach the Word of God through example and bring them into a full share of the material benefits God has given us, let us pray to the Lord.

Let us understand, O Lord, that of all peoples of this Earth, you have given Americans the affluence, time, leisure, and history of resistance to right our country and to place our genius, our wealth, and our energies to the service of humankind.

CU

We Have Trouble with Surrender

Convicted in the Catonsville trial and having had all appeals denied, Phil and his co-defendants remained free on bail. Eventually, they were ordered to report to the authorities on April 9, 1970, to begin serving their prison sentences. Rather than surrender, four of The Catonsville Nine (Phil, Dan, Mary Moylan, George Mische) decided to go underground and elude the authorities as a further act of civil disobedience. David Eberhardt was facing prison for the Baltimore action and also agreed to go underground.

Phil and David were apprehended by the FBI on April 21, 1970. In May, George Mische was apprehended. Dan remained on the run until August 11, 1970. Mary Moylan would eventually surrender to authorities on June 20, 1979. The following is a statement issued by Phil and David Eberhardt.

According to present information, members of The Baltimore Four and The Catonsville Nine must surrender to federal marshals on Thursday, April 9. For us, the appeals process had run its course, followed by entrance into prison.

Under a fiction of justice, the government will now exact payment for our "crimes." Crimes against paper rather than people, crimes of blood and fire favoring life and condemning death, crimes of protesting an $85 million daily waste in a brutal, futile war; crimes of speaking truth to a nation bewildered by affluence and torn by racism and violence; crimes of stating that politics are profits, and that the two-party system is, in reality, the Property Party. In a word, crimes of hope, relationship, community, justice, freedom.

We have trouble with surrender, even as we have trouble with official notions of crime or justice. Because this government refuses to represent the poor, or Blacks, or students, it does not represent us. If it were truly representative, we would not be sent to jail, nor would it suppress our Black brothers, our sisters; send to battlefield murder or to death our young brothers; suck dry, for profit's sake, our poor brothers and sisters here and abroad. And so, it becomes a problem to us as it has to the remainder of the world, placing us all in a common dilemma of survival.

As proof of this, one need only advise Americans to look around. Breathe the air, search for clear water, savor the slums, pay more for less and less, reflect on the peace (and the arms race spiral that keeps it), watch the war engulf all of Southeast Asia and slowly gain force in our Latin American provinces. The signs of the times suggest an American Nightmare rather than an American Dream, from which literally no one is immune.

We will therefore not surrender to the officers of this government. Rejecting its custody, we will seek the custody of peace people, and resist one last time before jail. Then we will speak to honest, serious people of their common state of oppression, and their common fight for survival. Speak to them also of hope and integrity and community and nonviolent revolution.

We do not fear its sanctions—its censorship, its genius of wealth and research, its jails. But we do fear its distortion of truth, its hypocrisy of law and order, its perversion of justice, its freedom (to join the death march or remain passive before it). These we fear, but we will withstand them, and we will call upon others to resist.

CU

The Sinless One Continues to Haunt Me

The following excerpts were written by Phil while in Lewisburg Federal Penitentiary and appeared in his book Widen the Prison Gates.

May 9, 1970

I get another whistle from Control. It's like a summons from the White House—one does not ignore it lightly.

The associate warden has a strike manifesto in his hand. Have I seen it?

"Yes. I read it two days ago."

"Did you write it, or do you know who wrote it?"

"No. It has been passed around—several hundred prisoners have read it by now."

He breaks the dialogue to refer to the manifesto's language (educated), its demands (very demanding), its tone (nonviolent).

I disagree somewhat—its language is affected, its spelling bad. But the demands are good. One thing becomes clear. The prison administration abhors strikes and has decided not to have them.

"How can we be sure you have nothing to do with this?"

I laugh at him, a gesture that is, in warden–prisoner relationships, tactically unsound and even dangerous. Wardens do not forget being laughed at by inmates.

I tell him, with smug good humor, that if I were to organize a strike, I'd take six months to do it, and it would be done right. But, say I reassuringly, "Penal issues are not my bag. It's the scene outside that occupies me."

He seems satisfied, and we part cordially. I leave complacent—always a bad position.

June 16, 1970

Great readings in today's Eucharist. Hebrews 12:4, "In your struggle against sin, you have not yet resisted to the point of shedding your blood." Indeed, I have not, either for my own sins or for the sins of others. The Sinless One continues to haunt me: "Who submitted to such opposition from sinners" (12:3). The yardstick against which I must measure myself is not, supposedly, weaker people but the innocent who die needlessly everywhere, and the Innocent One Himself.

What becomes clearer as insanity mounts and we take off our last hours is not just that many men will die, for they are dying now in increasing numbers, but that some will have to die voluntarily—to restage the Crucifixion. God alone knows how many. It is an inexorable divine and human law—no life without death, no resurrection without Calvary. We had better believe it.

June 1970

I am beginning to understand where life comes from—not just from parents or from the table or from the bulk of human knowledge kicking around, so much of it distracting and useless. It comes from God's Word, which brings a person to fullness, as sun and rain bring a plant to harvest. "The Spirit alone gives life; the flesh is of no avail; the words that I have spoken to you are both spirit and life."

And so, quite against inclination, I invest time in the Gospel daily. It's not just that I hope thereby to get the Book into my guts, or to derive from it an intelligence of the heart. It is to drive back some of the darkness within, to shackle some personal devils, to put under higher control those mysterious deadly forces so incomprehensible to me, so resistant to *my* control. "Lord, that I might see!" Lord, I believe—help me with my unbelief! "When your eyes are sound, you have light for your whole body; but when the eyes are bad, you are in darkness."

The disaffection of concerned people with institutional religion lies in the fact that the Christian Church claims privilege by the Gospel without preaching it or living it. If the Church were true to the Gospel, privilege would be its last desire. It would fear property, condemn war, and oppose power with its life and blood.

As it stands, however, the Gospel the Church preaches is a precise statement of the lie it leads—a degenerate stew of behavioral psychology, affluent ethics, and cultural mythology, seasoned by nationalist politics. It distorts the Gospel, as the state distorts the Declaration of Independence. In fact, both rely heavily on rhetoric and propaganda to anesthetize their followers and guarantee their support.

One is forced literally to rely on oneself, and upon a minuscule number among humanity, to reach the conclusion that Christ's morality was so intensely human that it could be both nonviolent and revolutionary. He was the political man par excellence. The values He taught and lived were revolutionary ones: faith in the Father rather than in human power, and integrity, justice, freedom, love. Sooner or later the ruling elite had to notice him, had to react to his threat by executing him.

July 6, 1970

Sunday morning Eberhardt and I had walked down with Tom Melville after Mass before he returned to the farm. "Out of bounds," a lieutenant tells us. Then we arrive early for dinner—again out of bounds. We explain, but he is adamant, writing us up on report. That means court on Monday.

Prison court is a burlesque, like many of the courts outside. It's a defendant's word against an officer's, with other officers constituting the jury. The captain reads the charges, we give our version, and then step outside to await the verdict. The verdict comes—a week's restriction to quarters. We're already restricted unjustly behind a twenty-four-foot wall. Two-thirds of our day is spent behind locks and bars and the few hours remaining are subject to arbitrary limitations, criticisms, persecutions.

Apart from the contextual injustice of restriction to quarters, David and I have been taking it up the rear exit since arrival. I can bring readily to mind a dozen painful injustices and, with a little pondering, perhaps a dozen more. Obviously, a line has to be drawn—we have to destroy the illusion that we are both likely and easy targets. We tell the captain that we are rejecting punishment. He orders us to return to quarters and to work. We tell him we won't work, and he says, "You want segregation, huh?" We say no, we just won't take his punishment.

My cell in segregation is larger—six feet by twelve feet—than the one I share with David back in quarters. I have a sink, commode, pallet on the floor, and western exposure—the sun sets directly into my window. I have a Bible to nourish me if no food. And I have more peace and freedom than I've had since coming here. It's good to smell a little battle smoke again.

July 13, 1970

As of this moment I'm high on Saint John. Don't know whether it's my empty gut [Phil was on a fast protesting the treatment of political prisoners] or the shining floor—I've just wiped it up—or the Holy Spirit. But the Lord makes powerful good sense.

John threw me some big questions. In Chapter 7 some of the brethren berate Christ because He will not go up with them to the feast "to manifest" Himself. He turns on them with something resembling fierceness: "My time hasn't come yet. But your time is always here, and the world cannot hate you. But it hates me because I testify of it that its works are evil." By the "world" He meant the wealth, interlockings, contracts, secret deals, police and armies by which people in power insulate themselves from the wrath of the masses and a fall from power.

The world "hates" Him because He uncovers its lies, postures, viciousness, death. Later the world kills Him, representing in His death all men, insofar as they desire to dominate others rather than to serve and love Him.

Why doesn't the "world" of today, mostly embodied in the Superstate as its politician, "hate" more Christians?

July 14, 1970

The captain calls us, and we go to his courtroom office, escorted by four huge guards, like two sailboats brought to haven by battleships.

We went nose to nose. It was inmate-to-cop all the way. The captain sneered about "playing games" by fasting in solitary. Then he charged that harassment was legitimate in light of my attempts to get contraband information in and out of this prison. I told him the attempts were in his mind—where was the evidence of moving contraband? He then accused me of wanting to make a deal. I said yes—either they let political prisoners alone or I hang on indefinitely. And I got up to return to solitary.

Back in the cell, I am nicely settled into some work when the guards squadron us again, this time to see the lieutenant. The warden has ordered us to move to the hospital, where we can be under "exact medical supervision." The fasting is getting to them, I reflect, especially in a bucko of my age and notoriety.

August 11, 1970

The news has just come in—no chance of rumor this time—that the FBI captured Dan this morning on Block Island, right off the coast of Rhode Island. They have taken him to Providence for arraignment, to be followed by quick transport here. Relief mingles with the shock and disappointment.

Quite spontaneously, I think of something from Scripture—"It is an awful thing to fall into the hands of the living God." Indeed it is: A person is a fool to ignore either His mercy or His judgment. But it is not necessarily an awful thing to fall into the hands of Caesar. One has normal human apprehensions about it, certainly. To risk Caesar's justice, or to experience it firsthand, is an enterprise that tests one's humanity, one's obedience to God and to man. A fear-full enterprise, from which most of us shrink. But to be Caesar's friend might mean, in these dolorous times, being God's enemy. Given America's crimes, keeping the law is rejecting Christianity.

Dan's faith told him this, and immediately he made the point clear. The issue was not fugitive status versus going to prison but resistance to Caesar, in whatever context resistance could provide.

August 17, 1971

Inmates dislike prison guards roundly, and in not a few cases hate them. There is a certain inevitability about this, flowing from the relationship between officers and prisoners. Society punishes inmates through their guards, expecting the guards to administer its disgust and rejection. Inmates, in turn, hold guards accountable for society's abhorrence. The result is an existential conflict, a quiet and sometimes not-so-quiet war.

WTPG

Following the Man of Calvary

On August 25, 1970, Phil was transferred to Danbury Federal Correctional Institute.

Dorothy Day has written that "we ought to fill the jails with our young men." One must remember that Dorothy's hope is in the Kingdom of Christ and not in any Great Society [President Lyndon B. Johnson's ambitious but ultimately unsuccessful plan to eliminate poverty, reduce crime, and protect the environment]. She lives her life around the belief that one builds justice by being just, and by allowing God to make of it what He will. There is no other way to eliminate injustice, she asserts, except by accepting it joyfully and positively and by giving it a chance to heal itself at every turn. Catholic Workers therefore have little interest in telling society what it must do. They consider it to be far more important to do what *they* must do.

But practically speaking, the government is not about to fill its jails with young men. It wouldn't even have the support to do so, since this war itself hasn't any popular support. Also, its jails are already filled, though not with war resisters. And building more jails might jeopardize the government's already diminishing popularity.

This is not to say that I want the jails filled from the anti-war movement or that imprisonment by itself is a mark of serious resistance. Perhaps we could say simply that no militant can solve the problem of consequences without accepting them in the course of events, that a person is truly of the Movement when his resistance has become indifferent to jail, separation, loneliness, humiliation, loss of financial security and career satisfaction.

There is jail on both sides of the walls. One treats the street as a jail, therefore, and acts to free it. One cannot avoid action in order to avoid prison, since one is already in prison. The thing is to act against prison wherever one encounters it.

The Lord's admonition inspires this ramble; the "for My sake" means for the sake of humans, because Christ is human; the Body of Christ is the body of humankind. To paraphrase: If you dare to be a human by taking the cause of humanity (the majority of people historically have been oppressed), you will be jailed, brought before officialdom, hated and perhaps killed. Why? Because you threaten the domination of the powerful, who have won their ability to dominate at the expense of the poor and the slavery of everyone. Especially themselves.

"Be on your guard"—the classic Gospel admonition of alertness, waiting for the Lord to manifest His need and the need of another, particularly for a suffering brother or sister, in the contemporary version of the prostitute, publican, and leper (Black woman, addict, homosexual, Vietnamese student). But waiting for the Lord requires not only alertness but also a clarity of mind and a resolution of will, an integrity in one's person that is capable of "telling the Good News" to the powerful—to those who live lies and punish with more lies.

December 1970

When Dan entered the Jesuits, he quickly superseded everyone else in the family in impact, becoming in fact a substitute father. It is impossible to explain in detail why this became so for me especially. I was searching for ideals and direction, and he supplied them. His life struck me as eminently worthwhile; it had a warm and lofty quality about it, yet it was not so remote as to be inimitable. I held him in awe, in the sense that the more I faced him, the more I had to face myself. The gap in quality between our two lives was so wide as to be intolerable. I could not endure myself and do nothing about myself.

After the army I entered training for the priesthood, the best formula we Catholics were familiar with for sacrifice, service, self-perfection. Moreover, Dan had tried it—and look at the man he had become!

No need to retread the ground walked on since. We have learned, I suppose, that following the Man of Calvary was more than we bargained for. We learned eventually that personal or institutionalized virtue was sterile unless applied in public; and on the other hand, that death to self was vain and pompous unless it invited ridicule, risk, prison, death itself. In sum, we learned that the virtuous man was also a public servant who articulated the fact that one might have to die for others to live.

WTPG

Resistance Is Essential

The following was written on the first Sunday of Lent, 1971, from Danbury Federal Correctional Institution. On January 12, 1971, while in prison, Phil had been indicted yet again on new charges by a grand jury in Harrisburg, Pennsylvania, for conspiring to sabotage government buildings and kidnap President Richard Nixon's National Security Advisor, Henry Kissinger. Also indicted were Elizabeth McAlister, Eqbal Ahmad, Neil McLaughlin, Anthony Scoblick, Mary Cain Scoblick, Ted Glick, and Joseph Wenderoth. Ted Glick severed his case from the others, leaving the remaining defendants to be called The Harrisburg Seven.

The spurious new charges were part of FBI Director J. Edgar Hoover's personal vendetta against the Berrigans. Part of this indictment and the subsequent trial would utilize personal letters between Phil and Liz, a further attempt at harassment and intimidation. If convicted of all charges, Phil would spend decades in prison.

Sometimes I write simply to gain fortitude. Writing helps me grip reality and sanity a little more firmly. Perhaps that's all fortitude is—a tenacious grip on sanity.

It has both a rational and a faithful aspect to it. Reason asserts that life has conflict and that one becomes most alive in nonviolent struggle *for* life and *against* death, *for* man and *against* his debasement. Faith asserts that Christ is human because He was first God, and that in Him humanity becomes possible. A professor of theology might put it that way. But I need to relate to experience. I am into my eighteenth month of jail, with recent confirmation of a six-year sentence overriding an appeal in Richmond. As further proof that my leaders love me, there is the prospect of an indefinite sentence, perhaps life imprisonment, if I am convicted at Harrisburg this fall.

So I submit to myself that it is one thing to know in one's head the ponderous vindictiveness of federal justice and another to live with it year upon year behind bars. Periodically my whole being rebels against such a present and such a future. I vomit it up emotionally and psychologically, trying desperately to swallow my nausea of spirit. I need to think that our technocrats enjoy only tenacious control (despite the evidence).

Today is the first Sunday of Lent. Lent recalls a number of happenings from sacred history: The forty days Moses spent preparing himself for the Law; the long Jewish exile in the desert; Christ's prayer and fasting before His temptations. And above all, Lent gives life to the grandeur and portent of Christ's prophecy. As Luke writes: "We are now going up to Jerusalem; and all that is written by the prophets will come true for the Son of Man. He will be handed over to the foreign power. He will be mocked, maltreated, and spat upon. They will flog him and kill him."

A question seldom squarely met (Americans, Christian or not, have perfected a facility for avoiding difficult questions): What does "going up to Jerusalem" mean today? And what of another passage, this time from Matthew: "This very night all of you will run away and leave me, for the Scripture says, God will kill the shepherd and the sheep of the flock will be scattered."

I take it that what Christ had in mind was that we be human, even as He was. But how does one act like a human—and not like a lemming—when humankind faces extinction, when there is a scarcity of humans? When one's country is the planet's Public Enemy Number One?

Common sense tells me (so does faith) that word and act are human only when they are one. Common sense tells me that the profession of life is an unalterable resistance to the high and mighty, who pose as patrons of man while they destroy him. Resistance, common sense reminds me, is essential. Without it one cannot realize humanity in oneself or in others, only illusion, euphoria, comfort, escape.

Resistance will outrage the high and mighty, who tolerate such convictions neither from Christ nor from any of us. Dissent they will ridicule smugly; impetuosity or passion is forgivable—at least the first time. If contrition is not forthcoming, however, an apparatus more frightening than ridicule is trucked out—indictments, exorbitant bail, collusion between prosecution and bench (conspiracy of common interest), an automatic conviction, punitive sentencing. If dissent remains inflexible and un-submissive, the power will invade even the penitentiary—monitoring rebellious thoughts and words, presenting the wretched rebel with new charges, new courts, new trials, new convictions, new sentences. In this setting Jerusalem becomes Atlanta, Leavenworth, Lewisburg; and Calvary becomes a permanent cell. And from these places one makes whatever resurrection one can.

So, we *do* have the naked character of American power to deal with, and we *do* have the Lord's words to offer the relevant questions. "We [the disciples and I]," the Lord says, "are going up to Jerusalem." But, "He [the Son of Man alone] will be handed over to a foreign power." If "He," why not the disciples as well? Again—is this government automatically our government, simply because we are citizens? Can this government be anything but a foreign power to a Christian? What is more normal for a Christian than to be handed over to a foreign power? Or what is more abnormal for a Christian than a truce with a foreign power, the illegitimate state authority?

So faith tells me. Which is not to say that it is ahead of, or behind, emotions or psyche. They are probably joined together. I perceive it and I labor to respond. Millions of dead Indochinese and Americans have a voiceless request—that we come alive and stop the murder, that we indeed live like humans by living for humans. And if that means rebirth through a prison cell, where life is incubated for succeeding generations—then, right on. How else shall we see the twenty-first century?

Until peace people master fear of themselves and that of other people, they have no hope of creating a movement, much less a revolutionary movement. When one fears himself, he fears others, oppressor and victim alike. Maybe this is why the Lord asked repeatedly, "What are you afraid of?"—implying of course that what you fear isn't there, it's not real. And it's not worthy of you, if you intend to be human.

Or look at it another way. When peacemakers fear dishonesty in their rhetoric more than they fear consequences, their fears will have become human, inspiring a clarity of passion and a style of genuine service. Camus put it well: "What is needed is a grouping of men resolved to speak out clearly and pay up personally."

But in the concrete, one cannot speak about fear without speaking of its focus in the Movement—fear of consequences. Everywhere one turns, in or out of jail, with prisoners, with Movement people, with militant clergymen, dove politicians, well-meaning bureaucrats of all denominations and hues, the big question is, "What will it [action] cost me?" Rarely is the question turned around to become "What will it cost me if I don't act?" The lunacy of present life inspires the question, and usually the answer.

WTPG

Withstanding the Attacks

April 1971

The government's libel concerning their ideas of the relationship between Sister Elizabeth McAlister and me is not in the least astonishing. It has the vicious consistency of all the efforts to fabricate a case against The Harrisburg Seven. Now the government brands two of the defendants as charlatans who stealthily denied their religious vows.

Our relationship lies, of course, outside the scope of the indictment against us. So it would seem irrelevant to "answer" such allegations. We have nothing to confess, nothing to deny, no cause for shame. We have done no violence to conscience, nothing to scandalize or injure others, nothing to violate trust in ourselves.

Had we in fact so acted, logic would have dictated that we abandon service and resistance and avoid risk in prison, that we flee the country before my incarceration and become safe spectators.

Pope John XXIII once wrote that governments are held to the same morality as individuals. Our lives speak for themselves. We welcome a comparison—by the Church and by the American people.

May 20, 1971

The big boys never learn; they finish one disaster and plunge into another. They blunder in their courts just as the military blunders in Indochina, bullies of "justice" and bullies of "goodwill." It is hard not to fulminate about the Ogre, his power, his "justice"; hard to cultivate an attitude more human than rage.

As national affairs deteriorate, as the country sinks into an uneasy stupor of shame and apprehension, the Ogre replaces bad leadership with worse, relying more and more on force to convince the people that the opposite of what is, is. And out of this comes a message that more and more Americans understand: "If you don't like the way we're running things, keep quiet, leave the country, or go to jail."

It reeks: abuse of the law and offenses against human rights—electronic and human bugging, intimidation of witnesses and defendants, smear tactics, strong-arm investigation and prostitution of the grand jury. One of our lawyers, experienced in political trials, confesses to being shocked at the excesses of the prosecution. "It [repression] is really happening here," he says sadly.

WTPG

Marriage with Liz

Elizabeth McAlister and I married on April 7, 1969, in Saint George's Episcopal Church in the Bronx [they privately exchanged vows]. In a conversation that evening we had become certain of a love we had long shared, and we accepted it joyfully and gratefully. We married for life and welcomed what life together might entail.

We accepted each other as adult, baptized Christians and exchanged our consent. And marveled at what God had given us, as gratuitous as grace. No one else was present, and at that time no one else knew of our decision.

I was free on bail then, following seven months in jail after a draft action. Resistance to the Asian war was not so much a passion as a way of life for me. Elizabeth perceived this, supported it, and shared it. Had her Order not threatened her with ejection, her involvement and conflict with the law might well have matched mine.

From the outset, therefore, there was a profound, largely unspoken agreement on the nature of our marriage. When we accepted each other, that included acceptance of our work in resistance and its consequences: discipline, risk, separation, jail. We understood this. It was unnecessary to discuss it or to make explanations, requests, plans. We had married each other, but before that we had married all who suffered in consequence of war, poverty, racism. Now, we believed the two contracts (to humanity and to each other) were complementary and mutually enriching. From the start we looked upon our marriage as a religious and political act.

Neither of us considered abandoning our vocations. We had great sympathy for those who had voluntarily left their vocations and those who had been forced to leave on discovery of love for another. But that was not for us. Why leave? We had a fundamentalist Gospel sense of Christian conscience, of freedom, of social responsibility. We had experienced firsthand the rigors and riches of celibacy, having lived it for many years. But we also felt that God had given us our love, not that we should sacrifice all we had known and loved and lived, whether Church, vocation, or community, nor that we should insulate ourselves from suffering jeopardy and jail. No, He had given us our love to open up for us vital new areas of conscience and service within our vocations.

That is to say, we tried to decide in favor of people, but no less in favor of the Church. It had nurtured us, educated us, giving us the Word and the Bread of Life. Neither of us, as our lives testified, was a stranger to freedom of conscience, and we owed even that to the Church, however imperfectly it realized freedom and practice.

In our view, and according to the rights of conscience, priests should volunteer celibacy, if they choose; or marry, if they choose. But marriage does not nullify their priesthood. By the same reasoning, a nun should be accorded similar rights. The issue is not marriage or celibacy but mature fidelity to the Gospel, in contemplation and loving witness.

We believe that the choice we have taken can contribute to a more intense service for the victims of war, exploitation, color. We believe that married love can embrace people everywhere, and that a wider love can renew and restore married love.

Our marriage, it seems to us, addresses questions to both the Church and to married Christians. To the Church: When will optional celibacy be accorded priests and nuns? When will nonviolent resistance to war (and not the constant preparation for thermonuclear war) be encouraged by official example? To married Christians: Is it Christian to exclude love for humankind and service of humankind because one has taken a spouse? Can one be truly married in Christ without being married to his brothers and sisters?

These were questions we believed we should face. Our decision to marry offered good Gospel sense to us, good human sense, good politics. We found it severely demanding, but profoundly rewarding as well. We denied ourselves frequent meetings, we never considered leaving the country or evading prison—even though such alternatives were tempting and possible. What helped us, without a doubt, was discipline—another gift from the Church.

As for the public, we wish Americans to reflect on the issues of freedom and peace implicit in our marriage. We love each other deeply, but that fact will not deter us from the sacrifices required for peace. So, we pray our country will choose peace, and will gladly and freely pay the price of peace.

The future remains obscure for Elizabeth and me. I am serving six years for destroying a few hundred Selective Service files—government hunting licenses to kill. Elizabeth is threatened with jail—how long a sentence, only time and the ambiguous character of American "justice" will tell. That "justice" ignores American war crimes, pins medals on those who kill, exonerates its Medinas [a reference to Captain Ernest Medina, U.S. Army, court-martialed for his role in the 1968 My Lai massacre in which U.S. forces killed approximately 500 unarmed civilians], gives immunity to the architects of genocide, and imprisons those who resist and refuse to kill.

If Elizabeth goes to jail, our separation becomes complete, relieved only by the "privilege" of writing (under government censorship, of course).

None of this will be news to us, none of it particularly unsettling or depressing. We foresaw it, anticipated it, and sought to prepare ourselves for it. But neither prospect nor reality has made it less costly.

Elizabeth and I have been separated over many months, and many others for longer. However long our ordeal, it is our present contribution to peace. The separations of war must be matched by the separations for peace; those profiting from war by those sacrificing for peace; those dead tragically by those alive responsibly; those licensed to kill by those imprisoned for not killing.

May 1971, WTPG

Smear and Ridicule

One of the ways really to learn basic civics is to be forced to feel in your bones and heart the corruption of government. Our leaders have done their utmost to smear and ridicule Liz and me; they have shadowed us, seized our correspondence, bugged our phones, sent their agents to gossip about us like hags over a back fence, leaked allegations to the press of our "squalid" affair. Despite their efforts, however, we had regained some measure of control over our love, in the hope of disclosing it later with dignity. Now control is ours no more. Friends, both defendants and reporters, have collaborated with our enemies and picked up their predatory habits. Our friends have done a bit of whoring. They have picked up with Mother State as one picks up with an ex-wife for a night of pleasure.

Where Liz and I go from here, in a way useful to Church and public, is anybody's guess. But we will find it richer for the experience of having been blocked. We will proceed hopefully with more wisdom regarding newsmen, and more love regarding defendants. In a real sense, security doesn't rest on much else.

WTPG

The USA v. Philip Berrigan

A public statement issued by Phil about the Harrisburg indictment.

I will not respond to this indictment as the government would have me. It is a potpourri of false charges, absurd allegations, and acts labeled crimes by the law, obligations by thinking men. As a legal document, this indictment is about as sane — or insane — as our government's Indochina war. In fact, one is the stepchild of the other: legal overkill following military overkill. Both are devious, ruthless, mad. The Indochinese desire their independence; we desire an end to the murder. That makes us criminals together, and Washington punishes us as criminals — they by American firepower, we by this indictment.

I will regard it, therefore, as a piece of legal pathology supporting our military pathology in Southeast Asia. And I will resist it as I resist the war.

May 1971, CU

Revolution, Berrigan Style

Dan and I have been led to different roads than others, ones that seem to us more at grips with this awful war and the insanity of our country. To stop this war, I would give my life tomorrow, and I can't be blamed if I have little time for those who want to run ads in the *New York Times* [some critics of the war ran anti-war ads in newspapers]. Both Dan and I are seriously dealing with clergymen and laymen, professionals and family people, who have come to the point of civil disobedience and the prospect of jail and are even foundering with the convictions beyond that point. We will either witness from jail, or we will go ahead with social disruption, including nonviolent attacks upon the machinery of this war.

In a word, I believe in revolution, and I hope to continue making a non-violent contribution to it. In my view we are not going to save this country and mankind without it. And I am centrally concerned with the Gospel view that the massive suffering of this war and American imperialism around the world will be confronted only by people who are willing to go with suffering as the first move to justice.

August 1971, *The Los Angeles News Advocate*

Obeying God's Word Can Get You Killed

I read Luke last night: "Happy are those who hear the word of God and obey it." It strikes me once again, almost as much as the first time, that obeying God's Word is very likely to get one killed. It accomplished that for Christ, who was God's Word, and whose actions were His Words. God's Word is a living force, and it will ensure life if it is lived. But it also provokes death, meets death in confrontation, and invariably if only temporarily loses. Let those who hear God's Word and try to hear it better, along with those who obey it and strive to obey it more perfectly—let them be forewarned. It can get you killed.

WTPG

We Constitute the Church in Chains

On August 6, 1971, the anniversary of Hiroshima, a group of federal prisoners at Danbury, Connecticut, began a hunger strike, which became a prison-wide work strike to protest the following: (1) the denial of parole to Dan and Phil Berrigan; (2) the operations of the federal parole board; (3) the fate of Vietnamese political prisoners, especially those confined to the tiger cages of Côn Son [brutal prison cages used by American forces in Vietnam]. Five days later, Philip Berrigan and ten other men participating in the hunger strike were transported to the federal prison hospital in Springfield, Missouri. There, under round-the-clock guard in isolated cells, they continued a liquids-only fast for a month.

During that time, the local bishop, William Baum, paid Philip Berrigan a pastoral visit and asked him to write a letter containing reflections on questions of priesthood and world justice. Bishop Baum was soon to attend the Synod of Catholic Bishops in Rome to discuss such questions. The following was written in August 1971 and later appeared in Commonweal.

Dear Bishop Baum,

Here are the few ideas I promised you. They are qualified, of course, by my status and by the two years I have already served. But I possessed them before imprisonment, my books are full of them, and it goes without saying, I believe them profoundly enough to stake my life on them. I have not found many people who can say that about their ideas.

So if you find the following negative, caustic, angry—remember that they come from one who has questioned domestic racism and modern war for ten years; who has resisted militarism and war-making repeatedly; who has experienced not only prison but also solitary confinement and long fasts; who has endured the charade of three political trials and who faces a fourth; and who probably will be in and out of prison for the remainder of his life. In sum, my experience has been out of the ordinary, and it comes purely from attempts to answer the question "What does Christ ask of me?"

Despite the fact that we come from different frames of reference, and that the Berrigan view of the Gospel (Dan's and mine) is radically different from the hierarchy's, we will not admit that our own responsibilities differ from yours. In fact, we might even suggest that the bishops have a deeper obligation to costly witness than we do because of the magisterium, their pastorship and charism. I tend to state the matter bluntly. On the issue of modern war, the hierarchy's default is very nearly total; it is so bad, in effect, that a nuclear exchange would find bishops unprepared to discuss anything but the morality of defending a fallout shelter with a shotgun.

Apart from these observations, which I offer only as an introduction, please convey our love and fraternity (Dan and mine) to the pope. It strikes me that we speak for those unable to do so, those sisters and brothers imprisoned around the world—priests, religious, laity—in Latin America, Africa, Europe, Indochina, the Marxist world.

We constitute the Church in chains—advocates of resistance to naked power, disproportionate wealth, racism, war-making. We want to express our fidelity to the Church and to the Chair of Peter, even as we sorrow over Christian myopia, hardness of heart, and even cowardice.

With these preliminaries, let me offer a few general observations as well. It impresses me that thinking in the Church today—now that we're over the Vatican II euphoria—is stereotyped, cautious, quasi-despairing. Bishops, theologians, and clergy are obviously operating under the housekeeping assumption: from top to bottom, from Rome to parish, more Synods, councils, democracy, and guitars will see us through present-world crises. We operate as though, under a divine and magical star, we will muddle through with minimal losses while grace and providence work for us—providing, however, we pretend hard enough that nuclear overkill does not exist, that genocide in Indochina has not been carried out, that the North Atlantic community does not control half of the world's wealth, that wealth and power are not identified with the White world, and poverty and desperation are not identified with the so-called colored world.

Those Catholics—clergy and laity—who have expressed disillusionment with such realities by leaving the Church altogether are leisurely marking time, maintaining a low profile, avoiding controversy, shoring up obsolescent structures, talking a species of ecclesiastical doublespeak, and rejecting any involvement in the social horrors of the day. Apparently, they take lightly the admonition of a witness like Paul: "Bear the burdens of one another, and you will have fulfilled the law of Christ."

Implicit in attitudes like these, shockingly pervasive as they are, is a dreadful and ill-defined fear—fear that we're not going to make it; fear that the Church will go down with the Powers of this world; fear of questioning, initiative, creativity, courage; fear of sacrifice, loneliness, criticism; fear finally of self, of neighbor, of Gospel, of Christ. I remember President [Lyndon B.] Johnson saying, with an off-the-cuff honesty quite foreign to him, "Peace is going to demand more than we counted on!" In the same manner, Catholics are discovering that Christ will demand more than we counted on. And generally the thought fills us with dread.

The Church in America—in fact, in the West as a whole—has accepted as religion a kind of cultural syncretism, culminating in near-perfect allegiance to the state. Not a few of its more prominent bishops have waited upon the presidency like court jesters. And now the culture is being violently challenged, and the state doesn't so much govern as rule by force. To whom do we turn?

A case in point is the Catholic response to the Indochina war. It is a classic case of burning incense to Caesar. After twenty-two years' involvement in Indochina; after millions of Indochinese deaths; after war expenditures of $300 billion; after documented ecocide and genocide; after all this, thirty-two American bishops have finally condemned the immorality of the war. In a tragedy of this magnitude, worldwide in its ramifications, the American Church, supposedly the most vital expression of universal Catholicism, has mustered thirty-two tepid episcopal voices, most of them recent. This, despite crushing evidence of the war's illegality. Why so long for episcopal word, why so late and feeble? So late, in fact, that few listen and few care.

Despite the clarity of [Pope] Paul VI's stand, despite constitutional protections, no bishop has challenged the illegality of the war in a serious fashion; no bishop has broken patently immoral laws (the apostles were martyred for refusing to obey the law); no bishop has advocated nonviolent resistance to the war. And only two or three bishops have visited Catholic resisters in jail, at least two of them virtually apologizing for their action: "This visit is a spiritual work of mercy, which I would perform for any of my flock." More to the point would be an explanation of why they themselves were not in jail.

Furthermore, no bishop has questioned the marriage of Big Business and Big Military and Big Government, and how the marriage results in government by and for the wealthy and powerful. No bishop has condemned the rape of the developing world, nor the arms race and its horrid weapons, nor American arms salesmanship, nor the division of the world by superpowers.

On the contrary, the American episcopacy has docilely and silently stood by while their countrymen and spiritual sons established the American empire and ruled it with ruthless might. They stood by as spectator, or advocate, while their country plunged into perpetual hot and cold warring, spent one and a quarter trillion dollars on war and weapons since 1946, and filled up Arlington National Cemetery with the dead of Korea, the Dominican Republic, and Indochina. And yet, the Church they lead, like the Savior, has come "to give life, and to give it more abundantly." What a gross irony!

Perhaps you might perceive my difficulty in speculating about the priesthood, and how it might serve man as physician and prophet. For who will finally legislate as to training, experience, freedom? And who will provide what is most crucial of all—example? The men and women who can address the subject realistically are concerned mainly with witnessing against institutionalized terror and death—and they are in severe jeopardy or jail.

Thinking Catholics make little distinction between treatment by church and state. They know that both desire malleability and conformity, that both are self-righteous and dogmatic. The understanding from this quarter is simply this: both church and state are vast, sprawling bureaucracies which share an insufferably arrogant assumption that they are the fundamental answers to the human condition. The understanding, further, is that, despite claims to the contrary, church and state have brought Western civilization to its nadir and have destroyed other civilizations in the process.

Critics have learned or are learning in swelling numbers from history as well as from the Gospels that nothing much makes sense except death to self and conversion to Christ and brother. All the virtues exemplified by the Lord—poverty, freedom and responsibility; the politics of community; willingness to risk jail and death for the exploited person, all these attack head-on the conceptions and realities of bureaucracies whether in church or state. The goals of bureaucracy are simply not the goals of Christ.

To apply all this seriously to contemporary problems of the priesthood—especially as an American—is enormously difficult, simply because we are so cut off from the mind and life of Christ. About all one can do is fumble with a few critical questions, and then labor with the complications of the responses.

The Catholic priest in America, and in the West generally, is more of a cultural phenomenon than he is a Gospel man. He is nationalistic, White supremacist, and uncritical toward affluence and its source. His training reflects nuances of these cultural fixations, but, beyond that, it schools him merely in neutrality toward life. By that I mean, he tends to take a purely institutional view of threats to life, whether they be its abuse or destruction. Indeed, if he is sensitive, he will go through immense pretensions to escape such brutalities. Or if he is hardened, he will advocate them or remain casual in face of them.

Therefore, the problem becomes how to instill conviction strong enough to resist dehumanization in himself, in others, in structures. How to instruct him in nonviolence as a way of life, as mark of the "new man," as instrument of human revolution and social regeneration? How to teach him the realities of power in all its nuances, from the will to dominate others to the will to exploit whole nations and peoples? How to toughen him so that he will understand and accept persecution, contempt, ostracism, jail, or death on account of conscience and above all on account of the suffering brother? How to acquaint him with such a sensitivity to human rights and dignity that he will test violence in every turn of his life—in himself, in the culture, in the state? How to convince him that Christ's man must integrate word and act, in full recognition that this might lead him to death, even as it did his Lord?

I don't know, because one can neither teach the above nor administer it. But the Church can beg the grace of God, the Church can provide the setting; even though it be modern catacombs, the Church can begin, realizing that her life must always constitute beginnings, and never endings. And if such fidelity means a vocation of opposition to Powers and Principalities as they operate in government and in the circle of prestige for which the government exists, so be it. If it means the outlawry of the Church, persecution, the Lord spoke of that too: "The time will come when those who kill you will think they are doing a service to God." But in the process, the Church will serve humanity, would even help to give humanity a future on this planet which it could not otherwise have.

As for the impending deliberations on world justice and peace, I have anguished questions about them. Do the American bishops accept the implications of their country's control over half of the world's productive capacity and finance? Do they realize that, despite our affluence, we have institutionalized poverty for perhaps one-quarter of our own people, plus millions in the developing world? Can they comprehend that war, particularly modern war, decides what nation or security block will control the profits? Do they understand that a few hundred American corporations, with hundreds of billions in assets and international holdings, are empires in their own right, exerting political and economic dominion wherever they are?

To deliberate justice and peace while overlooking such realities would be ignorant and dishonest. Just as it would be dishonest to deny that while most men starve, most bishops live in comfort and affluence, welcome the dividends of offending corporations, and remain discreetly silent before the excesses of capitalism.

In closing, I hope and pray this letter is a source of help to you, and not a cause for pain and shock. You are an unusual man and Christian—intelligent, open, compassionate. Obviously, you love the Church as I do. But before the tragedy and ruin of the times we must love the Church more—enough to criticize honestly and charitably, enough to pick up heavier burdens, enough to lose everything in order that others may discover life. In essence, what would the wretched of the Earth have us do to offer them hope, to lift from them the horrors of war and starvation, to extend a sense of dignity and destiny in God and human community?

Our prayers go with you. And our wishes for the light, the strength, the peace of Christ.

May 26, 1972, *Commonweal*, FTLW, CU

Fasting in Prison

I feel strong and clear-headed despite a weight loss of fifteen pounds. No big deal, I can afford it. Last night I dreamed of food all night—or so it seemed. This is my fourth fast of a week or more, and I don't recall such hunger pangs or such dreams.

The local bishop, William Baum, pays a pastoral visit. I bring him up to date, and he listens patiently. At one point he interjects mildly, "You see this as your witness, don't you?" Obviously, he didn't see "my" witness as his also, or possibly that of other Christians.

He is one of the new breed of bishops gingerly appointed by Rome. They generally know speculative theology, relish the Scriptures, are kind and not dictatorial men. But they are criminally ignorant of history, other cultures, the poor, entrenched power, human tragedy and triumph. Their mystique has no *politique* and is therefore doomed.

They recognize no flex in the Gospel, no pain, no dialectic. They know as little of naked power as the rich know of morality. And so they have little grasp of what underlies death or desolation in Pakistan or Indochina, no yardstick with which to gauge our common responsibility. Bishop Baum made it clear that he would publicize no judgment on me or our position. The genius of a successful churchman is to remain neutral even over life and death.

And yet Bishop Baum would and did visit me; most American bishops would not, given the opportunity. They offer a commentary on the American hierarchy more astringent than any I could possibly make.

September 8, 1971

We began eating yesterday; after thirty days it's bound to be a disturbing experience. Temperate as we were, some of us felt distress, and one or two guys were up most of the night, burping at both ends. We thought the doctors would descend on us like French governesses, clucking of soup and bland food. Just the contrary; they kept their distance and sent in the ordinary, heavy, greasy institutional food. But nearly everyone exercises faithfully and I expect will conquer the indigestion.

Liz [McAlister] and Bill Bender came yesterday, a particularly joyous sight for Ted [Glick] and me. One of their many services to us is a measure of tough, blunt talk about the trial's complexity, about the welfare of the defendants, about relationships with lawyers. Having Ted and me here fasting has activated some and weakened others. Whatever the situation, unity in the case is currently transparent and fragile.

Liz had seen Representative [Robert] Kastenmeier of Wisconsin, who heads a House subcommittee on prisons. He knew nothing, I mean nothing, of conditions in federal prisons, let alone parole board operations. But he appeared open and willing. Representative James Symington [of Missouri] is expected tomorrow. And on the weekend, Representative Bill Anderson [of West Virginia].

A lot of this work is attributable to Liz. It is not because of my being in prison or my dedication to these issues that she works so hard. Her performance is the same with any issue or project.

WTPG

Resistance, Liberation, and Fear

So, we spent about five weeks at Springfield Penitentiary in a segregated wing, and all the defendants [members of The Harrisburg Seven released on bail] visited us at least once, plus several of the lawyers. I think it is fair to say that everyone overreacted to our resistance and the official response to it. Yet the discomfort associated with a long fast, and the patience with which we heard our visitors out, seemed to us a source of reassurance and even liberation. In the end, all sympathized, and Eqbal and Liz worked like dogs to publicize our attempts.

Ours was the first challenge within memory to the parole board, which, the next time around, handed out paroles as if they were going out of style. Liz was instrumental in awakening a House subcommittee on federal prisons, and though its efforts at investigation were half-hearted and superficial, it was another first.

But most important, we acquainted federal prisoners with the idea that resistance to the parole board's psychological abuse was a good part of valor and a better part of politics. Before, it was unheard of to intentionally reject parole. Several friends are now doing it. They're saying, "Take your parole and stick it!"

Ted Glick and I returned from Missouri charged up, more than ever determined to confront nonviolently the disgusting conduct of government in this indictment. From somewhat successful measures to resist parole board repression we conclude that essentially the same resistance ought to guide us at Harrisburg.

The government is colossally wrong; the government is violent; the government is employing its courts as a legal force to back up its military force.

The government's barbaric war in Indochina needs Harrisburg. Its arrogance of power could end in an unresisted license to wage total war—and perhaps later, thermonuclear war. Of this we are convinced.

October 1971

The last World Series game is on; my conferees are out to watch it, leaving the dorm oddly quiet. I sit on my bunk and try to pray over the Beatitudes. They are a synopsis of all revelation, Christ's manifesto and life formula, His revolutionary doctrine.

The translation I'm using has the fourth Beatitude this way: "Happy are those whose greatest desire is to do what God requires—God will satisfy them fully!" My guts in my head react and tell me: Fine and dandy, if you want to die! Because desiring what God requires means doing what God requires.

What God demands are two dynamic processes. First, He requires the emptying of self so axiomatic in Scripture; and second, identifying with the oppressed. Moreover, the two are one, and must constantly nourish each other. Contemplation is essential for resistance, and resistance is essential for contemplation. The model in all this is Christ Himself.

Without question, I have desires that purely and simply oppose what God requires. These desires inspire fear; I fear their insistence, their clamor and tenacity. Above all, I fear their loss, and, because I do, I fear death. Death to self, death by violence; they are one, and I fear them.

The contrary of faith is fear. The Lord used to chide His little band, so timid and frightened despite their bravado and ambitions. He would ask them about their fears, exhort them to faith, give them evidence for believing. My problem is essentially the same as theirs—I fear death to self, I fear violent death done to me. I fear liberation. For death, properly understood, is liberation.

WTPG

Prayer, Risk, and Generosity

A public statement issued by Phil while in prison.

A reporter asked me if I thought the [Nixon] administration was successful in cooling down the war—winding down *news* of the war after supposedly winding down the war itself. I had to answer—Yes!

One problem intrudes, a very central one. Nixon is not winding down the war. Ask the Indochinese! He is merely substituting electronic gear for warm American bodies. He is creating the electronic battlefield. He is introducing sensors sophisticated enough to distinguish the army of the Republic of Vietnam from insurgents, different sweats from different diets, different uniform fabric from weapon material. The sensors trigger computers which get data to mortars, artillery, bombing squadrons—from which come an incessant rain of high explosives, hot steel, napalm, anti-personnel ordnance—upon this hapless land and people. Not only does our government still the domestic outcry over spilled American blood—infinitely more precious than Indochinese blood—but it maintains control far more economically.

Our technology can call in enough firepower to shred anything that moves—that's more efficient than young soldiers, who may get rebellious, may smoke dope, may frag Prussian-like officers, may come home broken and requiring expensive medical treatment.

Thank you from Dan, me, the defendants and our excellent lawyers. Let us combat discouragement and build peace in our lives and community. If the news is mostly bad, if the times are indescribably bad, we can nonetheless build hope by educating our sisters and brothers and by becoming people of prayer, risk, generosity; two things ultimately are needed—contemplation and resistance. Peace and liberation to all of you.

October 28, 1971, CU

The Strength and Faith of Liz

Today is Liz's birthday, her thirty-second. She visited us yesterday looking like a gamine, her hair short, her face piquant and animated. She is back from two bruising weeks on the road in Texas and the Midwest—four or five talks a day, Feds all over the place. And on her return, she encounters tough talk from me on indifference to the trial and sloppy priorities.

Like a cork in mid-ocean, Liz gets heavy seas from every side, most of it immeasurably more messy and painful than the weather. With me in jail, she has taken alone the veiled questions, arched eyebrows, and clumsy innuendos arising from our relationship. She expects, and gets, pressure and criticism from her Order, her family, the defense committees, friends, defendants, lawyers, audiences. And handles it beautifully, humanely, nonviolently, gently insisting that the issue is the murder of innocent people.

Only rarely does the strain show; her clarity and patience weaken. She has splendid stamina—capable of immense, sustained effort—and an intelligent resiliency of mind, cheerful and comprehensive.

She is a striking woman, spiritually and physically. I have no illusions about her, nor she about me. We have experienced too much pain alone and together for that. Like the official horrors we face and resist, our relationship is a fact, and we are fully confident in it.

My politics makes me difficult to know, even more difficult to know intimately. Sooner or later, tortuous questions arise, and most people flee from them. Besides Liz, what other woman could, or would, accept and support me, wait for me, while carving out her own identity and independence? What other woman could accept our separation as more normal than normalcy, face jail with optimism and courage, cling to the Gospel and to people with a rare tenacity of faith, all without compromise, sentimentality, or dread?

Here is a resistance woman, a true Christian revolutionary. I am very blessed in her.

WTPG

Renewing Wedding Vows

A fantastic day, unsettling but incredibly rich. Liz and I renew our vows, this time with Dan and all the defendants present. Everyone speaks to the event with hope and gratitude. All things considered, it was an audacious enterprise.

This morning federal marshals appeared and ordered me to pack for Harrisburg. When I protested that a meeting was scheduled and defendants were due from as far away as Chicago [Phil was back in Danbury Penitentiary], they said, emphatically, "Orders are orders." I refused to go, and they asserted that I *would* go, forcibly if necessary. The associate warden offered to call the others and tell them not to come. I backed down and went to pack.

An hour later, dressed and waiting for my captors, I hear that the defendants are here, giving me some small grace. And so it happened. In the teeth of my departure, my separation from Dan and an imminent, tortuous trial of three to four months, Liz and I renew our marriage vows.

Dan remarks that every significant juncture in his life has been marked by a marriage. Somebody else adds that such a sign of hope is a fitting preliminary to the trial, which must be a sign of hope to others. And another remarks that we ought to continue living life as it should be lived—that is, enough to embody the new society.

One of our friends in resistance is fond of remarking, "Hope is where your ass is!" I reflect ruefully that this is so, and that one's ass, to be hopeful, has to be pinched. A rule of life, so to speak.

January 13, 1972, WTPG

Truth and Peace Mean Resistance

From January to May 1972, Phil was transferred to Dauphin County Jail in Harrisburg, Pennsylvania, for the trial of The Harrisburg Seven. The following statement, written on January 23, 1972, was issued to the Harrisburg Defense Committee, a group of activists and supporters gathered in Harrisburg for the trial.

Peace and love from Dauphin County Jail; and gratitude to you for coming. I hope you're dealing with your lockup as well as I'm dealing with mine. I'm not trying to be flippant! I am trying to say that any American not in serious resistance against this government is in lockup. And in lockstep. I hope also that you're not worrying about us seven, or about Ted Glick. We're OK, getting it together, and will get it more together as the courtroom debacle develops. After all, we have one another, our lives and resistance, the best of lawyers, you and thousands like you. That's more than enough going for us. Instead of concern for us, how about using the trial as an occasion for giving rebirth to the Movement? How about giving movement to something that never really moved, or at least not in a sustained way? How about saying this time that our lives are truth and peace—both of which mean resistance?

Whenever one can share one's life, in jail or out, wherever people are, there is ignorance to be fought, fear to be dispelled, culture shock to be eased. Let's re-teach the ABCs to our sisters and brothers—the ABCs of compassion and resistance, of risk and expense, of courage in the face of the war-makers! Let's remember our Indochinese brothers and sisters—living and dead! Let's make our rhetoric very good and very real, but let's back up rhetoric with our lives. Let's conspire with truth and justice to withstand the real conspirators!

Let's build a real movement by building real people. Let's give one another hope and love, that's all people need, hope and love. Let's push back the darkness! That's what they said about Christ, you know—He pushed back the darkness—once and for all! Peace and love to you.

CU

An Enemy of the State

January 24, 1972

We begin trial today with selection of the jury.

This is my fourth political trial. The only ones who share that distinction are Huey Newton and Bobby Seale, but unlike me, they are multiple winners. I don't know how I would take a win. It would take some analyzing.

I sometimes ponder this ceaseless face-off with the state. Christ warned His followers that they would be hauled before kings and governors for His sake; He took his cracks at the Scribes, Pharisees and Herod; He tried to quietly teach Pilate something. But He ignored the state as such. He merely predicted that He would run afoul of the state, and that it would kill Him. And He warned them, if they were true, the same thing would happen to them.

Men generally know they ought to be better, but generally, too, they find being better a fearsome and mysterious task, one that they reject. From their refuges of mediocrity and smallness they create government to protect themselves from interpersonal excess and from the ambition of other states. The state merely mirrors and collects the failures of its citizens; it lies as they lie, fears as they fear, hates as they hate, fights as they fight. It is no more than a concentrated collectivization of national values—or human worth.

When, however, a few disagree with corollaries flowing out of *raison d'état* and say love is the law of life and man is more God than animal, a conflict readily and speedily develops. One becomes an enemy of the state.

WTPG

Our Acts Are Nonviolent

The following is a statement by Phil and read to the press by Elizabeth McAlister on Tuesday, January 25, 1972.

To Members of the Press Corps:

My warm and personal greetings to you. In this past year I have viewed some of the work done by the press on war abroad and repression at home with some appreciation. I hope your work of reporting facts to the public will receive the fullest cooperation from the defendants and members of the defense committee. We have nothing to hide. Our acts of resistance have been, and shall remain, nonviolent and designed to underscore publicly our opposition to a government which has lost accountability to the people.

We want you to know, the defendants and I, that we share your hope for adequate coverage of the trial in a completely open and free atmosphere, so that issues far transcending this unfortunate indictment might be aired. All of us owe the public that. People have been mocked and manipulated for too long. It is our deep concern that all of you be familiar not only with the history of this indictment, but with a history of anti-war activities.

I profoundly regret my sequestration from you. I mentioned this fact to the press yesterday—the enforced silence imposed on political prisoners is uncivilized and probably unconstitutional. The reality of men like my brother and me, plus hundreds of draft resisters, being powerless to voice our concerns for people, or for the government which has jailed us, is medieval at best. Tonight, President Nixon will announce a development in policy regarding Indochina. We hope for a decision of sanity which will remove all American forces, dismantle the electronic battlefield, and withdraw all naval and Air Force bombers from the area. If such a decision is forthcoming, it will terminate the cruel practice of employing POWs as pawns of presidential policy. Such a decision is a decade overdue. If it does not come, our national disgrace continues. So does our resistance.

CU

On Self-Pity While in Prison

Whenever self-pity grips me — it is the huge temptation of the political prisoner — I think of Côn Sơn [prison cages called "tiger cages" used by the U.S.-supported South Vietnamese to torture North Vietnamese prisoners] or the Passion. The first is the contemporizing of the second, perhaps the most terrifying example in the world of a man's hatred toward our species. The tiger cages at Côn Sơn are death prolonged and defined and denied its release.

The United States is responsible for the tiger cages at Côn Sơn. Without us they would not be open, without us more of them would not be built. Brazil has its torture chambers for political dissidents, Siberia its work camps, Spain its medieval cells. But none compare with the tiger cages, the horror of hell translated to concrete reality.

The first peacemaker, and the peacemakers since, often fall under human curse. But not I. Later, perhaps, but not now. In contrast, I have a tiny six-by-nine cell, complete with miniature table, sink, toilet and bunk. The technocratic meritocracy, as somebody calls it, affords me this. I have my books, other prisoners to talk to, commissary privileges, loyal friends. And though every move occasions caravans of marshals and guns, every word occasions paranoia and official smothering, my spirit flies free, like that of a young bird recently from the nest.

Moreover, I can sleep nights, as many a liberal and prospective juror cannot — by their own testimony.

I want to tell my friends: The further one goes in resistance, with faith in God and dedication to nonviolence, the less reason one finds for self-pity.

January 29, 1972, WTPG

What We Do to the Vietnamese, We Do to Ourselves

This is the opening statement Phil wanted to make at the Harrisburg trial but was denied permission to do so by Judge R. Dixon Herman, February 21, 1972.

Judge Herman, gentlemen of the prosecution and defense, friends of the press and courtroom; Most importantly, ladies and gentlemen of the jury.

I should at the outset express gratitude to the court for an opportunity to speak. Procedurally, I understand an opening statement by a defendant is exception rather than rule. So we thank the judge and hope this latitude will extend throughout the trial.

Next, a note of sympathy over your sequestration. As you know, the defense opposed it from the beginning. Forgive me, however, for thinking that I too am locked up; forgive me for concluding that all of us are locked up for a good cause. Possibly, that can console and strengthen us in the long weeks ahead.

We possess the utmost confidence that you can judge us fairly and impartially; that you can distinguish between conspiracy and acts of conscience; between plotting and responsible discussion—discussion allowed by the Constitution and which we judge a grave moral and political duty; between government war-making and our peacemaking. We have the fullest confidence, I assure you, that you can distinguish between these two realities—that we have never conspired to bomb or kidnap anyone, while the government has conspired to bomb and kidnap. In fact, it bombed and kidnapped—bombed Indochina until, as one of the pilots said, "It looks like lunar landscapes"; kidnapped millions of Indochinese by the simple expedients of bombing them out to forcibly relocate the survivors in refugee camps. It has virtually kidnapped millions of young Americans through its Selective Service Act—a certainly immoral and possibly illegal piece of legislation—coercing them to kill and possibly to be killed.

Facts like these are the dominating facts of this indictment, not the government's counts, not an enumeration of overt acts. We stand before this dock because we have nonviolently resisted our government's war-making in Indochina. That is the reason; there is no other. We are confident that you can perceive this and conclude it.

Please allow me to introduce myself. I'm Philip Berrigan, a Roman Catholic priest, a member of the Society of Saint Joseph, seventeen years ordained, in prison twenty-nine months of a six-year sentence for draft file destruction. I am the youngest of six boys—we grew up during the Depression on a farm, during a period of dire poverty and hopelessness. All my schooling has been Catholic—elementary, high school, college, seminary, graduate work.

Four of us served during World War II—one brother was in the Pacific before Pearl Harbor; another participated in the invasion of North Africa, Sicily and Italy; another went into Normandy on D-Day. Neither our parents nor we questioned the war—we considered supporting it our duty. And we went freely, even eagerly.

Consciously, I was an enthusiastic soldier; unconsciously, I learned from the destruction and horror of war. Four experiences with war helped educate me, helped lead me to resistance, to nonviolent civil disobedience, to federal prison, to this dock.

The first had to do with my second night in France during World War II. We were outside Brest, and the Germans began to shell us, lightly and intermittently—more of a nuisance than anything else. In any event, a light tank company in the next hedgerow panicked—they were green troops like us—and began to fire at shadows, sounds, and eventually one another. I saw dead and wounded men the next morning, and blood-splattered halftracks.

Later on in Germany, while the Battle of the Bulge raged southwest of us, I watched a convoy of American dead go by, perhaps a dozen trucks with 150 bodies. It was New Year's Eve, 1944. Bitterly cold—the corpses frozen, rigid arms and legs bumping on tailgates as the trucks bounced over the cobblestones. Where is the glory of war for these men, I thought, or the honor and reverence normally given the dead? They had been unceremoniously picked from the battlefield, blood frozen on their death wounds—perhaps near Bastogne—and transported like carcasses of beef to obscure and lonely graves.

Still later, in 1945, I returned to Germany an officer, having volunteered for infantry school outside of Paris. While being screened for officers' training,

I was warned that the combat life expectancy of a rifle platoon leader was something under several minutes before he was hit or killed. That made scant impression on me—I believed in the war, believed I had to do more to win it.

After commissioning in France, I went to Munster for assignment to a unit. The war had just ended—a personal disappointment to me. But Munster proved critical to my education—its devastation overwhelmed my senses. Saturation bombing had reduced a large and gracious city to dust and rubble. What sickened me the most, however, was not the unremitting, tedious destruction. It was the smell of the dead, the cloying, nauseating odor of those killed in the terrible hysteria of bombing. There they rotted in the warm summer sun—with no one to dig them out, no one to bury them—women and children and old men, a familiar pattern. And I thought vaguely and worriedly—must we win at this price? History tells us that the Romans salted Carthage after overwhelming it, so that a city could not rise again on that spot. I remember that fact from high school Latin and felt we must have had the same ruthlessness in bombing Munster as they did.

Some seventeen years later, I taught in the Black high school in New Orleans. Suddenly, in October 1962, the city went quietly rigid with fear, and people began to count up their sins. By an intuition I cannot grasp, residents realized that they were in mortal danger—within range of the Soviet missiles in Cuba—and that if nuclear war broke out, they would burn in the first wave of terror. As it appeared later, [Cuban leader Fidel] Castro requested missiles from [Soviet leader Nikita] Khrushchev as a defensive measure against the growing American hostility toward the Cuban Revolution—marked earlier by the Bay of Pigs invasion and by a complete embargo.

The crisis passed—to Castro's chagrin. Khrushchev backed down—wisely, as Americans thought. But what if he hadn't? What if he had insisted on his Soviet border? Thoughtful people in that city, in Miami, Atlanta, Birmingham and Gulfport realized two things: (1) Khrushchev probably saved them, and millions of others, by taking the saner course; (2) [President John F.] Kennedy bargained with their lives in a way reserved to God alone. I came out of those few awful days shaken, thinking despairingly that if this were the only way to keep peace, then unimaginable horror and doom would become inevitable.

I was impressively ignorant then, in 1962, as the threat of Cuba diminished. But I did know this—that the American and Soviet Cold War diplomacy was eerie, surreal, nightmarish, and colossally immoral. I also knew that my thirty-nine years had ill-prepared me to call into question the complexities of foreign policy; that I literally had to re-learn my ABCs, and that preaching the Gospel meant applying it to the main issues of life and death—war, poverty, racism, pollution, overpopulation—or reducing that Gospel to pabulum.

I began to read furiously, to hear every available expert on the arms race, to talk to anyone with an idea and a concern. From my own Church, virtually united behind inflated prosperity and war, there was no help except from Thomas Merton and my brother Dan, now in federal prison in Connecticut.

The next year my Order reassigned me in the north. Assigned to teach at our College in Newburgh, I joined tentative, general efforts to widen questions of our Cold War position, then hotting up in Vietnam. We began with a march or two, to debate on the war, letters to congressmen and editors, talks to small groups. But the uproar generated was sufficient to transfer me to Baltimore and parish work.

There in 1965, after a period of enforced silence, I again joined others to work for peace, and against the Vietnam War. We prayed, demonstrated, called rallies, staged debates, supported draft resistance, traveled to the nation's capital for the mammoth demonstrations there.

Meanwhile, I became acquainted with the men responsible for policy in Indochina. I talked at length with Secretary of State Dean Rusk, corresponded with [War] Secretary [Robert] McNamara and Walt Rostow, President Johnson's foreign policy advisor. I conferred with [Arkansas] Senator [J. William] Fulbright; with Alain Entoven, Assistant Secretary of War; with numerous congressmen, State Department officials. I debated experts from the great universities. I pursued all constitutional channels; I believed in the system; I believed our leaders were honest, decent, and humble men. I believed that peace would take time, but that it would come.

But I changed, as people we must change, under stress of conscience and event. I discussed with people as agonized as I the resistance of Socrates, of Christ, of Henry David Thoreau, of Gandhi and King and A. J. Muste. They all emphasized obedience to the higher law of God; they made clear distinctions between the rights of responsible conscience and the rights of the state. They called for, and practiced, nonviolent resistance to government—not as conspiracy or subversion, but to assert the democratic ideal of government of, for, and by the people, an ideal seldom reduced to concrete by men in power.

I committed civil disobedience and waited for arrest twice in Baltimore and at Catonsville not because I hoped that destroying draft files would arrest the American war machine, but because it was the only convincing way of saying that what we did to the Indochinese, we did to ourselves—as we ruined their environment, we polluted our own; as we killed their young, we killed our own at Kent State, Jackson State and at Attica; as we drove the Indochinese from their homes, so also we drove our young men into exile, or underground.

I waited for arrest twice because I was ashamed of young men taking the heat for me. They had nothing to do with the Bomb, or the Cold War, or

Indochina, but they had to fight, flee or go to jail. As for me, who had helped to build the terror (my silence was necessary for it), I lived in comfort and security.

I waited for arrest twice because a man must live what he believes and take the consequences. In Christ our Lord, word and deed were one—one life. He never said anything that he didn't do; He never believed anything that he didn't live.

I waited for arrest twice because it would be necessary to explain why we had defaced draft records with blood—for the blood waste in Vietnam; and destroyed them with napalm, for the burning of children. What I attempted to say—as did the other defendants as well—was simply this: I reject this war; I will neither support it nor remain silent in face of it.

For which pains I received an extravagant and vindictive sentence of six years. Lieutenant [William] Calley [of the 1968 My Lai massacre during which U.S. soldiers killed an estimated 500 unarmed civilians in My Lai, Vietnam], in contrast, is under house arrest for the premeditated murder of twenty-two civilians at My Lai—children, women and old men—while the other twenty-four charged with the massacre there never came to trial or were acquitted. Meanwhile, other veterans of a hundred other My Lais go free and proudly show their medals; and policymakers, who sent them to kill and destroy, run for reelection.

As for our part in the nuclear arms race, what has been euphemistically called The Dance of Death, we are now at a nuclear standoff with the Soviets and have been for nearly twenty years. And neither side can do the slightest thing to advantage itself except to take the moral course and to disarm.

This much is virtually certain—to continue the arms spiral, to build more and more horrible weapons systems, to rattle our nuclear sabers at anyone as admonition or threat is an act of insanity, a death wish extended on a mass scale.

Do people cook dinners and not eat them? Do they buy cars and not drive them? Do people ever build a weapon and not use it? Never—indeed, never. Otherwise, why build it? We build into our creations our intentions and purposes, which under certain circumstances we put to work. In reference to the Bomb, this means that when we want something badly enough, we will use the Bomb. They will then retaliate—action and reaction—a sure formula for annihilation.

My friends, I did not come to frighten you, shock you, alienate you. Americans experience great anguish in grasping such awesome phenomena. We have not suffered as other peoples—our power and wealth have insulated us from that. We tend to flee from shocking or unmanageable realities, to wish them out of being, to pretend they don't exist. We even tend to attack those who reveal them. I recall a scene in a Midwestern city five or six years ago, speaking on a panel, when an arms control and disarmament expert, himself a nuclear physicist, after giving his superb presentation of dangers like these, was verbally attacked from the audience, accused of fabrication, and treachery toward his country. The point is clear—we simply can't continue building a bigger and better Bomb, and not use it, or be victimized by it.

What provokes the Cold War most, however, and its arms race, is the Indochina war, which continues with undiminished fury in Vietnam, North and South, in Cambodia, Laos and even parts of Thailand. As long as Americans allow our government to follow a pattern of calculated genocide in Indochina, we will have no moral energy with which to suspend the arms race, unilaterally or bilaterally.

I hope what I have loosely presented becomes clear. Our government has played God with the survival of mankind for twenty-five years through its Cold War adventurism. And our government has assaulted the integrity, justice and unity of the American people since 1949 in Indochina.

Frankly, we came here to tell you the truth about ourselves and to share our lives with you. Central to those lives is the command given by Christ before He died: "Love one another as I have loved you." Notice three things about the new commandment: (1) it is not an ideal, it is a command; (2) Christ would not command the impossible, he would give his spirit to help us; (3) it transcends immeasurably the Golden Rule, since obviously no one was prepared to die for Him. But He was prepared to die for us, and did.

Samuel Butler once said that Christians are equally horrified to see their religion practiced, or to see it doubted. All over this land some Christians have been horrified by our lives. Which is their choice, except that most offer nothing real to stop the killing, to outlaw war before it ends civilization. Let them judge us, let any court or government judge us when they have a better idea. For this government has no intention of ending the killing, ending the Indochina war or the arms race.

When peace comes—we are confident it will—when the Indochina war preoccupies historians rather than soldiers, when this indictment and trial have faded from memory, then may present anguish and division heal; then may we all pick up work to secure the peace. Thank you!

CU

The Plastic Goliaths

The following prison journal excerpts were written during the Harrisburg trial.

Monday through Friday of this week was introduction to Psych Warfare, or the Imposition of Shame as Repression. Liz and I sat rooted for five days and just endured while the informer [Boyd Douglas, a fellow inmate and government informant] wove his lies and fantasies about us and Mr. Lynch [the prosecutor] read our letters—*with proper emphasis*. We sat rooted while our hopes and affections and lives were stripped layer by layer—sat there impassively helpless, lest the jury and press interpret reactions as guilt. Privacy was shattered, nonviolence ridiculed, everything about us reduced to a caricature—a hideous, incompetent, frantic plot, worthy of only the irresponsible or the mad.

People conclude the following is probably true: [J. Edgar] Hoover forces the government to indict, which it duly does. The government in turn must then build a case, which it attempts, with limitless manpower and money. The plastic Goliaths in government can no more stomach defeat in Harrisburg than they can in Indochina.

March 14, 1972

The price tag on this escapade has been highest for Liz. I have been insulated from public conjecture by jail. So in addition to all the other burdens, there has been this one, taken without a murmur or second guessing or the slightest recrimination.

Cross-examination drags on; people not exactly sure that it should take this long. The insulation that the court drapes around our friendly informer is shameful, and he responds with a combination of arrogance and/or amnesia.

But we should end tomorrow, and we should witness a different phase of the government case on Thursday.

March 17, 1972

Saint Patrick's Day. I have a natural jaundice about the Irish thing, but today was good. Liz in her typically impudent way brought in green carnations for all the defendants and lawyers. And lo, in troops the jury also wearing them. It brought the house down.

March 30, 1972

It is 6:30 P.M., the jury is deliberating, and I write this from back in the marshal's cage. A strange day. The judge opened with a charge for the jury; it went fairly well until the last fifteen minutes, when he launched into a review of the government's evidence, defendant by defendant. We had become *used to* his malice and incompetence, but it shook us nonetheless. Sort of one last putrid bone on a pile of putrid bones.

It will soon be Easter. One of the Psalms, the 28th I think, puts it well: "Even though an army encamp against me, I will fear not." If David, or somebody, could sing that without the empty tomb, I guess all of us can take *any* verdict with dignity and equanimity.

April 2, 1972

A strange week—hopeful, ominous, interminable. It was as though time had imposed on us a cage of its own, enclosing us all in waiting.

We discover that sum and substance have suddenly evaporated from this case—that our fears have had no basis. The trial itself, which once imparted the eerie feeling of being devoured and digested, now impresses one as having the consistency and value and smell of gnat shit. These last months have been life at its drabbest and meanest, "sound and fury, signifying nothing."

Our bloated Goliath of a government has been hamstrung by building an imaginary case to appease Hoover's ego, by relying credulously on a confidence man who conned it into prosecuting, by a notoriously inept and malicious prosecution, and by our decision to arrest the defense.

The jury deliberates for its sixth day. I pray for them as I pray for the marshals that guard me—that truth invade their neutrality.

WTPG

Acquittal

The Harrisburg trial ended with the jury unable to reach a verdict. Phil and Liz were found guilty only on contraband counts (smuggling private letters to and from prison). Eventually, the government quietly filed for a dismissal of that remaining charge. The government's failure to convict the Harrisburg defendants made headlines around the world. Nevertheless, Phil still had to complete his sentence at Danbury for his nonviolent actions at Baltimore and Catonsville.

It's a truism to say that everything seen from jail takes on a different perspective, yet it needs saying over and over. This applies especially to nonviolent resistance and specifically to the trial we have just endured. One is in jail — jail is *the* penalty, and jail holds no special terrors. One has lived it, built community, seen the power of nonviolent resistance in jail, experienced both peace and dread, enlarged one and controlled the other. Most important, one has seen the dominators stripped of malevolence by determined, nonviolent effort. All this deepens one's understanding of a trial, and one's hopes for it.

Let me illustrate how imprisonment enriches understanding — of life, of resistance. I have done two stretches in solitary — one for two weeks, one for four — and two long fasts because of political resistance. A prolonged fast in solitary is a profoundly liberating experience; inevitably this question arises, What more can they do to one? And the answer is, Nothing! The current legal arsenal was empty, the ammunition exhausted, and Goliath, with his scabbard bare, looks bewildered and defenseless.

Such experiences helped me immeasurably when the government indicted us. Conviction on the charges in the first indictment carried a possible life sentence. The only real position one could take toward life imprisonment was to accept its possibility — it could happen! The government had our letters and they had Boyd Douglas. So I thought at that point, well, if it comes to it, I'll take it day by day, just as I'm doing now. Millions have died in this war, and some have died to stop it. A life bit isn't too great a price!

There are certain givens within this living tradition — light in struggle against darkness, good against evil, truth against falsehood, nonviolence against violence, conscience against the state, life against death. One sees them define life, knows their truth, connects them with similar manifestations in self and society, takes them into one's chemistry, lives them to liberate oneself and others. Within this living tradition one knows that Amos, Hosea, Jonah and Christ have meaning today — indeed, they live in those who give them meaning. One says Yes! to them: The same witness, the same stand-up, the same resistance is necessary today against personal and state evil.

Life has not changed, one discovers — only its accidents have. Christ's resistance against the hierarchy and empire of His day is essentially the same as resistance against a dominating technocracy led by the rich, with an entourage of cheerful, generously endowed bishops in attendance, that we have today. Both systems are fundamentally totalitarian, both stink of lies and death. In the face of such, what was required then is required now — truth, love, courage — all taking root in nonviolent resistance.

June 21, 1972

Religious power is the power of God moving gently into a person, dominating as it frees. It is not like human power, with its illusion-breeding violence, always aiming at control, always springing from desire. It permeates a person, paradoxically liberating as it masters, extricating her/him from intellectual myopia, emotional tyranny, volitional flabbiness. But every advance in liberation presupposes submission to the spirit — to the desert as the soul's climate, to crucifixion of pride and fear, to leaps of faith into risk, into financial and physical helplessness, into imprisonment, and possibly into death.

WTPG

To Create Hope Is to Wrestle with Death

Silence is one of the keenest pains a political prisoner must endure, since, in effect, imprisonment strips one of opinion, of judgment, of public concern for people.

The ironies provide some lively contrast. One has been jailed because of a statement against violence and mass-produced death; because of a plea for the living and the unborn. But prison ends that abruptly, choking off word or effort for others. It is like being dropped into an abandoned well — bystanders might hear a fading cry, a thump perhaps, and then silence.

Be that as it may — I am not here to spout brave noises, to issue a polemic against the government, to champion the defense or denigrate the prosecution, to glorify myself or any defendant as above weakness or criticism. None of that. I would rather talk about hope at a time when many sensitive people see almost no hope. I would rather say something about our obligation to be hopeful, and to be hope to one another.

Hope is an elusive quality, having to do with promise and reality. Promise because people need to be sisters and brothers before they need to be selves; reality because a few always become those for others — the one small race, the one tiny family, the handful faithful to God and to people. These few become what we would all prefer to be; they offer lucidity and purpose and strength; they embody living evidence that indeed, we can all make it and survive.

Even more surely, people die without hope. They contract and shrivel up and calcify inside, suffocating their spirits. One can see death in the faces of so many today — a hardening of features, fear, even terror, cruelty, and a profound unhappiness. Recently, we spoke to a middle-aged prisoner one evening on the compound — one notorious for hedonism and brutality — now condemned to anonymity, contempt, a sterile old age. He failed to grunt, even, at our greeting, preoccupied as he was in his misery. Someone with me remarked pityingly, "He died when he was twelve years old."

When he won the Nobel Prize for Literature in 1970, Aleksandr Solzhenitsyn prepared a lecture only recently slipped through Soviet censorship and published in the West. In it, he wrote almost despairingly of violence sweeping the world like a plague. Not a plague, one might add, with a plague's ordinary sign and horror, but a plague immensely more lethal, with 1,000 enticing faces, all as beguiling as Circe's nation-state rivalries, imperial ambitions, corporate greed, ideological fixations, quick and easy profit, class and racial division, war as technological and political science.

How can one be aware of this threatening and violent torrent without despair? That is the question for millions of decent and sensitive people. The evidence would seem to indicate a universal conspiracy to ruin and empty the planet—a conspiracy led by the superpowers. The evidence would seem to indicate that nihilism was life, as we become more entrapped by tyranny of ego and structure.

There is one revealing characteristic of violence that Solzhenitsyn refers to, calling it the spirit of Munich. Notice he does not apply the term to leaders allegedly preoccupied with appeasement as the price of peace. He does not speak of Neville Chamberlain as the classic example, or as some would today, of George McGovern. Rather, he applies it to "those who have given themselves up to the thirst after prosperity at any price, to material well-being as the chief goal of earthly existence."

Solzhenitsyn's spirit of Munich is, I suppose, no more than the mild paraphrase of Christ's ominous words in Luke's Gospel, "But how terrible for you who are rich now; you have had your easy life: how terrible for you who are full now; you will go hungry!" (Lk. 6, 24, 25).

One might inquire if there has ever been a time in our history when so many serious and dedicated Americans have gone into exile, or plan it? Who can dismiss out of hand their search for sanity, for community, for desperately needed change, and their failure to find it here? They have, for the most part, worked hard at responsibility—trying ideologies, leaders, parties, causes, organized protest. Yet little changes for the better—air and water grow more foul; slums expand and crumble; a country of stunning beauty becomes scarred and blighted. But the crushing burden for them is one of perpetual war, the cynical, incessant, senseless killing of people. On the one hand, they cannot endure it; on the other, they cannot stop it. As their perception grows, so does their revulsion. And their hearts fail. They become people of mourning, and misery, of hopelessness and escape.

However much one shares their anguish, one must search for better alternatives than silence, dropout, or exile. I have in mind a singular example of hope and courage.

On August 6, Hiroshima Day, eleven prisoners at Danbury began a fast against their countrymen to stimulate nonviolent resistance to the Indochina war. As it happened, another gallant community joined them by a similar fast in New York City. I'll mention only the prisoners here, since obviously, I am more familiar with them.

The prisoners felt deeply that they must hope in themselves—prison did not discharge them of responsibility for the war. They felt they must hope in their sisters and brothers, hope in their sense of justice and social generosity.

In their case, I think, hope was both measured by sacrifice and sustained by it. People would eventually learn what it cost a federal prisoner to fast in protest—shipment 1,000 miles to a medical center in Missouri; isolation from other prisoners, separation from family and friends, official pressure to break the fast. Several were draft resisters—apparently, they refused to rest upon the act that first imprisoned them.

Since then, one has contracted heart complications; one has had a stomach hemorrhage. All have suffered grievously from hunger, weakness, and loneliness. But they continue, convinced that Americans will listen, will awaken to the agonies of a war-stricken people.

Some will judge them naïve, others fanatic or masochistic. But I can attest that love for their countrymen, and for people in the war zone, motivated them. The bare little that they had as prisoners—visits from relatives, indifferent food, hope of early release—all these they freely gave up.

Apparently, some Americans understood. One lawyer inquired, when hearing of their effort, "What's wrong with us, that prisoners must show us how to resist this war?" And the mother of one of the prisoners, a non-resister, said, "Not only did my son educate me, but it's clear he'll never go back to prison for the wrong reasons."

Basically, what did these people attempt to say to us with their fast for life? Very simply—that we have made a false peace if we are not doing our humane utmost to end this war; that we cannot claim reconciliation with God while having no reconciliation with the Indochinese; that affluent and overfed as we are, we are starving for God's nourishment—truth, justice, compassion, personal and social risk; that some demons, perhaps demons of delusion like indifference or cynicism, are exorcised only by prayer and fasting; that true hope is both a grasp of reality and a nonviolent plan to communicate it.

Those prisoners offered hope, I say, with a large and painful portion of their lives. Remember the Lord's gratitude for a revelation made to "merest children," and withheld from "the learned and the clever"? (Mt. 11, 25). Perhaps we need to re-learn wisdom today from the poor, from the victims of raw power, from prisoners.

Perhaps the hope we embody—that is to say, the hope we offer others—is the same as the effort to kill slavery to ourselves and to inhuman structures. To create hope is to wrestle with death. And since we all desire life, we must desire, as well, a struggle with death. That struggle constitutes our hope.

September 29, 1972, *Commonweal*

Dealing with the "Blahs" in Prison

A letter written on October 1, 1972, to Phil's brother Jerry and Jerry's wife, Carol.

Dear Carol and Jerry:

Woke the other morning leaden, depressed, enervated. As someone once remarked, "It was a morning of debate—one sits on the bed's edge and decides whether it is or isn't worth it."

Have had a lot of similar mornings lately—too many. It began to alarm me, so throughout the day I tried to analyze the blahs. Excuses I had plenty—classic and repetitious screwings by the Powers; spasmodic support from the Movement; jailhouse blues; waste—waste of time, talent, effort, one's life—these all occurred to me. But they were too superficial, too wide of the mark.

Then it hit me, like a good bolt of truth. I was quitting, picking my shots, ignoring the need around me. I was dying, ceasing to live. The struggle of life was convincing me, insidiously and subtly, that life wasn't worth it. And I was, in effect, playing the death merchant game, for this is their hardware, and their sales pitch—hedonism, falsehood, murder—packaged plastically and labeled LIFE.

I knew—but not well enough—that God's greatest gift is life, and that every day is another manifestation of that gift, that truth applies no matter where one is—in jail or out, in Fun City, Harlem or the Sierra Nevadas; in Hell or in R&R in Honolulu.

The misery in any American jail is appalling—prison compounds shriek and moan of failure. Not failure to make it in the man's asylum, but failure to be a man, that same termite which eats out the foundations of Super Fortress America. It is the old choice of death over life, the old choice enticing me. And this much is sure—if I buckle and kiss the man's posteriors, if I knuckle under and program to get out, if I school myself to like the stench of dead thoughts and dead deeds—there will be less hope among men here, less cheerfulness, less generosity, more despair, violence, death. The 10,000 worldwide who die daily of malnutrition and starvation silently witness my lassitude and indecision; so do the kids of Vietnam, 50 percent of whom don't live beyond five years; so do the young men fed into the war thresher by our grim, elderly reapers. They had life and clung to it piteously until the rip-off came. They can hardly relish my vacillation with a supreme gift.

There are Soviet political prisoners who hardly remember being free; Greeks and Brazilians and Vietnamese who will not leave prison alive or will leave it permanently crippled. I will greet each day promising to live, and to welcome any struggle that attends. "Though an army encamp against me, my heart will not fear; though war be waged upon me, even then will I trust" (Ps. 27, 3).

Peace and joy to you and to Freda [Phil and Jerry's mother] and the children. In short, every good and perfect gift from the Lord.

CU

Thanksgiving 1972

This is my fourth Thanksgiving in prison. I remember the first, in Baltimore City Jail with Tom Lewis in 1968. A pretty violent and depressing experience — several in our cellblock were quite torn up by being away from their families. Thank God, these years have not hurt me — quite the opposite, in fact. And I am as thankful that they haven't hurt others — or if they have, the hurt was unintentional.

WTPG

Finally Free . . . for a While

Phil was released from prison on December 20, 1972.

I regret nothing that I have done, nor do I resent anything done to me. Government is what it is (we understood it well); government people are what they are (we knew many, and the stripes are similar); both had to do what they did to me, to Dan, and to other resisters. But the fact of *that* and our recognition does not remove the conflict, nor does it pacify or domesticate us. Our dialogue will continue—from without and within jail.

I have no answers but a search for God, for sisters and brothers, for love of the first so that I might love the second. And a search is essentially a question.

Such a search is rare enough to be perilous. But eminently and stunningly worthwhile. To the extent that it is, I dare to suggest it to my sisters and brothers—everywhere. As a question, not an answer.

Of such, I believe, is Christ's reign—His truth, peace and freedom. I wish you all these as I do people everywhere.

WTPG

PART III

Community, Plowshares, and the Bomb

1973–2002

Perhaps our imprisonment will give weight to the following reflection: If we want peace, we will have to stop making war. If we are silent, we are making war. All this government needs to lead the world to nuclear ruin is an irrelevant vote every four years, a sizable slice of our income for war, and silence.

—PHILIP BERRIGAN

Paying Dearly for Our Love

A statement written by Phil and Liz and released to the public on May 28, 1973.

Elizabeth McAlister and Philip Berrigan have known one another since 1966 and have worked together in the peace movement since almost that time. We became aware of our love in the spring of 1969 and by mutual choice married one another in trust and gratitude.

For nearly eighteen months, we kept our marriage private, without the knowledge of families or intimate friends. We formalized our union in January 1972 at Danbury Prison; it was witnessed by the Harrisburg defendants, by Sister Jogues and by Daniel Berrigan.

Our love has deepened through the past four years—we've paid for it dearly, as have our friends. We have considered our relationship a service to the victims of American aggression, to other Americans, to our family and friends and to one another. We have lived these four years married in every sense but lifestyle (having no common home) and public knowledge.

From the outset, we agreed on certain lines of commitment: a guarantee of freedom in the service of resistance with its requirements of discipline, risk, separation, jail. We have refused to allow personal considerations to interfere with our dedication to Gospel and to people. So we met infrequently, and never considered abandoning our work or evading its consequences. At the same time, we saw an opportunity to share our marriage with the Church and with the public.

By 1969 resistance to the war had become a way of life for Philip (three political trials and a six-year sentence). Elizabeth had pledged her life to her religious community as a college educator or a resister. Our lives converged in community and nonviolent resistance, particularly to our country's war-making in Indochina. Community and nonviolent resistance defined the religious life to us.

The Church has made celibacy the spirit of religious commitment, if not its heart. We had hoped that a time would arrive when religious communities would invite both celibate and married people to a situation of mutual support and service to the Gospel and to suffering people. But present Church vision, policy and leadership make that impossible. Nonetheless, we cannot but question and resist the priority of celibacy over mature conscience and the spirit of the Gospels. We have tried to live responsibly since our contract—in separation, in jail, in legal jeopardy, in official attempts to disgrace us. Separation from our religious communities has not been our choice. For we believe that in our case, as with others, celibacy is not the issue. Responsible freedom is.

We see our marriage as a radical assertion of our faith. With God's grace and the support of our friends, we hope to continue to live the Gospels in poverty, community, and nonviolent resistance, convinced of the contribution of religious resistance to humankind.

We realize that many friends will be disappointed and hurt by what we now reveal. We owe an explanation as to why we have kept this truth from you for so long.

At first, we wanted our relationship to clarify itself without pressure; in the midst of that process, Philip went to prison in April 1970. At that point, public disclosure was impossible since it would have put the total burden of explanation upon Elizabeth. Later in the year, we did speak to friends and family, and their pain at our secrecy revealed an error in judgment on our part. As the Harrisburg trial approached, we contemplated disclosing our union. But we felt that a free admission on our part would confuse both the substance of the trial and our relationship. Following the trial, and up to the point of Philip's release in December, the separation of prison further prevented any public acknowledgment of our marriage. Since that time, we have sought opportunities to publicize it and to share it with our friends.

As we evolved our plans over the past five months, some friends encouraged us to announce this day (May 28) as the beginning of our marriage. Such an uncomplicated course would be easier on us and on the public. But we decided against this, feeling that it would serve neither the truth nor others whose love is apt to be tested, as ours was, by separation, by trial, by prison. Finally, we felt that such a decision would fail to serve the public, who all too infrequently hear the truth—without ambiguity and varnish—from any public person.

Today we celebrated our marriage with our families, and with those—defendants and lawyers—who shared the events of the past three years: civil disobedience, the separation of thirty-two months of prison, and the Harrisburg trial. (Later, in June, we will hold a general celebration for friends.)

The future still holds the possibility of a year's imprisonment for Elizabeth followed by three years' probation. Philip remains on parole until September 1975. In the past few months, we have worked with a small group of friends working at nonviolent resistance. We are presently seeking a center out of which that ministry can operate.

We hope that our ministry will serve the victims of war and serve the Gospel. We also hope, with all our hearts, that at some future date the Church will accept our marriage, as well as our efforts for nonviolence and peace. And we continue to be profoundly grateful for the great gifts of that Church, and of our respective religious communities.

FTLW

Religion and Politics

From Phil's journal, written on September 17, 1973.

I subscribe to the view, both evangelical and Gandhian, that religion and politics are complements, two rhythms of one organism. Religion is the interior of politics, politics the exterior of religion, with an interdependence at once reinforcing.

Very simply, religion cultivates the interior relationships which make a human community rather than a Darwinian jungle. All relationships — to neighbor, enemy, self, material world — hinge on love of God, who alone can empower us to love creation. Religion therefore begins with love of God, making possible love of neighbor, love of enemy and love of everyone as Christ loved everyone.

The ultimate political person is one in whom the love of God flames — toward neighbor, enemy, toward every person since Christ loved all and died for all. In fact, a truly political person is one who loves the victims sufficiently to resist their victimizers; to resist the powermongers of state. After all, to submit to them is to make an abstraction of the state. It is to say that the Gospel has no mission to those unfortunates of wealth and power. It is to allow them to be devoured by their crimes. It is like standing by with silent applause for a local version of a rampaging [Lieutenant William] Calley [of the 1968 My Lai massacre].

Americans have a peculiar genius for keeping love remote, vague, abstract. In doing so, they weave a cocoon of insulation about themselves: It relieves them of the responsibility of bringing truth home, of applying it, of living it. Practically, this allows lives that are devoid of meaning while both individual and popular consciousness is preoccupied with the loftiest ideals. Both religion and politics require loving means, which in turn requires the acceptance of sacrifice, suffering and risk.

A national paradox is this—most Americans will choose the suffering and essential risk associated with spiritual blindness, intellectual confusion, public docility, and a living mediocrity, rather than to choose the ennobling suffering and slight risk connected with being a person for the victims. Suffering in the darkness is always more painful than suffering in the light.

CU

A Ministry of Risk and Liberation

On Sunday, May 12, 1974, Phil gave the following lecture at the New England Life Hall for the ordination of Philip Zwerling, passing on to the newly ordained priest Phil's beliefs of what a ministry can and should be.

Dear Sisters and Brothers, I would like to open with two passages from the Last Supper Discourses of Christ. I quote them under the assumption that they are addressed to me, and to some or all of you: "A servant is not greater than his master. If they persecuted me, they would persecute you also. If they kept my word, they would keep yours as well" (Jn. 15: 20). "I have told you this that your faith may not be shaken. They will expel you from the synagogue. And indeed the hour is coming when anyone who kills you will think he is doing a holy duty to God" (Jn. 16: 1, 2).

Let us imagine the context. We might imagine those words spoken between the washing of their feet — "You call me Master and Lord, and rightly; so I am. If I then, the Lord and Master, have washed your feet, you ought to wash one another's feet" (Jn. 13: 12–15). And the crucifixion the next day — "A man can have no greater love than to lay down his life for his friends" (Jn. 15: 13).

How does this apply to a ministry and church of liberation? Both must build lives; both must work continually to unlock minds, to discipline emotions; to deepen intelligence and wisdom, to instill love and courage. The last acts of Christ's life were a rising crescendo of compassion and love — the washing of feet, the last instructions and encouragements, the Eucharist, the Cross. "I shall not call you servants anymore, because a servant does not know his master's business. I call you friends" (Jn. 15: 15).

What do people need from their minister and their church? Many things too numerous to list. But above all, a ministry of risk, which rests upon a mature and self-sacrificing love. The goal being, of course, the liberation of the people themselves, by themselves. Liberation from what? From the tyranny and egocentricity of government; from fetters of interior violence and structural oppression. Minister and Church must concentrate on awakening God in the people, where God joins them in their liberation.

Not just a ministry, but a ministry of risk. What passes for ministry today is more social service than ministry. And social service we have aplenty—both voluntary and paid, both professional and clerical. In fact, we have so much social service in this country that it has become an industry of sorts, caught in the hopeless task of salvaging a few of the victims of a society careening out of control. Under these conditions, it is increasingly difficult to distinguish clergyman from social worker.

But a ministry of risk, that is another thing, radically. It rests squarely upon the love of God as the Lord of Creation; the author of harmony and right order; the master of life and death. It reflects the compassion of a God who loves us with all the power of being, who did not hesitate to sacrifice his only Son for us.

More than that, a ministry of risk goes unerringly to the side of the victims, to those threatened or destroyed by greed, prejudice and war. From the side of those victims, it teaches two simple, indispensable lessons: (1) That we all belong in the ditch, or in the breach, with the victims; (2) That until we go to the ditch or into the breach, victimizing will not cease. Neither will war nor the crimes of overlords. Furthermore, to align oneself with the innocent, one has to resist the death merchants—the false politicians, the word hucksters from Madison Avenue or from the Oval Office; the platitudinous clergyman, the hot and cold warriors.

Again, we must turn to Scripture to give clarity and urgency to this ministry. The prophecy of Ezekiel tells us of the Jewish sentry who was commissioned by God to warn the people of the approaching sword (a metaphor for violence), who is indeed, the custodian of every life. The text makes this emphatically clear: "But if the sentry sees the sword coming and fails to blow the warning trumpet, so that the sword comes and takes anyone, I will hold the sentry responsible for the person's death" (Ez. 33:6).

The sentry, therefore, takes his risk—he stands between the people and official death dealing. He must not only sound the alarm from uncompromising truth, but he may have to bear the brunt: may have to, in fact, sacrifice freedom and/or life in resistance to raw power.

Christ complements the Jewish concept of sentry with his metaphor of shepherd. The shepherd is not only the gate of the sheepfold, but one who lays down his life for the sheep. He/she stands in stark contrast to the hireling (most clergy are hirelings) who is of neither the sheepfold nor shepherdhood, who runs away at sight of the wolf, which snatches and scatters the sheep. "That is because he works for pay and has no concern for the sheep."

Obviously, without a sentry to warn them, without a shepherd to protect them, the people have virtually no chance for adulthood. From birth to death, they remain sheep, bewildered by propagandists, betrayed by leaders; blind people led by the blind. Maturity becomes closed to them; they never leave the helplessness of the sheepfold to assume protection of the helpless.

Next—a ministry of risk and liberation runs risks with its people. When has it been popular to remind people of their immaturities and petty crimes? How can it be popular to tell Americans that, by and large, they are spiritually flabby, emotionally undisciplined and fragile—tending to reflect and to entrench the racism and war-making of their institutions? Since when has it been popular to remind people that those of faith are those for others—the bombed, imprisoned, starved, and ostracized?

The risks of ministry, however, are only minimally with the people, while overwhelmingly with the state. It is the state, not the people, which has historically taken the sword as sign of authority and vehicle of power. It is the state which lies to the people, betrays their trust and mandate; wages perpetual, foreign war; brings that war home and turns it against its people; escalates the doomsday weapons race; coddles the oil, arms, and agricultural barons. Generally, the state has proven itself the very enemy of the people it is sworn to serve. That state must be resisted.

A ministry of risk discerns the hydra-headed forms of violence, in people and in the state. It cries out like the sentry; it protects like the shepherd. It leads and exhorts people to an adulthood of faith in God, and to compassion for the victims. Without a vanguard of example, without serious risk to good name and liberty and life, others have no embodied alternative, ideal or challenge. Only a common denominator of mediocrity, sterility, and practical despair.

Let me share with you a similar scene from my own history. Roman Catholic clergy have a tradition of First Mass. At mine, in 1955, an ex–Air Force chaplain of impressive academic and military credentials preached. He told me bluntly from the pulpit, "If you're not prepared to suffer, you will become a poorly disguised hypocrite. If you don't like egg on your face—and worse—you have no business with Christ." I took him with some seriousness—he was myopic politically, but a Christian of generosity and integrity. And he was right.

The ministry you join, Philip Zwerling, and the history of this Church, has a noble partisanship for the weak, the poor, the exploited and oppressed. That pales somewhat, however, before the critical challenges of the present and the dilemmas of a society which traffics chiefly in death. In face of this, our joint task may be that of survival before the threat of runaway militarism, of mass starvation in the world, of the twin poles of corruption—Watergate and Saigon. We may yet have to, as Gandhi did, fill up the jails and resist.

Fidelity will rest assured, Philip Zwerling, if you hold tenaciously to the role of sentry and shepherd, in fair weather and foul. Without these essentials in the Church, the people will not grow out of the sheepfold, will not become shepherds and sentries. "For the servant is not greater than the master. If they persecuted me, they will persecute you also. If they kept my word, they will keep yours as well."

CU

Disarm or Dig Graves

On November 26, 1975, Phil was back in prison with Dan and others for digging a symbolic "grave" on the lawn of the White House.

I speculate on the relationship between law and conscience from the District of Columbia jail, a Great Society spa lavished on me for my part in the digging of a symbolic "grave" on the White House lawn on November 26, employing the stark theme "Disarm or Dig Graves." I write from that and from nine indictments, six convictions, and years of prison for resisting American military escapades. Predictably, I come down on the side of conscience.

Some may call that bias, but I disclaim bias. To me, conscience means corporate knowledge, knowledge of the welfare of all. To me, conscience obtains maturity from two sources: revelation and life. Both revelation and life summon conscience to responsible freedom. Revelation provides the inspiration which results in conspiracy for others. My case for conscience over law rests on the Gospel, nonviolence and contemporary reality.

The Beatitudes constitute the Gospel spirit and heart. They are its synopsis, its order of necessity, if you will. Christ reveals His character in them and, therefore, that of the faithful disciple also. They are a creator's, or a brother's, vision of what we are and what we are called to become. Let me dare a paraphrase: "You will be happy/blessed if you are poor in spirit, meek, merciful, persecuted for my name's sake." The Beatitudes, so widely rejected, imply struggle against the fall and embodiment of His risen life, imply presence in the world while standing against its crimes, imply championing life and resisting death.

The Beatitudes illumine the primary and essential law—the law of love which is at once the law of conscience and of life. Keep this law, Christ says, and you will be a poor person, a peacemaker, a victim of power as the prophets were victims. Keep *this* law, and you will sift the state and the state's law; you'll be familiar with the state's political police and the state's jails. A rich brew, the Beatitudes, too heady for most.

The case for conscience over law rests secondly with nonviolence, Gandhi's Satyagraha. Gandhi drew on Hinduism and Judeo-Christianity to offer the harmony of a way of life, a revolution in the four key relationships: to God, to neighbor, to self, to creation. Life for him revolved around the momentous question: What is truth and how does one live it? Satyagraha (truth force) resolves itself eventually in Swaraj (self-rule) rule, which rejects domination of one's life by any worldly other and rejects domination over any other person. (No submission, no exploitation.) Reductively, Swaraj draws on the Beatitudes for its politics not of law but of a free-spirited people, who will to sacrifice to revolutionize hearts, lives and, finally, the system itself.

The case for conscience over law lies finally with contemporary realities, dominated by the grisly, inexorable swell of lunacy in the world: nation-state and imperial rivalries; war and doomsday weaponry; affluence against starvation; humanity sliding to catastrophe like a drunk on a ski run. Lead downhill lurcher is the United States: number one in genocide (Indochina), number one in weapons systems and scenarios of mass annihilation, number one in war-budgeting and war-making, number one in political prisoners recently in Indochina and now in Iran, Indonesia, South Korea, Chile and Brazil, number one in domestic homicide.

If one had no religious tradition, if one knew nothing of Satyagraha, sanity would still require breaking the legalities guarding the state's monopoly of force. Without that, an insanity happens—one becomes digested by the state, becomes complicit in its crimes.

From a biblical view, the state is chief idol, false God in the American soul. The Bomb and the law are others. The state needs the first for superpower credibility, the second for legitimacy. The rule of law has permitted the state to bankrupt the present and future for Americans and millions more. Law refuses to try American war criminals; law slaps the wrists of Watergate hoodlums; law goes blank before what [Ralph] Nader calls "a corporate crime wave"; law subsidizes [former President Richard] Nixon at San Clemente. But law also fills kennels like this one with "criminals": the poor acculturated to desire property like all good Americans, and then denied access.

Obviously, the law betrays a tragic vulnerability. Without the restorative of conscience, law degenerates into a legitimization of the pharaohs. Camus used to speculate about the affinity of silence to terror—silence causing terror;

terror reciprocating by reinforcing silence. Look at public silence today. Look at official terror! And Thomas Merton, with similar incisiveness, reminded us that white-collar, not blue-collar, crime is the issue threatening the very existence of humanity.

Nonetheless, the tragedy of our times is not official terrorism. It is, rather, the self-induced death of conscience. When human conscience awakens, as it must, under the impulse of God's spirit and under awareness of our collective peril, it will target neither law nor institution. Rather, it will discern evil, whether personal or structural. It will discern the many faces of death and move to resist them.

One can dream of when peace criminals will supplant the poor in the prisons and, by sheer numbers, force them out. Such a contagion of conscience will burst the prisons from within, rendering them obsolete and useless, even for arch-criminals. Such a contagion might break up the superpowers, dismantle the Bomb, outlaw war. Such a contagion might redeem the times and save the race. But the dream depends on each of us, on our fidelity to God, our love of life, our hatred of death. It depends on something like Ovid's *principiis obsta*—"Take a stand from the start!"

National Catholic Reporter

Resisting Nuclear Suicide

The Indochina war was and is a traumatic episode in American history. It is traumatic not because it marked a sharp deviation from normal American policy but precisely because it revealed to many people the true thrust of that policy.

But around the country voices spoke up against this immoral and illegal use of power. There was organizing of all sorts, there were demonstrations and marches, anti-draft campaigns and tax-refusal campaigns, refusal to register and refusal to be inducted, exile and desertion, draft card burnings and draft board destructions. Many risked prison and many spent time in prison for raising their voices and resisting. A symbol of their resistance was a Call to Resist Illegitimate Authority which a group of people issued in the midst of the war. The call to resist was made year after year as the war continued, and year after year more people responded to the reality of the war. Now *that* war is over. But is the need to resist illegitimate authority over?

Perhaps the question is better put this way: In the age of the nuclear arms race, is there any option to resisting? Since World War II the United States has spent $1.5 trillion of our tax money on war-making, or about $3,200 per year for every taxpayer. What say have we had in this use of our resources which are so badly needed here and abroad to feed, clothe, and house millions of human beings we call our sisters and brothers? The nuclear race is accelerating the misuse of these resources. We possess enough nuclear power to destroy the world several times over, yet we are adding to our stockpile of death more than three nuclear warheads every day. Added to this is the Pentagon's announced need to build whole new weapons systems to carry and deploy these warheads, systems such as the B-1 Bomber and the Trident submarine. At present the

Pentagon has on the board or in production 140 weapons systems costing $150 billion. When do we the people say: Enough! No more resources for death!

One such experiment in resisting the nuclear arms race and breaking the silence began on the steps of the Capitol in Washington at noon on Monday, July 21. Replicas of the atomic bombs dropped on Hiroshima ("Little Boy") and Nagasaki ("Fat Man") were placed on the steps, and people kept a 9 to 5 vigil Tuesdays to Saturdays in an attempt to awaken all of us to the threat facing all of us. Everybody was asked to join the vigil there—tourists, congress-people, media people. This was just one step, joining those who have bravely resisted the nuclear race for years, and sounding the cry again: Disarm or Die!

The Community Church News

A Leaflet at Christmas: Christ or the Bomb

"The prophet Elijah hiding in a cave is told to await the coming of the Lord. First, a strong and heavy wind comes by—Elijah remains in the cave. Then, an earthquake passes—Elijah stays. Then, a tremendous fire approaches—Elijah does not come out. Then, a tiny, whispering sound is heard . . . Elijah covers his face with his cloak and stands at the cave entrance awaiting his Lord" (1 Kings 19: 9–13).

"While they were there, the days of her confinement were completed. She gave birth to her first-born son and wrapped him in swaddling clothes and laid him in a manger, because there was no room for them in the inn where travelers lodged" (Lk. 2: 6–7).

The Lord comes to us as Elijah, or as Mary. The Lord comes as a tiny, whispering sound, or as a helpless child born to powerless parents. The Prince of Peace comes silently and peacefully. But only to those of silence; only to those of peace.

Christians, like others, long for peace. They long for peace while Angola yawns like Vietnam's tunnel; while the Middle East simmers; while Irish kill Irish; while Portugal teeters on the verge of civil war; while the great powers huckster their arms, plot bloody intervention, and lead the lunatic nuclear arms race. They long for peace while the tumult of bloodshed and violence drowns out the whisper of God's birth. Christ finds no room in the noisy, mad inn of the world.

We might long for peace, but for a cheap peace that will cost us nothing. Our noisy, violent spirits have no room for Him—we scramble to commercialize His birth; we hunger for more bread and circuses; we fear and hate and pre-judge; we shut our eyes to the victims; we honor an almighty and criminal

government. Christ wants a birth in us. But we give Him the trivial purposeless-
ness of our lives, and an hour's stony worship. We cherish our noise and petty
violence—much more than the promise of His silence, love, and courage.

What will the new year bring to us Christians? Will 1976, Bicentennial
though it may be, bring us more of 1975, with its wars and rumors of greater
wars? Will it inch us closer to the greatest crime, the ultimate crime—nuclear
suicide? If we cannot hear Christ, how can we hear the Bomb as it ticks closer
to humanity's midnight?

Christ's birth summons us to rebirth, to the Cross after the manger. There
will be no peace unless Christians accept the Cross. It summons us to a revolution of values, to a resurrected life, to peacemaking after war-making. It
summons us to banish the war in our hearts and to resist the war-making of
our government. It summons us to search for Him in silence, in action and
in peace.

The spirit of His birth is listening to the tiny, whispering sound of Christ's
spirit.

The spirit of His birth is sisterhood and brotherhood of all.

The spirit of His birth is resistance to the Bomb and to any government
which menaces with it.

The spirit of His birth is the struggle against death, an insistence upon
life—for oneself and for all.

All life is Christ's. And He, not the Bomb, will rule. With or without us.
What is our choice?

CU

A Time When No Leader Can Buy Us

So, the bureaucrat's case is a general one, so is the journalist's, so is the prisoner's. Like all of us, they are products of the mass phenomenon of American society—mass education, mass media, mass religion, mass ethos and values and social purpose, all adding up to mass culture. And ending in mass control. Most of us have our price; we consent to selling ourselves or being bought, while failing to perceive that such merchandising is slavery.

Essentially, the journalist or prisoner or bureaucrat differ only in degree from [former President Richard] Nixon, the classic bought/sold man, "surrounded" by a gang of zealots and thugs who shook down companies for millions of dollars, bought elections, sold services and decisions of the government, conducted illegal wars, harassed so-called enemies, committed burglaries and forgeries, provoked violence, engaged in spying on fellow Americans, ordered mass arrests in violation of the Constitution, and assisted organized crime in evading legal punishment. All possessed an ethical neutrality stemming from the dominance of "job" in a mass culture. In their case, "job" bought silence in public passivity. In Nixon's case, "job" justified high larceny and mass murder.

A few worries and questions. What buys the scope of silence which allows the government to spend with impunity $1.3 trillion on war-making since 1946? How many lives must the rich hold in bondage before they hold government in bondage also, now existing virtually for them? One can only guess in response, while comprehending, nonetheless, that the main traffic is not in goods or services at all. It is in the lives and spirits of Americans. *They* bring a rapturous jangle to the cash registers.

Nothing particularly new here—Scripture said it all before. Recall excuses in the Gospel for absence from the wedding feast—a new wife, a farm, oxen. Currently, as for three decades, the murderous war policies of Washington call for sustained public resistance. But the excuses remain—a "job," the sweet life, bloodline responsibilities, fear of separation and prison as the disaster. Such a lack of spiritual fiber is stupefying in its implications—it normalizes merchandising of the spirit; it sells freedom cheaply; it abandons innocent people to the powermongering of official ad men, or to the *Junkers* of the superpower; it reduces human survival to a blasphemous conjecture.

Somewhat to the point, Christians could ponder the dialogue between Christ and Pilate in John's Gospel. "Reentering the Praetorium, Pilate said to Jesus, 'Where do you come from?' But Jesus made no answer. Pilate then said to him, 'Are you refusing to speak to me? Surely you know that I have the power to release you and I have the power to crucify you?' 'You would have no power over me,' replied Jesus, 'if it had not been given you from above; that is why the one who handed me over to you has the greater guilt'" (Jn. 19: 10, 11). Which is a profoundly tactful way of saying to that ancient functionary, "You don't have any power over me at all" since your power doesn't come from God; your power isn't moral.

Similarly, the power of any leader (Hitler, Nixon, Ford) to implicate a people in the crimes of empire is only what people allow, only what is in their heads. If we claim that Nixon's power was illegitimate because of foreign genocide, nuclear sovereignty over life and death, or domestic corruption, we are saying in the same breath that his power, or that of his marionettes in the domestic management apparatus, is immoral, non-objective, nonexistent. They possessed over us only such power as we gave them. The same holds true today.

Finally, there are our idolatries and their part in creating the leader and making him necessary. In a biblical sense, idols are what we love when we fail to love God with all our being, and our sisters and brothers as ourselves. It is our idols which substitute ersatz for real, plague us with doubt and guilt, ready us for official magicmen who will verify our lies with greater lies, who will secure our toys and security blankets, who already hit us for mass rip-offs like Indochina, Watergate and #1 status.

That is what supergovernment is about—the protection of our idols. That is why we sell ourselves—to possess idols. And that is why the destruction of idols, and liberation from their brassy, demonic charms, is also to resist the leader— his pomps and circumstances, his deceits, minions and bombs. There may even come a time when no leader can buy us, a time also when we won't sell.

Catholic Agitator

The Kenosis of Christ

This ten-day jail sentence stems from the digging of symbolic "graves" on the lawn of Secretary of War Donald Rumsfeld's home on August 28, 1976.

Our second day here — Vince Scotti and I. Despite overcrowding — twenty-two prisoners in a sixteen-person dormitory — the jail is better than many. The food is substantial, if leaning heavily to meat; the prisoners amenable and considerate; the staff prompt to act on legitimate requests.

Vince and I spent an hour or so on Philippians 2. It struck me once again how the Bible cleanses through garbage to fundamentals and real substance. It is the letter of a prisoner (Paul) to us prisoners: "Never act out of rivalry or conceit; rather, let all parties think humbly of others as superior to themselves . . . your attitude must be that of Christ Who though he was in the form of God, emptied himself and took the form of a slave . . . obediently accepting death, death on a cross" (Phil 2, 3 seq).

The kenosis of Christ (self-emptying) is precisely what Christians find most threatening. Perhaps for two reasons: (1) we must destroy false gods like ego, property, attachments to others (domination of them), and eject the demons who afflict us with false gods; and (2) we must substitute the real God — Christ with His infinite compassion, fearlessness, and freedom. We find both sides of the process abhorrent, because toppling the false gods leaves us with no familiar anchor. And because the incomprehensible freedom of Christ leaves us trembling and revolted.

In similar vein, who thinks of others as superior to self? The psychological illusions permeating our culture state that self is first; self alone is overriding. Such distortion — also at the heart of capitalist self-interest — is tremendously

bewildering and destructive. God loses sovereignty and Lordship; others supe-
riority/equality. The God who abused Himself/Herself by becoming human,
and who welcomed abasement further in assuming the condition of a criminal and a criminal's cross, loses meaning. Christians search for a will-o'-the-
wisp —their true selves through selfishness.

The Church, for its part, will neither preach kenosis nor practice it. In such
a climate, the state becomes Church, and assumes the Church to itself, making it a whore. Consequently, a handful of believers encounter the spectacle
of an exterminator/state, armed with weapons of mass extermination, and a
flabby, unfaithful Church. Both are blind leading blind; both are purveyors of
confusion and fear. Together, they may bring down the world—the Church
through omission and default, the state through fateful arrogance of power.

Note —this ten-day jail sentence stems from the dig-in at Secretary of War
Donald Rumsfeld's home on August 28, 1976. Mrs. Rumsfeld testified against
us—Scotti and I cross-examined her to a minor degree, Hizzoner declaring
most of our questions "irrelevant to the crime." He fines us $100 or $10 per
diem. We refuse to pay the fine and go to jail.

Next court appearance, January 21, for the December 28 action at the
Pentagon.

CU

Fools on Christ's Account

Phil's statement for trial and sentencing for his action on December 28, 1976 (Feast of the Holy Innocents), where twenty-nine people were arrested, some of whom had poured blood on the pillars of the Pentagon.

In pondering a few words for this occasion, I happened on to Paul's First Letter to the Church at Corinth. Let me share two brief passages from the early chapters with you: "Let no one delude himself. If any one of you thinks he is wise in a worldly way, one had better become a fool. In that way, one will be truly wise, for the wisdom of this world is absurdity with God" (1 Cor 3:18). And again: "We are fools on Christ's account" (1 Cor 4:10).

I know people who treasure their roots in a long line of fools, beginning with Brother Fool, Christ himself. The apostles were fools, died for their foolishness. So were the women and men who filled the pages of the martyrology, like Anastasia, Agnes and Ignatius. So were the witnesses through the centuries, many of them persecuted by church and state alike. So were the Bonhoeffers, Delps and Jägerstätters of the Nazi era, for their resistance to Hitler. All were fools on command, the command being: "Love one another as I have loved you."

Clearly that commandment makes such people fools. But so do the wise of this world — the Herods of history — the Stalins, Hitlers and Nixons of our own time. So do the high priests of science — the Fathers of the Bomb, whether American or Russian. So do the *Junkers* of the military bureaucracies; or the cozy, ambivalent functionaries of the major faiths; or the corporate chieftains and their trafficking in goods, services, and people. So does the judiciary and its legalizing of white-collar crime. The commandment makes fools of such people; but so do the buyers and sellers of death.

In a modest fashion, I have sought membership in this company of fools. This is my seventh indictment for anti-war resistance; it will probably result in my fifth conviction. One indictment for foolishness allowed life imprisonment upon conviction. Through over thirty-nine months in prison, through long fasts and bouts of solitary confinement, through two indictments while in jail, I have been reckoned a fool, by pharaohs and friends alike. My brother is a fool, barely tolerated by the Jesuits and by the public. My wife is a fool, as incorrigible as I. (It is our passionate hope that our two tiny children will avoid the paths of the wise.) We live in a community of fools, unregenerate and stubborn, frequently judged by family and acquaintance as feeble-minded or fixated. Furthermore, a dear friend, a younger fool, serves sentence in a federal penitentiary, somewhat unique in his imprisonment for post–Indochina war resistance.

Let none find our foolishness puzzling. It is as simple as honoring the Fifth Commandment and rejecting official legitimations of murder. It is obedience to the truth and compassion of Christ; or recognizing no enemy in the world. It is as simple as the struggle that children might live; or that everyone might become what they are—daughters and sons of God. It is as simple as respecting the planet as common property, as common gift and heritage. That is the idiot vision—that is the summons and task. For that, as Paul promised, one risks becoming the world's refuge, the scum of all (1 Cor. 4, 13).

CU

Thoughts from Alexandria Jail

Phil was incarcerated for the pouring of blood on the pillars of the Pentagon on December 28, 1976.

Something for the record, my tenth bust and seventh conviction for talking back to Caesar. The tally grows, but the toll remains negligible in light of the stakes. Some few years back, the nuns used to tell us that we were on this Earth to save souls. Today, that's a challenge, the Bomb being *Alter Christus* for so many Christians.

It occurs to me that every new weapons system deployed claims a proportionate number of victims. The Soviet SS-18 and the American Minuteman III have their counterpart in spiritual cadavers. More and more people die inside as we threaten with more and deadlier technologies. It is in this area of spiritual strangulation that the real storm gathers, with a force that can assault all life and reduce it to radioactive ash.

The action went smoothly enough, the police can outnumber us two to one and still be powerless to protect sixteen pillars from blood. The police tackled us, threw us to the steps, handcuffed us behind the back with plastic thongs, throwaway handcuffs. Hoses appeared, and a powerful stream of what looked like water, sand and detergent sluiced down the pillars. A carmine flood washed the steps, over the sidewalk and into the parking lot, the object being to get signs of broken covenant and slaughter out of sight.

I stood under guard with the others and watched faces—disbelief, revulsion, shock. Unrequested, we introduced conflict—service within that awful building obviously requires bloody work without its ever being identified as bloody work. The job ethos holds nonetheless—military, civilians and police sidestepped the grisly traces and got about their work. Within forty minutes, they know, police efficiency will have whisked away everything discourteous or offensive—blood and us. And then a blessed normalcy could return.

Five hours of legal burlesque in the courtroom—boring, predictable, interminable. I have a recurrent vision, as I always do on trial, of all the official cutthroats since history's dawn huddling uneasily under an umbrella marked THE LAW.

OBBI

Philip Berrigan in uniform during World War II with his uncle Father Edmund Berrigan, 1944.

Newly ordained as a Josephite priest.

Phil with his parents, Thomas and Freda Berrigan, August 1958, Syracuse, New York.

The Baltimore Four. On October 27, 1967, Phil and three others entered the Selective Service headquarters in Baltimore, Maryland, and poured their own blood on draft files as a symbolic act of nonviolent resistance to the Vietnam War.

The Catonsville Nine. On May 17, 1968, Phil, Dan, and seven others entered the Selective Service office in Catonsville, Maryland, and burned draft files in the parking lot with homemade napalm. (Getty Images)

On April 21, 1970, Phil was eventually apprehended by FBI agents after refusing to report to prison, having instead gone underground and become a fugitive from justice.

Phil and Liz with daughter Frida, 1974, at Jonah House.

Phil under arrest and handcuffed during an action at the Pentagon, August 6, 1977 (Hiroshima Day). The pillars behind him are stained with a broken bottle of Phil's blood, symbolically splashed there.

Phil with toddler Frida at a protest in 1975.

Phil, Bruce Friedrich, Lynn Fredriksson, and Rev. John Dear incarcerated after a December 7, 1993, Plowshares action at Seymour Johnson Air Force Base in Goldsboro, North Carolina.

Phil speaking at the Pentagon, 1995.
He returned there often for actions.
"Meet me at the Pentagon."

Phil in prison jumpsuit
with visitors. From left
to right are Kate, Liz,
Phil, Frida, and Dan.

Phil and Liz, 2002.

In loving memory of

Philip Berrigan

October 5, 1923 - December 6, 2002

"Peacemaking is not only a central characteristic of the Gospel,
peacemaking is the greatest need of the world today.
We are the daughters and sons of God,
and that means we are called to be peacemakers."

Philip Berrigan prayer card used for
his funeral, 2002.

Phil's handmade casket carried through the streets of Baltimore, 2002. More than 600 people followed the procession for the memorial service held at St. Peter Claver Catholic Church.

Liz on the day of the funeral, 2002.

The Berrigan children—Kate (*left*), Frida (*center*), and Jerry (*right*)—at Peace House in Kalamazoo, Michigan, in 2019.

Phil at Jonah House, 2002. (Art Milholland)

Prophecy and Life

Written for convocation at Manchester College.

Sisters and Brothers:

As my share of this general topic "Prophecy and Life," I've been asked to say something abstractly and concretely about sustaining struggle, about maintaining stamina in struggle, and about a deepening commitment as one's life advances. Maybe the question is misplaced, however. I think probably the biblical paraphrase would be "How does one grow up? How does one become a mature person, become an adult—a person of deeds and works in the New Testament sense?" Most of you can recall our Lord pointing to His works, the things He did, and saying, "You don't have to believe in me, but how are you going to handle these works? Believe in them, if you will."

I'd like to share with you a poem of my brother's. He is that kind of rare combination of writer and poet and activist. You'll notice his preoccupation with the concrete. He says this:

For every ten thousand words,
there is a deed
floating somewhere
head down
unborn.
Words can't make it happen.
They only wave it away
Unwanted

And then he uses a metaphor, and he calls the deed a child.

Yet child,
necessary one,
unless you come home to my hands,
why do I have hands at all?
Your season,
your cries,
are their skill,
their reason.

We draw deeds out of our persons the way a midwife or an obstetrician draws a child from its mother's body. Our hands are meant to make the deed happen, otherwise why do we have hands at all? The time for the deed is urgent—like that of a baby urgent to be born. It provides skill and reason to hands.

Remember the Pauline observation "When I was a child I spoke like a child, I thought like a child, I reasoned like a child; when I became an adult, I gave up childish ways" (1 Cor. 13:11). This matter of Christian growth has two sources, the first from God and the second from the human community (which we as Christians believe is under the inspiration of God). This is because the Christian is by definition daughter or son of God and sister or brother of all people. That statement, in itself, is no more than a reflection of the great commandment that you will love the Lord your God with all your strength and that you will love your sister or brother as yourself. God therefore sponsors the deed.

So, we have to ask the question, "What does God require of me?" You remember the Fourth Beatitude taken from Matthew's treatment. Paraphrased, it says this: "Blessed are those whose greatest desire is to do what God requires, for God will satisfy them fully." What does God require? Very simply, that we are reborn in His Son. It means we are to be reborn into the works of Christ, which is the telling of the Truth. Everything begins with that.

He lived the Truth. He healed and comforted and liberated people from their slavery to evil—deeds again. His words had importance only insofar as His deeds matched His words. In reflection the people said, He has done all things well.

He loved, which is to say He sacrificed—our flesh always shrinks from sacrifice. He laid down his freedom and life for his people: us. He Himself said the night before He died, "Greater love than this no person has, than to lay down his or her life for a friend." And everybody, of course, was his friend.

Is this sacrificial love to be taken literally? Certainly, it is! If one's greatest desire is to do what God requires, it is to be taken literally. Gandhi took it literally and said this at one point in his career: "Millions sacrifice themselves in war, without any guarantee that the world will be better as a result or even that the enemy will be defeated. Yet who does not fiercely resent the suggestion that anybody die in deliberate nonviolent sacrifice?"

The maturity of deeds also has its source in the human community which is operating in obedience to God. The community is under the inspiration of the Holy Spirit and as a result the community conspires. Conspires: If you were to take the word apart, it means "to breathe together." This is no more than the paraphrase of what we call life, which has its source in God, who is one, but is also community. He has three persons.

The first act of the public ministry of Christ was to form a community. And reflecting back upon the experience before He died, He prayed that "They may be one in us, Father, as I am one in you, and you are one in me." The first move of the Disciples following the ascension of Christ was to form the churches, to form communities. Out of this, Christians must understand that they must embody the unity of God and the unity of humanity—and that that embodiment is community. We must think as a community, live as a community, be accountable to a community even as we are accountable to God.

The constant deepening of the desire to do what God requires in Christ is contemplation, and the constant public expression of the desire to do what humanity requires is resistance. So, one endures, one keeps going, one continues, sometimes against all human hope, in fidelity to a vision that comes mainly from the Sermon on the Mount. A vision that sees we are one in God and that we are one in each other. I don't mean that in a rhetorical sense; I mean that in the most highly concrete, practical, and lived sense.

One knows that the central characteristic and the final summation of biblical light is peacemaking. As our present pope says, "Well, you have peace, or you have nothing." That's putting it boldly, but that's pretty close to the truth. The Bible was *centrally* preoccupied with the building and erection of peace. Christ wished the Disciples peace both before and after His death, implying that they were to carry this ultimate gift, His Truth. His reconciliation, His resistance, to every living person.

Thoughtful people know that our civilization is doomed as it stands now and that it has doomed itself. Thoughtful people, including some scientists who have become the prophets of apocalypse today, warn us of all this. Yet thoughtful people think and talk, but they don't act. Also notice that scientists have always spoken out against something that they were instrumental in developing only afterward when it was safe to speak out. And they never acted.

Not, however, the biblical person, who is light years removed from the thoughtful person. The biblical person will think, certainly, but will act as well. As Gandhi put it, "God never appears to you in person, but only in action." A very pungent way of putting this. Or as Christ would say, "You will know others and yourself by their fruits." Their works, their conduct. The biblical person supports contemplation and he or she will digest the Bible into gut and spirit; but he or she will also act risking freedom, and even life, for the victims. The biblical person will use faith and common sense and will render to Caesar what belongs to Caesar—and that is virtually nothing—and to God what belongs to God—and that is literally everything!

The biblical person will realize, finally, that not to resist the warfare state, not to know the state's indictments, courts, prisons, is to join the spiritual death already rampant. It is to worship idols and to reject God. It is to abandon sisters and brothers to the probability of the greatest crime since the Crucifixion: mass suicide. That's what we're faced with today. I guess my few stumbling words are an exhortation to deeds, to conduct that is worthy of you.

Bulletin of the Peace Studies Institute

Hostage to the Bomb

A letter sent to the Saint Theresa Catholic Worker House, The Little Way, and published in May–June 1977.

Letter from Prison

Have been locked up for December 28 action at the Pentagon, since January 31. Liz is over in the women's section doing ninety days. [Liz participated in the same action at the Pentagon.] Other sisters and brothers in West Virginia and Pennsylvania. Came from Plains to do ten days in Rockville, Maryland, for an action at [Secretary of War Donald] Rumsfeld's house, where they dug symbolic "graves" in his front yard and now sixty days here.

Yes, the times are very critical. The credential for nationhood is the Bomb. Proliferation is a fact; everyone in the world is a hostage to the Bomb. As for most people, they are Bombed out; there's a very profound demonic factor there. They will literally pay taxes for their own destruction. As for us, the struggle is not only for the race/family. It is for our souls. To do nothing is to choose the Bomb rather than Christ.

We all have the arid times, the dark nights of soul. But they are probably more profitable than the graceful times. To struggle, to pray in the times of dryness, to meditate on the New Testament daily, to summon the Holy Spirit out of his/her silence—this is fidelity, this is maturity. And above all, to live faithfully to one's present state of conscience.

Peace in the struggle, Phil Berrigan.

The *Catholic Worker*

Back to the Pentagon

Phil's statement for sentencing on April 28, 1978. He and others had returned yet again to the Pentagon to pour blood and spread ashes.

In considering a brief statement for sentencing, a verse from Paul's Letter to the Romans struck me as suitable: "Instead, give yourselves to God, as people who have come back from the dead to life, and surrender your whole being to God, as weapons for justice" (Rom. 6:13).

So, I pondered, what does it mean to come back from the dead? What did that awesome experience mean to the little daughter of Jairus, or the widow of Naim's son, or to Lazarus himself?

To be sure, Paul speaks of a different death. So did Christ in his conversation with Martha before raising Lazarus. In fact, He raised the dead simply to show Himself as the life of the world, as the paradigm of human life — as life itself. And therefore, as victor over death — the death of the spirit which Paul isolates in the same letter: "Because people refuse to keep in mind the true knowledge about God, he has given them over to corrupted minds, so that they do things they should not. They are filled with every kind of wickedness, maliciousness, greed, ill will, envy, murder, bickering, deceit, craftiness. They are gossips and slanderers, they hate God, are insolent, haughty, boastful, ingenious in their wrongdoing. . . . One sees in the people without conscience, without loyalty, without affection, without pity" (Rom. 1: 28–32).

Here I have no intention of sermonizing or turning this court into a pulpit. Nor can I in justice indict "they," "you," while exempting myself from infidelity toward God and from betrayal of people. I as well as you have felt the turmoil of Paul's deadly litany in my life. I as well as you have submitted to death in myself rather than to the works of justice and of life.

In a word, I stand indicted with you—we all stand in the dock before God and humanity. (And the dock is not this courtroom.) The symbol of our death, our refusal to live, is the Bomb. What society, daring to call itself civilized, can prepare the incineration of tens, possibly hundreds, of millions? Ours can! What nation, daring our Declaration of Independence and our Bill of Rights, can cancel out its own right to live by moving inexorably to mass suicide? Ours can! What people, daring to call itself Judeo-Christian, can enlist God in scenarios to poison His creation and to atomize His people? Ours can!

The Soviets can also, that I'll admit, but not with our contradictions—not under our avowals of justice and peacemaking, not under our rhetoric of inviolable human rights, not under our fervid moral and religious profession.

To return to Paul, and this admonition: "Surrender your whole being to God, as weapons for justice." He writes as a Jew, who now accepts another Jew as Lord and Savior. And he writes from a dominant theme of his tradition—what we call the Old Testament—that one cannot know God until one does justice. The God of the unjust is not God at all, but human illusion, a concoction of idols, a lie. It is this lie, this injustice, which has made comfort stations of our churches, which legislates weapons rather than bread, which transforms the world into a huge time bomb, ready to explode.

Others in this society, or in this courtroom, may embrace other means to live spiritually and to break enslavement to the Bomb. I'd like to hear them, in all openness and respect. But for Ladon Sheats [Philip's co-defendant] and me—the means are resisting the Pentagon, asking sisters and brothers there, or the brother in the White House, or the brothers on the Joint Chiefs of Staff: "What are you doing? Do you want to loose hell upon this Earth to keep the U.S. number one, or because of a job, or because of a misbegotten concept of patriotism or law, or because of an ideology centered on our Way of Life? Are you going to murder any less certainly with a 20-megaton bomb than with a club or a Saturday Night Special?"

As I say, we returned to the Pentagon to register a nonviolent question, breaking the law because the law legalizes the murderous intention, the annual billions for war, the scenarios for irradiation, the overkill, the counterforce weapons, the first-strike policy, the prospect of mutual suicide. It's the only obedience we know, the only way we've discovered to face our own injustice, and the other injustice threatening to engulf us all. It's the only way we know of "coming back from the dead to life."

CU

We Cannot Be Silent if We Want Peace

A letter written from the Richmond jail, May 28, 1978.

Friends:

On April 28, Judge Oren Lewis of the Federal District Court, Alexandria, Virginia, sentenced Esther Cassidy, Ladon Sheats, John Schuchardt and me to one year in prison, with six months suspended, followed by two years' probation. We joined in prison Ed Clark, with a similar sentence, and Carl Kabot, O.M.I., serving one year. All six of us are from the Jonah House Community in Baltimore.

Lewis forbade a statement at sentencing, gave us successive sentences despite concurrent dropping of charges for exactly similar offenses in his and other federal courts, and disregarded Esther Cassidy's pregnancy of three months, her recovery from a serious Easter Sunday auto accident, and her first-offense status.

We'd poured blood on the pillars and floors of the Pentagon, revealing its bloodletting covering three decades. And we scattered ashes, as a symbol of mourning and repentance, and as a warning against a world in nuclear ash.

At Catonsville we said that the genocide stops here. Now we say that the preparations for mass suicide stop here. To prepare for mass suicide is to be guilty of it. We will not pay for the conspiracies and mass destruction weapons of this or any government. We will not contribute our silence. Rather, we will testify against official waste and madness, simply because the price of complicity is unconscionably exorbitant. If physical freedom is bought only by complicity, then we will discard complicity by breaking the law.

The court sentenced us purely because we broke the law and offered to withdraw sentence if we promised to honor the law. But in our view, the law clearly legalizes the state's lawlessness. If we are cremated in mass nuclear destruction, we will have the consolation of knowing that it was legal.

Perhaps our imprisonment—in my case added to forty-four months already served for nonviolent resistance to war—will give weight to the following reflection: If we want peace, we will have to stop making war. If we are silent, we are making war. All this government needs to lead the world to nuclear ruin is an irrelevant vote every four years, a sizable slice of our income (for war), and silence.

We trust that sisters and brothers will awake—as the Gospel entreats. And respond in time.

Fraternally in Christ, Philip Berrigan

CU

Letter from Prison to Dorothy Day

Dear Dorothy,

Have meant to write for some time. In any event, all of us—John Schuchardt, Ladon Sheats, Fr. Carl Kabat, Ed Clark and I—send greetings, love, peace.

You might have heard that Carl Kabat, a priest from Jonah House in Baltimore, is finishing up a year for civil disobedience at the War Department, and that the rest of us are serving six months, six-month suspended sentence, and two years' probation. Once again, the government tries to neutralize us. It's an automatic response when people begin to resist their murderous policies.

A little more history—our Jonah House friends from Baltimore have been going to Washington, D.C., to the White House, Pentagon, since the fall of Saigon in April of 1975. Our concern, of course, was the Bomb. Since then, there have been dozens of civil disobediences, hundreds of arrests, and considerable jail time. For example, most of us here have been arrested twelve to seventeen times and have served many months in jail. This term will take me over four years' imprisonment—between Vietnam and the Bomb.

Elizabeth and our two children, Frida and Jerry, are superb. Liz has just finished a ten-day workshop/campaign at the Pentagon. There were five arrests on Wednesday, July 5. I just heard from Mike Harank, an old friend from Holy Cross. And Dan tells me that the Catholic Worker was represented at the UN sit-in on June 12. Thank God for that!

You're familiar with Allenwood Prison, I know—a huge, government beef, swine, and dairy farm. We do easy time here, despite the overcrowding and limited facilities (like library and workspace). But the staff is generally low-keyed, and the food is good.

Our prayers that you're well. Please remember us in your prayers. Christ's peace be with you and His spirit's light and life. Love from all of us,

In the Lord, Phil Berrigan

Catholic Worker, CU

A Call to Faithfulness

For complying with our government, giving us a false reverence for
    peace, forgive us o lord.
For the greed and power that enable us to construct our weapons of
    death, forgive us o lord.
For our continuing neglect of the world's poor and needy, forgive us o
    lord.
For the involvement of our church institutions in nuclear madness,
    forgive us o lord.
For the past, present and future victims of ongoing militarization,
    forgive us o lord.
For the enslavement of and violence to Blacks and other minorities,
    our sisters and brothers, forgive us o lord.
For our children who are absorbed in our lust for a war mentality,
    forgive us o lord.
For the myth of deterrence as a policy for peace, forgive us o lord.
For the hideous and immoral military budget from which our world's
    ghettos and starving result, forgive us o lord.
For our passiveness and neutrality in allowing the promotion and idol-
    atry of the Bomb and its terror, forgive us o lord.
For our selfishness and overconsumption in the face of starvation,
    forgive us o lord.
Because of the frivolous life we have created for ourselves with our will
    for war, forgive us o lord.
For our failure to urgently pursue alternative forms of energy, forgive
    us o lord.

To this temple of death, the Pentagon, we say, let us disarm.

Because of the death and suffering of long-term nuclear victims who are dying even today, let us disarm.

For the multitudes of broken people who live in despair, let us disarm.

For those victims and our timeless destitution, let us disarm.

For the continuance of life, where the living must envy the dead, let us disarm.

To halt the further testing of our death technology, let us disarm.

For our diplomatic threats to use atomic and hydrogen bombs, let us disarm.

For the children who suffer from cancer and leukemia from nuclear fallout, let us disarm.

Because of threats posed by the radioactive waste from nuclear power plants, let us disarm.

To the lust of corporate greed and war profiteering we must say, let us disarm.

To our complacency with falsehood and our acceptance of blood money as a way of life, let us disarm.

For our commitment to peace that comes through God's love, not weapons, strengthen us o lord.

For the living resurrection and spiritual awareness, strengthen us o lord.

To resist the Pentagon's misuse of our tax dollars, strengthen us o lord.

For the building of humane communities as our alternatives to death, strengthen us o lord.

So that we may lay down our fears, strengthen us o lord.

To hope in the face of despair and brokenness, strengthen us o lord.

For the spring of resurrection which is yet to bloom, strengthen us o lord.

Lord, remember Christ your Son who is peace Himself and who has washed away our hatred with His blood. Because you love all brothers and sisters, look with mercy on us. Banish the violence and evil within us by this offering. Restore tranquility and peace through Jesus our brother.

CU

Naming the Beast

The Holy Spirit reminds us that until we name the Beast, i.e., expose its lies and curb, however modestly, its destructiveness, it names us, defines us, enslaves us as accomplices in its colossal crimes.

OBBI

Tribute to Liz

Liz has gone to Washington and California for speaking engagements, invited by Dick Carbray in Seattle, Sam Tyson in Modesto, The Catholic Worker in Los Angeles. She has [their daughter] Frida along as companion. Given the interest in those areas, a grueling schedule results, even without a twenty-two-month-old to tend to.

We seldom speak or write of our marriage, our friendship, even to those closest to us. Not because we have privatized it, so to speak, but because God has normalized it by His grace. Why thump the drum for the normal? (We realize such an explanation might not be helpful to others.)

Maybe we assume too much in a time when the "soft" institutions like church, family and school are enduring a piecemeal destruction. That is why I laboriously write this little tribute.

I still wonder at the resources that allowed Liz to survive thirty-two months of prison separation, including the Harrisburg indictment. Or the tent-like existence of the Jonah House Community with its simplicity of life far eclipsing that of our respective religious communities. Or resistance—action after action—arrests, courts and jails, all accepted uncompromisingly for ourselves and our children. I wonder at her selflessness—with interminable and endlessly repeated meetings, with cleaning and cooking, with correspondence, with study and lecture preparation, with the bewildering human and physical needs of children and community. I wonder that she views this as natural and normal—this hand-to-mouth struggle, this unpredictable skirmishing with Mother State. She is very nearly unique, like Ruth and Esther and Mary, that rarity that God places among us as a sign. I recall David Eberhardt's modest compliment, when she ran herself ragged for us while we were underground: "That Liz! She is so amazing."

We understand, I think, even as evidence deepens understanding, that a marriage lived for others will engulf the married with its blessings. By standards of indulgence, we have nothing. By and large, society views us with contempt and fear. But we have everything. As Tolstoy's angel says in *What Men Live By*: "It is not given to man to know his own needs. . . . I understood that God does not wish men to live apart, and therefore, He does not reveal to them what each one needs for himself/herself; but He wishes them to live united, and therefore reveals to each of them what is necessary to all."

Liz comprehends that elusive, self-evident truth. She learned it from the Gospel, the Eucharist, the Church. She loves Christ and holds herself in constant tension with His summons and His life. I recall the many times we pondered His reminder of the Last Journey to Jerusalem. "Listen," He told the Disciples. "We are going up to Jerusalem, where the Son of Man will be handed over to the chief priests and the teachers of the Law" (Mat. 20:17–18). The question is, what is the Last Journey for us? That is obscure, of course, but it has something precisely to do with resistance to the pharaohs. Even as it did for Him.

I have never seen a person with less insulation between Gospel and life. It almost seems that in her case, belief in the Word attacks insulation, overwhelms it, throws it into retreat. That preserves her clarity; saves her from psychologizing; frees her for humor, movement, life. So she works like a slave, but effortlessly, in cheerfulness and balance. She stays alive. She has no time for anything smacking of death—complaining, indulgence, self-pity, negativism, irritability. There is service to offer, resistance to be planned, peace to make, life to live. So, I revere her, love her, remain in no little awe of her. The *Digitum Dei* is on her; the Lamb's mark on her forehead. She is a Christian, one of the holiest (wholest) of the handful I know.

OBBI

Liz in Prison

Liz writes me from the Alexandria jail, where she begins a six-month sentence for dousing the Pentagon with blood. There is some chance of a reduction to four months.

Liz and I are fairly unique in this respect—we had our marriage of May 1969 interrupted by thirty-two months of prison for me. In this one, as well— we have Frida (thirty-two months now) and Jerry (twenty months now)—but obviously not with us. Rather, with friends at Jonah House—our sisters and brothers in resistance. Which fact runs smack-dab counter to mass thinking and practice—to church, state, culture—every value our unhappy society tries to make stick.

CU

Beating Swords into Plowshares

On September 9, 1980, Phil, Dan, Dean Hammer, Elmer Maas, Carl Kabat, Anne Montgomery, Molly Rush, and John Schuchardt walked into the General Electric Nuclear Missile Re-entry Division in King of Prussia, Pennsylvania, found a room with unarmed nuclear nose cone missiles, and hammered on them to fulfill Isaiah's oracle that someday people will "beat swords into plowshares, and their spears into pruning hooks, and study war no more." They also poured blood on blueprints and papers nearby. They were quickly arrested, jailed, faced ten years in prison for this action, and became known as The Plowshares Eight. A tumultuous trial ensued. Theirs was the first of hundreds of subsequent Plowshares disarmament actions carried out by activists around the world.

Empty parking lots, shards of light, the patter of our footsteps climbing stairs. The plant spreading squid-like and ominously quiet. We race past a security guard, to a door, a sign: "This is a non-destructible testing room." Inside, we find nose cones for Mark 12A warheads, the world's most advanced reentry vehicle for ICBMs. These warheads carry an atomic package of 336 to 350 kilotons; the Hiroshima bomb carried twelve-and-a-half kilotons.

We go to work, beating swords into plowshares, ruining two Mark 12A nose cones before screaming security guards rush into the room. We lay our hammers on a table. No one resists. Our arms are yanked behind our backs, and we are shoved from the room. But not before I manage to pull a vial of blood from my back pocket and splash it over classified blueprints.

The Plowshares Eight—Dan Berrigan, Philip Berrigan, Dean Hammer, Elmer Maas, Carl Kabat, Anne Montgomery, Molly Rush, John Schuchardt—have no illusions about the warfare state. Congressmen and women won't visit us in jail, the Pentagon isn't going to invite us over for a chat, the president will never call to ascertain our motives for invading General Electric's plant at King of Prussia.

Nothing of that matters; we aren't attempting to reform or overthrow the government. We don't care who sits in the White House, or who walks the hallowed halls of Congress. The King of Prussia action and Plowshare actions that will follow are not attempts to offer an alternative policy to nuclear madness.

We pour our blood at GE in order to proclaim the sin of mass destruction. In the words of my brother Daniel, we are confronting the "spiritually insane." Confronting not with mere words, but through symbols. Our blood confronts the irrational, makes megadeath concrete, summons the war-makers to their senses.

The authorities react to us with apprehension, even hatred. We fill them with fear and dread, as though we carry a plague. We are taken to jail and locked up. An hour passes, then two. No one speaks to us. We are given no food or water.

Then we are herded into a van, driven back to the General Electric plant, and ordered to disembark. When we refuse, guards roll a wheelchair up to the door and slam one of our group into the seat. One by one they force us to enter the plant. I ignore their threats. They decide not to drag me from the van.

The others are paraded, some walk, others are carried, before a gauntlet of angry GE employees. Blood-stained papers marked "Top Secret" are scattered about the room. The culprits are identified, indicted, and convicted on the spot.

We are returned to jail, stripped of our pants and shoes, and are ushered again into the jail to await our fate. We know the wires to Washington are humming. We have invaded one of the government's atomic temples, offended the high priests of megadeath, poured blood over the national security state's idols. Lord Nuke will exact revenge.

No food or water. Around 6:00 P.M., we are ushered, still in our stocking feet, before a judge who charges us with thirteen felony counts. Bail is set at $250,000 for six defendants. Dan and I are held without bond. The charges are ludicrous, the bail absurdly high. Our active disarmament harmed no one. We scattered our blood on an evil system, not on the men and women who work at GE. We beat on nose cones, not human beings.

Daniel Berrigan, Anne Montgomery, Dean Hammer, and Molly Rush agree to accept bail in order to organize support and defense committees for The Plowshare Eight. Outstanding defense committees were organized in places like Pittsburgh, Norristown, Philadelphia, New York City, and Baltimore. We shortly enjoy the volume of support that went far beyond expectations.

The courthouse sent messengers across the street to make us an offer. We could leave jail on our own recognizances, no bail required. A promise to show up for trial would suffice. A rather remarkable offer. Five months before, the government refused to set bail; now, it was offering to release me, and other King of Prussia defendants, with absolutely no bail. We turn this offer down, stating our intention to remain behind bars until our trial. Desperate to see us leave, the court ordered our jailers to kick us out, to literally eject us. That was the first of two occasions when I've been tossed not in, but out of, jail.

We come to trial in April 1981 before Samuel Salus III, a judge so inept and incompetent that his own associates had considered disbarring him. He was absolutely one of the worst judges I have ever encountered. Our attorneys were Ramsey Clark, Charles Glackin, and Michael Shields. All dear friends who served us well. We were familiar with court and had no illusions about the judicial system. We weren't expecting to find justice in Judge Salus's courtroom. The judge perched on his throne, his black robe swollen with importance. And why not? He understood the game being played out in that room. He was sworn to protect the empire, regardless of what his masters might be doing, or planning to do, to all of Creation. He was sworn to crush the weak on behalf of the powerful. He was there not to arbitrate justice, but to perpetuate violence.

Salus ranted and threatened, charged us with contempt of court, hurled invective and insults at us. We tried to talk about the necessity defense, which was not allowed in this trial and would not be allowed in subsequent trials of Plowshare activists. In other words, if a house full of children is burning, it is necessary to break the door to rescue them. This, in essence, is the necessity defense. At the Plowshare Eight trial, and future Plowshare trials, the government refused to allow this defense, arguing that we could not prove that nuclear war was imminent. We explained that nuclear war could happen at any time. It was imminent because the government was designing, building, and deploying nuclear weapons. It was imminent because our air, water, and food supplies were being poisoned with radioactive isotopes; because atomic testing had already killed millions of people worldwide.

At one point, we walked out on the farce, leaving Salus to fume. We returned to General Electric plant number nine at King of Prussia and attempted to continue our civil disobedience there. Bishop Parilla from Puerto Rico, an outstanding resister, accompanied us, but the guards kept us outside. The next day, we boycotted the court again, returning to plant number nine, where sheriff's deputies had arrested us. In Great Britain and Northern Ireland, IRA defendants would often show their contempt for corrupt court proceedings by turning their backs on judges. After many futile, frustrating, humiliating days, we turned our backs on Judge Salus. He ranted and threatened; we ignored him.

The state has death as its *modus vivendi*, while a Plowshare action insists on the primacy and sacredness of life. A Plowshare action states that we are all sisters and brothers, one race, one people, one family. The Scripture says, "One royal priesthood." That's what God made us, what we are attempting to realize through our lives. A disarmament action states the truth, makes it incarnate, makes it real. Life will always conquer death, as typified by our Lord's resurrection. Sooner or later, life will prevail, and disarmament will come about.

Several of the jury were highly sympathetic to us. One man, an auto mechanic, was apparently on the verge of acquitting us but voted guilty instead. Later, he was attacked and beaten for expressing his sympathy with us. We turned our backs on the jury when it brought in a verdict of guilty.

Like other judges who presided over Plowshare cases, Salus made it difficult, if not impossible, for the jury to rule on the merits of our arguments. He told them, as his colleagues would tell other Plowshare juries, that citizens have no standing to invoke international law in relation to foreign policy. Whether the government was planning to kill hundreds of millions of people, a clear violation of international law, was not the issue. The Nuremberg principles were not the issue. Testimony by experts in the field of international law, scientists who had worked on atomic weapons, theologians, and historians must be disregarded. The Gospels and the Word of God must be ignored.

The defendants had broken the law, damaged property; that alone was the only issue the jury should consider when deciding guilt or innocence. By narrowing their instructions to the jury, judges stood the Nuremberg principles on their head, arguing that citizens are obligated to obey the state, even when its leaders are planning mass murder.

We were convicted of burglary, conspiracy, and criminal mischief, and Judge Salus sentenced Daniel and me to serve three to ten years in prison. Other defendants received shorter sentences. We weren't surprised. The prosecutors pursued our case with great vigor, the judge was biased and incompetent, and the jury felt it had to follow Judge Salus's instructions. We might even have been rather grateful for the outcome. This was the first act of disarmament since the Cold War began, a direct challenge to Lord Nuke's authority. We hardly expected that our message—that in the name of God and the human family, the arms race must end—would be well received. The national security state had shown its contempt for the ecology in countless ways. The Atomic Energy Commission had been concealing for years the effects of radiation on human beings. Fifty thousand radioactive waste sites were scattered across America, and no one knew how many were leaking into the water supply of millions. We could hardly expect compassion from a government that would deceive and poison its own people.

FTLW

Liz Resists the Arms Race, Again

On Thanksgiving Day, November 24, 1983, Liz McAlister, Jackie Allen, Clare Grady, Dean Hammer, Vern Rossman, Kathleen Rumpf, and Karl Smith entered Griffiss Air Force Base in Rome, New York. Hammering and pouring blood on a B-52 bomber, they were arrested and imprisoned. They were called the Griffiss Plowshares. Phil writes of the group's brave actions, their trial and confinement, and how he and Liz attempted to explain to their three young children what was happening and why.

Elizabeth McAlister, in support of these early Plowshare actions, decided it was time for her to act. With her characteristic purpose and clarity, she set about helping to gather a community, and eventually seven remarkable people came together to explore nonviolence, community, and another Plowshare action. Before every action, Plowshare activists grapple with their doubts. Fear speaks to us, attempting to beguile us with the many rewards of silence. Just acquiesce, says fear, and things will be fine. Don't rock the boat. Don't upset the apple cart. Play it safe. Accept a life of quiet desperation.

In the Gospels, Jesus exhorts His disciples to transcend their fears. He encourages them to leave status, security, friends, and family behind. To embrace the world, with all its pain, danger, and contradictions. To live in community, serve the poor, challenge injustice. We can't deny our fears, any more than we can ignore the poverty in our neighborhood. But fear need not dominate our lives. Indeed, weapons of mass destruction express a deep human terror, a desperate, failed effort to conquer human fear.

Our critics say that attacking atomic weapons with ball-peen hammers is an act of violence. Destroying property, they insist, is a form of violence. At best, it is a curious argument, one I've heard many times before. Warheads whose sole purpose is to vaporize cities are hardly to be thought legitimate property. Bombs that indiscriminately murder millions of men, women, and children are not "property."

Liz knew that she and her friends might well be entering a "deadly force" area, where guards were under orders to shoot intruders. In fact, Liz was "shot" when the group role-played a walk into Griffiss Air Force Base. Liz spent time praying, deep breathing, being still. She dreaded being taken from her children. She loved tucking the kids into bed, reading them to sleep and hearing their rhythmic sighs, joining friends in the kitchen for a bedtime snack. She might well spend years in the penitentiary far from her children, unable to snuggle with them at night, to hear their happy chirping in the morning.

She also understood that, like the raids on draft boards during the Vietnam War, Plowshare actions provoke controversy and stir anger and condemnation. We pour our blood to symbolize the death of innocent human beings. But our actions are meant to be more than symbolic. We pound on bombers and submarines with hammers, intending to damage and, if able, literally to disarm them. At Jonah House, our faith in God helps us control our fear. We are saying no to our government's atrocious war-making. We are trying to be just; the effort flows from God's enjoining justice upon us, and our knowing that God is just. Faith in God, and in the ultimate goodness of other human beings, helps us control our fears.

Shortly before the Griffiss action, one network aired "The Day After," a film in which nuclear missiles were launched. Farmers, housewives, children look toward the sky, knowing they have only a few hours to live. And in one very poignant scene, a woman frantically cleans house. She straightens the curtains and carefully makes the beds, determined to deny the impending disaster. Liz and I watched the movie with our children. And like millions of others who saw this film, the children were upset. We listened to their concerns and told them that we didn't want the bombs to go off. As parents, we had a responsibility to see that that didn't happen. We told them that their mother might spend time in prison for acting to end this madness.

They understood and, I think, felt less fearful, knowing that Liz was going to resist the arms race. Frida and Jerry were willing to take this risk, even if it meant being away from their mother for a long time. Katie was two years old and, though a very bright child, couldn't fully understand. Her older brother and sister agreed to help her through the difficult separation from their mother.

And so Elizabeth and six others climbed through a barbed wire fence and walked into the Strategic Air Command Base in Rome, New York. They entered a hangar where B-52s were waiting to be retrofitted with cruise missiles, small first-strike weapons designed to fly by sensors on automatic pilot. Each missile has the force of fifteen Hiroshima bombs, and each B-52 carries twenty missiles. The seven protesters—Liz, Dean Hammer, Claire Grady, Jackie Allen, Kathleen Rumpf, Vern Rossman, and Karl Smith—poured their own blood on the hangar floor and over planes, pasted photos of children on the sides of bombers, and hammered on bomb bay doors. No one was at hand to arrest them, and they walked onto the tarmac, unfurled a banner, prayed, and sang for nearly an hour.

A security guard approached. It may be Thanksgiving, he said, but they must leave the base. They replied that he should look at Hangar 101, where they have just done a disarmament action. Soon they were kneeling in the mud, hands cuffed behind their backs, M16s pointed at their heads. A bus arrived, and they were ushered inside, ordered not to talk, and given no food or water for the next eight hours. When Kathleen Rumpf broke the silence, she was pulled from the bus and deposited, hands still cuffed behind her back, in a pool of water.

At the Syracuse public-safety building the resisters were stripped naked, ordered to squat and cough. Fingers and flashlights probed their body cavities. They were led to a shower, told to scrub clean, and given a rulebook to memorize before they reached the cell block. On the evening news, a reporter announced that "The maximum sentence for the Griffiss action could be 25 years."

One week before Christmas, Frida answered the phone; it was her mother. She is out of jail and will be home the next day. "You mean it's all over?" Frida asked. "Oh sweetie," Liz said, "I wish it were, but I'm afraid this is really only the beginning." We had a fine time between Christmas and the trial in May. Liz was home again, and though we knew she would be leaving soon, each day was a celebration. Not with streamers and balloons, but through reflection and preparation for the trial. Liz will undoubtedly be sentenced to prison. She has acted out of love for her children, and for the children of the world. The national security state considers her a dangerous person.

The Griffiss Plowshares defendants appeared before Judge Howard Munson, federal court judge, Northern District of New York. On behalf of the seven defendants, Liz presented an argument, "On Freedom of Religion and Contemporary Idolatry." She argued that nuclear weapons constitute a religion and that this violates certain freedoms guaranteed by the Constitution. She stated, "Nuclearism is the ultimate fundamentalism of our time. Above all, this is the idolatry against which we stand and because of which we stand in this court. And the modern state is the child of the nuclearist religion. . . . It amounts to a congressionally established religion."

The jury found all seven Griffiss Plowshares defendants guilty. Liz was sentenced to three years in prison. Things certainly could have been worse. Dan and I received three to ten years, respectively, for our parts in the King of Prussia action. Judges in the Midwest would impose draconian sentences on Plowshares activists—up to eighteen years for pouring blood and pounding on a concrete missile silo. Comparatively speaking, a maximum of three years wasn't terrible, though that would mean long months of separation from community and family, particularly from her children.

This was a rough time for our children. They missed their mother very deeply, and yet they were struggling to understand the statement she was making: that through her action at Griffiss and her willingness to go to prison, Elizabeth was expressing her love not only for them but also for all of the world's children who were threatened by this hideous arms race.

Elizabeth was confined at Alderson, a federal penitentiary for women about a six-hour drive from where we lived. Once a month I gathered food, kids, and friends, praying that our car wouldn't break down in the West Virginia mountains. Ellen Grady was living at Jonah House with her husband, Pete DeMott, and they often came along, singing, telling the children stories, helping the miles fly by. We spent weekends at a guest house for relatives of prisoners and were able to see Liz on Friday night and on Saturday until 3:00 o'clock in the afternoon, and again on Sunday morning. Then we started for home.

Precious time, with many hugs, kisses, and tears. Liz piggybacked the children about the prison grounds, rocking them in her arms, telling them giggle stories. During every visit she spent time with one of the children alone while I played games with the other two. When the weather was good, we spread a blanket on the grass and a picnic lunch. Our children suffered terribly when these weekend visits ended. They wrapped themselves around Elizabeth, reluctant to let her go. One last kiss and they would leave their mother, knowing that another month must pass before they could see or touch her again. They wept, as children do, with a heartbreaking passion.

On the way home things would calm down a bit. We didn't pretend. Their mother was in prison and she would not be coming home soon. But she was alive, she was well, she loved her children, they loved her. And what a gift to see her, to hear her voice, to feel her warm spirit, even if only once a month. We were extraordinarily blessed to have Elizabeth as mother, wife, and friend. We felt her presence with us in the car, she would be with us at bedtime, and in the morning around the breakfast table. The state might keep Elizabeth behind bars, but it would never imprison her spirit.

Frida and Jerry were at a difficult age. To urge them to share their thoughts, we almost had to know what they were thinking. If we wanted to understand their feelings, we had to know what they felt. They lived in community, but weren't about to accept a substitute mother, although Frida did develop a close little sister–big sister relationship with Ellen Grady. Katie was only two-and-a-half years old when Liz went to prison. She was cute, cuddly, and able to express her needs, which were almost always met. For example, one night Ellen was cooking in the kitchen when three-year-old Katie rushed in. "I *need* you to read me a story right now," she cried. Not "Could you, would you, or I want you to" but "I *need* you to read me a story right now." Everyone in the community gave Katie time, attention, and devotion. She was ill for quite some time while her mother was in prison, and Liz and I wondered if she might be going through a stage of mourning. But then she bounced back, cheerful, open, friendly and loving.

One morning I was trying to get Katie ready to go to Head Start. She was running through the house, laughing, shouting, refusing to get dressed. I picked her up, sat her on the bed. "Katie," I said, "you're making it difficult not just for me but for everyone in the community. You have to think about them, not just yourself." She listened quietly for a while, then said, "I know it must be very hard on you, Daddy, having Mommy in jail." Liz and I have often laughed over this episode, marveling at a child's ability to turn the tables on adults.

Liz wrote to the children every day from prison, telling them stories, often accompanied by drawings, always about things she thought might interest them. Katie learned the alphabet through her drawings: "A" for Noah's ark. "B" for bear. "C" for cat. The animals danced and sang for Katie, and the stories cheered our children when they were feeling downcast. These letters were bridges over loneliness and unhappiness, a place where Liz and the children could meet to share love and joy.

During our twenty-six-year marriage, Liz and I have often been separated. Altogether, we've spent ten years apart while one of us was in prison. I've spent over seven years in jail, Liz about four. During all that time I never needed to question her moral, psychological, spiritual, emotional support. Nor did she need to question mine.

Our children grew up in a resistance community. Their parents and friends poured blood at the Pentagon, attempted to disarm airplanes and submarines, attacked missile sites with hammers. When we were tried and sentenced to prison, our children were in the courtroom. They listened to the prosecution, heard our testimony, and learned how the judicial system works. We hid nothing from them, nor did we demand that they follow our path. Jonah House is a community, not a cult. Children are encouraged to think critically, to discuss and debate and come to their own conclusions. Resistance shows the violence and criminality of the American empire. Through resistance, our children learn to deconstruct the myths and counter the lies of their culture. They were empowered to distinguish between truth-telling and obfuscation.

The Plowshare movement began, and it must continue, because the government has no intention of disarming its nuclear arsenal. Atomic weapons protect the rich and powerful. That's why they were designed, built, tested, and deployed. That's why the establishment is willing to threaten other countries, and our own people, with atomic annihilation. The biblical view of the law, the courts, and the state is profoundly radical. The Bible looks upon the state as a kind of rebellious artifice; it is spurious, a human creation and a rebellion against God.

Plowshare activists maintain that there are two great historical commentaries on the law. First, Christ was condemned in accordance with law. The Judean leadership told Pilate that, according to their law, Jesus must die for declaring himself the Son of God. Our Lord was completely innocent. He spent his life teaching the good, healing the sick, and feeding the hungry. He preached nonviolence, urging his followers to love their enemies.

Second, in our day the law legalizes nuclear weapons. The slaughter in Hiroshima and Nagasaki was legal. The spread of nuclear weapons has been legal. Atomic warfare that threatens to spawn a nuclear winter, destroying life on Earth, is legal. The poisoning of millions of human beings, and the contamination of our air, food, and water supplies are legal.

FTLW

Disarming the Nuclear Navy— and Ourselves

On Easter Sunday, April 3, 1988, at Norfolk Naval Station in Virginia, Phil, Andrew Lawrence, Sr. Margaret McKenna, and Greg Boertje boarded the battleship U.S.S. Iowa and disarmed two armored box launchers for the Tomahawk cruise missiles, hammering and pouring blood and unfurling banners. Called The Nuclear Navy Plowshares, they were tried and convicted of trespass. Phil received the maximum sentence of six months.

The Navy deploys 37 percent of the U.S. nuclear arsenal on nearly 200 ships. None of these weapons, except submarine-launched ballistic missiles, fall under any arms limitation agreement. Moreover, their use is directed by Ronald Reagan's lunatic Maritime Strategy, which advocates penetration of Soviet waters in times of international crisis to destroy their fleet, naval bases, command centers and onshore installations, and particularly to destroy the Soviet submarine fleet, their second-strike force.

Our Navy readies itself for the unthinkable by incessant maneuvers off Soviet waters, by some marine penetration of ports and naval areas, by intelligence gathering in the Black Sea, by scores of collisions and some nuclear alerts. Of course, the Soviets try to retaliate in kind. A deranged superpower nuclear "chicken" game results, one which a U.S. admiral has described as "exhilarating." Worse still, nuclear roulette on the high seas is sufficiently obscured, distorted and offended by Reagan's propaganda machine as to pass virtually unchallenged. None of our vaunted checks and balances there, yet experts claim a higher likelihood for nuclear war starting at sea than in the Third World.

There were reasons as well why we chose the *U.S.S. Iowa*, the symbolic

"Big Stick" of imperial diplomacy. This armored behemoth, nearly 900 feet long and displacing 60,000 tons, had recently returned from "police" action in the Persian Gulf, and before that in Central America. It flaunted nine sixteen-inch cannons, twelve five-inch guns, plus a nuclear armament of forty-four cruise missiles fired from Tomahawk and Harpoon launchers. Each cruise missile warhead carries the nuclear equivalent of ten Hiroshimas, giving the *Iowa* enough destructive capability to set a continent aflame.

Reasons finally why we chose the Sunday of Christ's Resurrection? He emerged victorious over sin and death. That is to say, victorious over all the human arrangements to lie, bribe, exploit and murder, over armies, navies, multinationals, nation/states, empires and security blocks, over war as institution and politics.

Hundreds of tourists had crowded the *Iowa's* main deck that day, permitting us to quietly desert a tour group and ascend to a third deck overlooking the ship's stern. There, four ABL's (armored box launchers) awaited us. First, blood on two of them, for theirs is a bloody business, by intent and in actuality. They and their missiles (and their Soviet counterparts too) starve the children now, kill the poor now, kill the radiation victims now, and have locked the rest of us in a nuclear Death Row, now. Our blood merely unmasked the blood they hide under the drab gray paint.

Blood on these devilish appliances also reminded one of the new covenant in Christ's blood. That is to say that those who would spill their blood to expose bloodshed in any form were also bound never to shed the blood of another. But rather, to keep the new commandment protecting the new covenant: "Love one another as I have loved you" (John 13:34). Blood as symbol clarifies a public responsibility: to expose bloodshed while rejecting it utterly oneself.

Next: hammers. Hammers made those hellish weapons; humans must unmake them. Between the making and the unmaking, however, lurks the lethal intent, which resists the unmaking. Isaiah's prophecy (2:2–4) makes one vital point: We become God's people only when we disarm ourselves by disarming the weapons. In other words, given the nature of annihilatory weaponry, we will survive as God's people, not as genocides or as global suicides. Disarmament, therefore, is a work of life, and it is a life's work. As long as weapons, nuclear or conventional, enliven the institution of war and threaten us all, then our reality as daughters and sons of God, as sisters and brothers of one another, is nullified and mocked. Between the arming and the disarming of these infernal things is our refusal to become as fully human as we really are.

We had three or four minutes to act before our clamor alerted the security and the tourists. But in that time we freed the symbol of disarmament and made it public, cutting grounding cables, hammering shock absorbers, gauges and hatch covers. In those few minutes the symbol became real and the launchers became inoperable.

A young Marine interrupted us, the very embodiment of fright and fury. Within seconds other Marines arrived, covering us with riot guns. Still other security persons handcuffed us and led us to a security station in the guts of the vast ship.

The Navy moved fast. Admirals poured aboard, and by the time the FBI arrived, decisions to cool it with us were included. The head agent showed himself an obedient son, saying to me, "We know what you want, Berrigan, felony charges as long as your arm, a showcase trial, a long prison term and plenty of publicity. We won't give you any of those things!" I reflected that the Navy had learned from our peerless president the wonders of public relations.

On May 19, a federal magistrate tried us in Norfolk on one misdemeanor of trespass. Friends staged a rousing Festival of Hope the evening before. As expert testimony, we had on hand Dan Berrigan, Ramsey Clark, Paul Walker and Eric Markuson. The judge allowed us to speak, but none of them. Another political railroading, one for each of the twenty-five Plowshares actions! We terminated our defense, offering a brief explanation—"This court affirms that the government is a law unto itself"—and turned our backs to the court. So did most of our friends in the courtroom.

The judge became unsettled, likening us to tax resisters who killed IRS agents. Disclaimers arose from several friends; the marshals ushered them out. The judge hurriedly convicted us. A chant began: "The state is guilty! The state is guilty!" The marshals muscled us back to the tank. Our sentencing will be in late July. Jail has been prayer, study, community with the poor, a deeper resolve. Twenty-six, fifty, a hundred Plowshares!

Peacework: Twenty Years of Nonviolent Social Change

Empire and the Super-rich

The following is an address given at the Community Church of Boston in 1993.

What is the social and political role of the military? Empires are always status quo societies, which resist change, resist justice and democracy. The U.S. is no exception. The inequality of power and consumption that empires achieve abroad is ultimately enforced at home. We see this in startling fashion today in a government representative of the super-rich. We see it in the slow destruction of the American middle class. We see it in homelessness, large-scale destitution, unemployment, urban decay, and blight. Indeed, empire has added the Third and Fourth Worlds to our desperate urban tenderloins. I see them in Boston, in Baltimore, and Washington, D.C., everywhere. By definition, empires must expand or go into decline, but they are never about social relief, justice and change, and ours fits the stereotype.

The military enforces the status quo. It protects what the plutocrats call "balances of power"—that is to say, it confirms and secures present levels of wealth and power, keeping them in the hands that now possess them. Our military contributes this to the super-rich, the 1/200th of our people who sit on 37 percent of American wealth, while they are exempted from paying for protection. We pay for the protection of the super-rich because they pay almost nothing proportionally by way of taxes. That may or may not change—maybe it won't.

In other words, the rest of us pay for the American military juggernaut, a machine which makes us nuclear hostages for the super-rich, ensures their swollen holdings, privileges and consumption. This is why the warrior mandarins of D.C. are terrified of peace. Peace would eventually mean a redistribution of money and resources which could address ecological blight, urban decay, housing shortages, lack of employment, discrimination against women, Blacks and Hispanics. Peace would eventually bring a redistribution of wealth, and given the quality of our one-party political system, that can't be tolerated.

[President Dwight D.] Eisenhower said to the effect that if people insist on peace, governments will have to step aside and get out of the way. We have to re-learn the richest tradition of nonviolent resistance in the world, which we have as Americans. We must re-learn how to say, "No!" to a government unrepresentative and lawless. "No! Not in my name, not with my money, not with my bloodline!" We must speak our "No!" publicly out of a deeper "Yes!" for life, a "Yes!" that reveres life, that will not take life or be complicit in taking life.

The Jewish–Christian scripture puts it very, very well: Love your neighbor as you love yourself, love your enemies and do good to those who hate and persecute you. There is a comparable Buddhist formula: "I will not kill, and I will prevent others from killing." We have no trouble with the first part because we won't kill—you won't kill, and I won't kill—but we do have trouble with the second, preventing others from killing. That's where the rub lies. Including governments, multinationals, fanatical groups, cults—we have real trouble with that one. That is a big order, but it must nonetheless become clear that nothing happens that will enhance human life in this country until we stop the killing. Everything revolves around that commandment: "Thou shalt not kill." Love and justice and everything else are not possible until that commandment is kept.

I would like to say a word in closing about the Russian scientists of Leningrad [now Saint Petersburg] because the world desperately needs people of their caliber, and their quality is possible to all of us. We should never say to ourselves, "It is not for me, I am not up to that, I can't do that." In the winter of 1942, the Nazis laid siege to Leningrad, surrounding the city with tanks. For 900 terrible days, the citizens endured artillery fire and bombing, but the worst was starvation. Before the blockade lifted, starvation had killed 600,000 women, men, children. Those who survived ate grass, sawdust, rats, anything they could find. At Leningrad's Vovilov Institute, a botanical and agricultural research center, thirty-one scientists remained to guard the unique collection of plants and seeds gathered meticulously from their places of origin all over the world under the direction of the legendary biologist, geneticist and plant explorer Nicolai Vovilov.

Vovilov and his colleagues (he had been imprisoned by [Soviet leader Joseph] Stalin for "sabotage of agriculture") were less concerned about the expansion of Nazi Germany or Stalin's expanding Gulag than about the expansion of industrial civilization into those areas of the natural world that contained the unique genetic resources that govern the world food supply and genetic diversity. They ignored the Nazis, they ignored Stalin, and they concentrated on their work because they knew that the survival of humankind depended on it in very large measure. Because these areas were under a siege of their own, the specimens at the Institute represented for many species of food crops the only remaining link between the past and the future.

Even during the bombardment of Leningrad, Vovilov and his colleagues bravely planted new generations of crops in order to freshen their genetic stock. When hungry rats learned to knock the metal boxes of seeds off the shelves in order to get at the contents, the scientists took turns standing watch to protect their genetic treasures. And surrounded by edible seeds and sacks of plants such as rice and potatoes, fourteen of the scientists died of starvation rather than consume their precious specimens. Dr. Dmitri Ivanov, the Institute's rice specialist, was surrounded by bags of rice when he was found dead at his desk. He is reported to have said shortly before his death, "When all the world is in flames of war, we will keep this collection for the future of all people."

We need to be inspired by their example and to refresh and renew ourselves in light of what they did.

The Community Church News, Community Church of Boston

Free Enough to Go to Jail

On December 7, 1993, Phil engaged in another Plowshares disarmament action at Seymour Johnson Air Force Base in Goldsboro, North Carolina. Joining Phil in the Pax Christi–Spirit of Love Plowshares action were the Rev. John Dear, Lynn F. Fredriksson, and Bruce Friedrich. The group hammered on bomb pylons, the cockpit undercarriage, and other flight equipment on the nuclear-capable F-15E fighter plane. They were charged in federal court with two felonies: destruction of government property and conspiracy to commit a felony. They were all found guilty. Phil spent eight months in North Carolina jails and, later, time under house arrest at Jonah House. The following reflection, written from Robeson County Jail, Lumberton, North Carolina, was published in January 1994 in The National Catholic Reporter *and republished in* Fighting the Lamb's War.

I recall intense discussion ten years ago. The question in the air went something like this: How do we remain faithful to the Gospel in a climate of nuclear terrorism, military interventions and public confusion and indifference? Around the circle, people had their say. Finally, a woman, legendary for her thirty years of anti-war resistance, for numerous demonstrations and jailings, offered this: "We must risk jail without, of course, seeking it. Then we must wonder the value of being there. As far as I can understand, things are that simple."

Our friend was confirming Gandhi's observations that "The truth seeker should go to jail even as a bridegroom enters the bridal chamber," that "social betterment never comes from parliament or pulpits, but from direct action in the streets, from the courts, jails and sometimes even the gallows." Or Dorothy

Day's statement that "If Christians seek a better life for the poor and relief from the tyranny of nuclear weapons, they must fill up the jails." Dorothy's "filling up the jails" is her translation of the nonviolent revolution of the Gospel. One accepts jail as a consequence of resistance; then the jailed one reaps a paradoxical benefit. As Tom Lewis puts it, "I have to be free enough to go to jail."

Filling up the jails also clarifies the struggle, as Saint Paul reminds us, not against flesh and blood but against Principalities and Powers. The struggle is for possession of our own soul and the souls of others. It is a bill of divorcement drawn up against false gods. It offers deliverance to the poor, something quite other than feeding and housing them. It pits the realm of God against the murderous deceits of the technocratic state. Its character, finally, is a quest for liberation. Paul again: "It was for freedom that Christ has set us free."

Christians of every age are confronted by the question of Christ: "And you—who do you say that I am?" Much depends on our answer, much more than we are commonly prepared to admit. And whether our image of Christ is the Suffering Servant, the Man of Sorrows or the one who refused the sword in favor of the Cross, the same imperative follows on the answer, whatever form it takes: "Follow me." The "Following me" becomes the fundamental problem. He leads, and we so often renege. We are slow to follow Jesus in living the Gospel and building community, slow to follow, resisting, as He resisted illegitimate power, slow to follow into jail as He was jailed. Slow and then a halt. Follow Him in torture and death?

I write this from jail. On December 7, 1993, four of us—Lynn Fredriksson, Jesuit Father John Dear, Bruce Friedrich, and I—disarmed an F-15 fighter bomber in North Carolina. The F-15 was the winged workhorse of the Iraqi war. It brought death to thousands. More, it is, as the jargon has it, "nuclear-capable."

As a consequence of our crime, the government refuses to set bail. According to the judge, we are a danger to the community. So, in all likelihood, we will remain in jail until trial and undoubtedly afterward.

From the standpoint of most, jail is irksome, boring and absurd. But we have another view. Jail for us is a way of subverting a society that needs more and more jails. Jail is a way of disarming a society that builds nuclear weapons and indulges in perpetual war-making. Jail unites us with the poor, confronting a society that manufactures destitution and homelessness. Jail is subversive of a society that in one way or another manages to shackle the conscience of even its favorites.

None of us likes jail. No one in his right mind would seek it. But God's Word and a strenuous work of community are sufficient for us. We transcend this pit of misery, we shrug, grin and bear it. In measure, we help humanize it. Meantime, in the so-called real world, the Clinton administration sounds the war tocsin against North Korea. According to this "august" hypocritical exercise, the vast American nuclear arsenal and the considerable nuclear development of South Korea are equally beside the point. What then is the point? A perennial worldwide search is on for that all-but-vanquished species, a veritable Loch Ness monster, the "enemy." Purportedly, in some mirage or other, Cuba and Libya together with desolated Iraq have been cited by the mad clairvoyants.

As for slavish concessions to the Pentagon, President [Bill] Clinton outpaces former President [George H.W.] Bush by a mile—in arms sales, fiscal support, new weapon systems and a belligerent ideology to match. The rich are reassured. The weapons are in place. The great Democratic hope has lately been hailed as "the best Republican in memory." In this morally polluted atmosphere we believe that imprisonment could hardly be more to the point. We shudder under the blows of a society permanently mobilized against peace. Duplicity, propaganda, media indifference, institutional betrayal mark our plight. Our people are confused and hopeless.

Let us not give up. Let us continue to nourish one another by consistent and prayerful presence at military installations, in courts and lockups. Indeed, we need to be free enough to go to jail. We need to fill up the jails. Nonviolent revolution will come out of the wilderness, as it always has. And be assured, dear friends, one formidable wilderness today is an American prison.

FTLW

Commemorating Martin Luther King Jr.

On January 15, 1994, supporters of the Pax Christi–Spirit of Life Plowshares held a prayer vigil outside the Robeson County Jail in Lumberton, North Carolina, to mark the birthday of Martin Luther King Jr. They asked Phil to mail them a statement which could be read aloud. The following is Phil's written statement from prison about Dr. King.

Thank you for your presence here. Nothing is more to the point than keeping alive the memory of Dr. Martin Luther King Jr., simply because he was an American, because he was Black or African American, and because he was a modern prophet. Let me say something about each in turn.

First, Dr. King was an American. Because he was, he knew his country, he did his homework, [he knew] the half-truths and outright lies of the politicians. The spin doctors in Washington did not fool him. He knew we were an empire and that empires exploited the poor abroad and ignored the poor at home. He knew that [the] government in Washington represented not the American people but rather the rich and the super-rich, who control our country's wealth. He knew that the American killing machine, which has kept us at perpetual war since Pearl Harbor Day, 1941, exists simply to enforce the status quo, to keep the poor poorer and the rich richer. He knew that we were the greatest purveyor of violence in history and that our violence threatened to plunge the world into nuclear destruction.

Second, Martin Luther King was an African American. Because he was, he saw the real world from the vantage point of oppression; he saw reality from below, with the eyes of his people. He knew that any people who enslaved another would carry a terrible wound in its collective soul. He knew that the

Civil War was fought not to free the slaves but to preserve the Union. He knew that Hitler learned his racism from reading American racists. He knew that emancipation for Black people was merely a new kind of colonialism. He knew that his people, 10 percent of the national population, supplied one-third of the combat troops in Vietnam, and one-third of the casualties.

Finally, Martin Luther King was a prophet. He was what all of us are who try to live the Gospel of Jesus Christ. There is nothing exclusive or elitist about Christian prophecy; it is speaking truth to power, as the Quakers say. It is exposing the crimes of power, it is holding power accountable to the people. It is staying in the streets, breaking the unjust laws, filling up the jails until the war-makers are flushed out, until the American people come to their senses. And the bottom line of prophecy is this: "Stop the killing!" Dr. King spoke truth to power, spoke from the streets, from the courts, from the jails, spoke truth to power by giving his life.

Remember this, if you will, Americans will not stop killing one another on the street until we disarm our war machine. There will be no stopping the little guns until we disarm the big guns. We cannot be ready to blow up the planet with our nuclear guns and protect life at home.

So let us honor Dr. King's memory by sharing his prophecy, by becoming prophets ourselves. And our message is simply this, from the streets, courts, and jails—"Stop the killing!"

1994, from the Files of Rev. John Dear

Isaiah in North Carolina

On December 7, 1993, Lynn Fredriksson, John Dear, Bruce Friedrich, and I (the Pax Christi–Spirit of Life Plowshares) walked onto the Seymour Johnson Air Force Base in Goldsboro, North Carolina, and symbolically, yet literally, disarmed an F-15E nuclear-capable fighter-bomber. Imprisoned in northeast North Carolina, convicted of felony destruction of government property and conspiracy to commit a felony, we await sentencing the first week of July. We face up to twenty years in prison.

Why choose the F-15E for the forty-eighth Plowshares testimony? Because this enormously flexible and powerful fighter-bomber is the darling workhorse of the U.S. Air Force, responsible for the deaths of thousands during the Iraqi war, including the infamous decimation of Iraqi soldiers fleeing from Kuwait on the "Highway of Death." Moreover, the Pentagon will replace F-111s in England by deploying F15 Es, a more versatile and deadly nuclear carrier. They will be fueled, loaded and ready to go.

Plowshares takes its vision from the second chapter of Isaiah, where, deductively, our status as daughters and sons of God (climbing the Lord's mountain) depends on our becoming sisters and brothers of one another. Our weapons prevent sisterhood and brotherhood; they destroy any true relationship. And so, the prophecy of Isaiah demands disarmament.

Our weapons, whether nuclear guns or Saturday night specials, reveal a dark and terrible spirit of hatred and contempt. They create enemies of people who have what we covet, or who have a darker skin, or who believe religiously in a way repugnant to us. As long as the weapons infest our country and our world, as long as we pay for them, or manufacture and deploy them, as long as they have our names on them, how can we relate to a just and merciful God, who came to us disarmed in His Son? In preparing for war, or going to outright war against our "enemies," are we not making an enemy of God Himself? Are we not going to war against God?

One can go deeper still into the matter. The greatest assault on the environment comes from military sources. The greatest poisoning of our air, soil and water comes from war and preparation for war. Can it be that our hatred for one another, represented by nuclear and conventional weapons, puts us at war with the Earth, making us wasters and despoilers of the Earth? Exactly so.

War preparation and warfare are not just killing us spiritually and physically, not just killing our neighbors as violence explodes on the streets. War preparation and war kill the Earth as well. Indeed, if we fail to disarm and to outlaw war internationally, we will hand over to our children an uninhabitable planet, one on which they can do little but sicken and die.

If Isaiah's prophecy asserts the ancient covenant of nonviolence between God and us, the Sermon on the Mount confirms it and goes beyond it. God commands us not only not to kill, but to love our enemies. That is to say, refuse to have enemies. And refuse to allow any group or government to fabricate enemies for us.

Loving one's enemies deserves another look. The Good Samaritan saved his enemy's life, the life of a hated Jew. In effect, he tended him and rescued him from death. Christ, the Good Shepherd, protected the sheep (us) from the hireling, thief, and wolf, finally ransoming us with his life. So when official haters or exploitative governments identify an enemy and go for his jugular, we must protect that enemy and withstand the government. Does this apply these days to Bosnia, to ethnic cleansing and to bloodshed? Of course. The most grievous atrocities there do not excuse military intervention. How about North Korea? Of course. A worst-case scenario with a functional bomb is no excuse for military intervention. The United States can justifiably check the North Korean nuclear development by just one course: disarming itself.

A simple choice beckons: Are we going to be people of perpetual war with darkened souls and bloody hands? Or are we going to be people who dare to be the sons and daughters of our nonviolent, just, and compassionate God, who face the world's lunacy disarmed? On December 7, we emphatically stood for the second.

Governments never disarm, only people do. Governments disarm only because their people insist on disarmament. National interests, about which all wars are fought, are in reality the interests of the rich, for which most people must pay and for which some people must fight.

There will come a time when the American people will reject the tyranny of the 5 percent who swallow 40 percent of the nation's wealth, when they say "No!" to killing and war and insist on peace.

Who can imagine what it will mean to have the money and skills of war reinvested for peace?

Blood and hammers were the symbols employed by us on December 7 to make a simple, seminal statement: "Stop the killing!" Our blood because the covenant of disarmament is sealed in Christ's blood; hammers because the people must, at some point, convert nuclear and conventional swords into plowshares.

"Stop the killing!" is now the most urgent cry in history. "Stop the killing!" Becoming human begins with that. There's been enough killing in the twentieth century, the bloodiest of all centuries. The killing is killing us. "Stop the killing!" is the sane choice. Let's stop the killing, beat our swords into plowshares, and study war no more.

Simplicity (newsletter of the Norfolk, Virginia, Catholic Worker, Spring 1994, Vol. 5, No. 1)

Hellholes, Courts, Jails:
A Triple Source of Resistance

Some ten years ago, I attended a lecture on the biblical evaluation of law and the courts. One of the main points offered was this: In political cases, the courts *are* the society condensed and crystallized. So, if one can imagine society — packaged, addressed, and delivered — that's what the courts are. The jails are not the barometers of society, as Emerson claimed. The courts are.

During the weeks of April 10 and 17, Lynn Fredriksson, Bruce Friedrich, John Dear, and I went to trial, for the second time, from jail, charged with a felony (destruction of government property) for disarming an F-15 nuclear-capable fighter-bomber at Seymour Johnson Air Force Base in Goldsboro, North Carolina, on December 7, 1993. Prior to that, in preparation for our first trial in February, we fundamentally clashed with Judge Terrence Boyle, a federal district judge in eastern North Carolina. Boyle forbade the rest of us to meet with Lynn Fredriksson and with a lawyer/advisor, making it virtually impossible to prepare for trial.

We viewed Boyle's oppression as the tip of the iceberg, abuse which promised to multiply. So we decided to not cooperate and prepared a statement exposing Boyle's suppression of our rights. After Lynn Fredriksson read this statement in the court, we turned our backs on the judge, joined by twenty-one friends from the courtroom. Judge Boyle smothered the uprising with contempt charges, citing ten people in all and sentencing them to six months.

In the two months between trials, the suppression grew. Judge Boyle took measures to intensify control and avoid another mistrial. He approved an *in limine* motion (gag rule), forbidding us to speak of divine or international law, nuclear weapons, U.S. foreign policy, recent American wars, the necessity defense, alleged crimes of the U.S. government, etc. (As one wag put it: "You can't sneeze without contempt!") He severed us into four separate trials, and named standby counsel, a measure anticipating troublesome conduct and suspension of our *pro se* defense.

When we finally went to trial, it became an agonizing ordeal, as exacting and painful as disarming an F-15 fighter-bomber. I've never experienced its equal, not even in a court permeated with the neuroticism of Judge Salus at the King of Prussia trial. Our efforts to expose the court as complicit in the government's addiction to war and nuclear terror were met with a flood of objections and threats of contempt charges. As for rights—human, legal, or other—we didn't have any. We couldn't finish an opening statement unhampered; we couldn't cross-examine witnesses from Seymour Johnson Air Force Base without constant interference. We couldn't even testify in our own behalf, attempting to list the incidents which led us to that technological hellhole, without repeated interruption.

Under these onerous circumstances, a fair trial or possible acquittal became an illusion. Experience with some forty Plowshares trials had convinced us that imperial courts (they are all imperial—federal, state, and local) might accidentally allow a hung jury, as they did with the Epiphany Plowshares, but they would never acquit. [The imperial courts] suppressed jury nullification, the necessity defense, and divine, international, and constitutional law. In a word, they were distorted to protect the government from its people instead of the other way around.

What did we learn from this exasperating and painful exposure? Mainly this, that Seymour Johnson Air Force Base, Federal District Court, and Chowan County Jail are all resistance settings. The hellholes, courts, and jails are all sites of resistance, all essentially linked and continuous. Trial and jail follow hard upon action. The empire railroads its resisters, thereby camouflaging its crimes and protecting its weapons. Judge Boyle's court is Seymour Johnson Air Force Base with a judicial face, the jail a civilian stockade for those daring to interfere with the legalizing of death. Both courts and jails sanctioned to the hilt the insane conduct of the military. Everything the military does—from irradiation at Hiroshima to genocide in Vietnam to a "Turkey shoot" in Iraq—the courts and jails declare legal. Anyone who challenges this madness, this holding people and the planet on the edge of a nuclear knife, becomes illegal.

The Bible is full of political trials, from those of the great prophets to those in the acts of the Apostles. Mark connected numerous court scenes with the Passion and Crucifixion of Jesus. And John depicts Jesus as constantly on trial, indicted and tried by the world.

Undoubtedly Christians contribute to the terror and madness of today's world by their absence from imperial courts. We are not present at that cosmic setting where God's nonviolent sovereignty and the world's duplicity and murderousness meet and clash. It will be in the imperial courts that human fidelity is measured; where the fate of the world is decided; where, indeed, God's reign will be proclaimed. Or rejected.

PeaceWork, from the Files of Rev. John Dear

Suffering Servanthood

From Phil's handwritten notes in 1994.

Let's begin by saying that jail is the bottom line. Most American peace people never come to grips with that. As we know, this attitude arises from idolatry, a superficial grasp of nonviolence, from willingness to offer excuses for the system, from ignorance of its lying and murderous character, from lack of vision as to the new society that needs building, from lifestyle and some of its corollaries, like security, career, income, future, etc.

All of us would agree that no one belongs in jail. A state has no authority to deprive a human being of physical liberty. How does one square this with jail as the bottom line? If nobody belongs in jail, we don't belong in jail. This becomes true only in an ideal order of things. But even then, we must win our freedom, and the means to freedom is suffering servanthood. The Cross always becomes central, and it entails offering our physical liberty, even our lives, if necessary. History proves this very emphatically. Justice comes from nonviolent resistance at the hellholes, in courts and in prisons. No other way. The disciple defends the victim; and the state, intent only on victimizing, makes the disciple an outlaw.

In nearly every chapter of the Acts of the Apostles, we have a record of harassment, ostracism, torture, flogging, imprisonment, and execution. Like Christ, the Disciples preached and lived a new way of justice, peace, love, freedom. The status quo, the powers, the pharaohs found this intolerable and threatening.

Thus goes our tradition. It aims at the centrality of "Thou shalt not kill!" A commandment upon which everything in the moral universe depends. Love inspires the commandment, love becomes possible because of this commandment. Which is to say, unless one draws the line on killing the unborn, prisoners, the elderly, everyone, then every other moral act is subverted, compromised, nullified. Moral ambivalence on killing certainly assaults the image of God and the creation of God and other human beings. But more directly, it is an attack upon Christ, who is brother to all sisters and brothers, who took our nature, who became us.

When one resists the state's right to kill, whether in war or in capital punishment, one subverts, threatens and declares "doomed" the state itself. The state, through its functionaries, will then protect itself and put you out of business. That usually means jail.

In court, and before the burlesque of a "fair trial," one faces not only the crystallization of the imperial society but also the imperial judgment on disobedience. Both must be resisted. One resists by facing it with truth and fortitude. The weapons have already been exposed by plowshares. Now the courts, which legalized the weapons, must be exposed also. One does that by insisting on the moral/political/historical/truly legal "Why?" By insisting also on the sovereignty of God's law and any decent human legal derivative. For example, Nuremberg's insistence that underlings are legally bound to resist immoral orders is a human and legal derivative.

In jail, the resistance takes a different form, continuing the appeal to hearts, minds, consciences that began with the action. This takes two forms that occur to me. First a powerless identification with the powerless, with prisoners, with the poor. And service of them. "I'm one of you, I'm with you!"

The second has an extra-institutional appeal to the wider public. "I've risked my life and donated my physical freedom for very good reasons. Look at them! And do more than look at them. Do something nonviolent against the imperial crimes." This appeal from jail is extremely powerful; it is in fact necessary for the building of any movement for justice and peace. It built the Church, it built the movement in India; it built it here during the Vietnam War; it built resistance dozens of times in the course of American history.

What do we have to offer in all this? Certainly, our love, justice, our sacrifices, anguish, loneliness, tears, our nonviolent truth, our suffering servanthood. Gandhi states that these are the realities that have being, life, substance. While the things we appease are non-life, non-being, delusions, chimera.

Here we are a testimony against them, even if everyone outside forgets us. Our presence is a living testimony against the criminality in high places. "They will imprison and kill the innocent to be able to continue their crimes."

Imprisonment presents inescapable questions like this one: "I know this person, why are they locking her up? What are they doing? What are they hiding?" Questions that otherwise would not surface.

In jail, none of us need feel captive to stagnation, boredom, self-pity, feelings of discouragement and uselessness. We must say often to ourselves and believe it to conviction: "This is the best place in the world for me. I can do no better work than this!"

DP

Working for the Long Haul

Critics of the Plowshare movement point out that we've been arrested count-less times, and yet the United States refuses to disarm its arsenal of nuclear weapons. We've prayed and pleaded, poured our blood and pounded upon atomic weapons; and yet our government continues to kill people, here and abroad, in the name of peace and justice. Conclusion: Our actions are useless. According to such critics, the outcome of conscientious activity must always be measured and quantified: *A cup of success, a spoonful of failure. Two hours of success, one week of failure.* There must be a scoreboard to determine who is winning or losing.

Yet it is impossible, we maintain, to measure results stemming from integrity. We act because working in a nonviolent way for justice and peace is right, proper, essential. Moreover, our actions do make a difference in people's lives.

How many lives, how much of a difference? We can hardly measure that. But it is clear from the many friendships we've formed over the years that some are influenced, perhaps even inspired, by our nonviolent witness.

Moreover, by our refusal to be complicit with the war machine, we have avoided becoming a cog in the military industrial gearbox. The killing has not been, will never be, in our name. We leave it up to others to measure our success or failure.

My justification for nonviolent revolution stems from what I and other Plowshare activists believe is fact: that Christ embodies God; He is the image, as Paul says, of the invisible God. Looking upon Him, listening to Him, fol-lowing Him, is to be in union with God.

This God is nonviolent to us. He allows His sun to shine upon the wicked and the good; allows the rain to fall upon the just and unjust. He is benevolent, loving, and compassionate. Never retaliatory, never revengeful. He never punishes us; we punish ourselves. When we sin, or are unjust, and exploit one another, we punish ourselves.

It is the will of this God, the God of Jesus Christ, to humanize us to become children of God; we are daughters and sons, sisters and brothers of one another. And that's the biblical basis for nonviolent revolution. That's why we have it, and why it must continue throughout history.

The Christian who follows Jesus must be a nonviolent resister and revolutionary. There is no avoiding this truth. A Christian must take risks for the Kingdom of God, the New Jerusalem, the new sisterhood and brotherhood. Christians are obligated to resist collusion between church and state, and to fight nonviolently against tyranny, injustice, and oppression.

I see no point in working within an evil system. Christ was never a reformer. He didn't advocate voting for one corrupt politician over another. He never urged people to embrace the state. He told parables about putting a patch on an old garment that would soon unravel. He preached that we should dismantle, not attempt to patch, the state.

The Cold War may be over, but we cannot cease insisting on the sovereignty of God and the Lordship of God over creation. The state is a usurper, attempting to seize sovereignty from God. Dan, Liz, I, and many others like us have clung to our Catholicism. In fact, we have arrived at a formula which might serve to define us as: *We are Catholics who are trying to be Christians.*

FTLW

My Roots Are in the Church

I never had the slightest temptation to leave the Catholic Church, and I am extremely grateful for everything the Church has done for me, not only in the early years of my life but also in later years. After I was excommunicated in 1973, several other Christian bodies asked me to join them, and to minister under their aegis. I refused, because I have never considered myself anything but a Roman Catholic trying to become a Christian. My roots are in the Church, and in spite of all the prostitutions and betrayals of the institutional Church, these roots are lifegiving.

My brother Daniel has often said that many priests and nuns learned their politics by confronting the Church and resisting it, through calling it to the accountability of the Gospel. The transfer to resisting the state from that experience was automatic.

FTLW

"From Prison, Old Militant Struggles On"

As quoted in the New York Times, *November 29, 1997.*

You have to struggle to stay alive and be of use as long as you can. You have to sacrifice yourself. I don't want to make a big deal about it, but you have to pay your dues. I wouldn't have it any other way.

DP

Reliance on Community

A frequent controversy arising in peace communities centers on the "rights" of individual conscience against those of a collective conscience. Virtually nothing seems written on the subject—foreign to the experience of most biblical or nonviolent scholars.

Steadfast resistance to war-making requires a profound reliance on community, and this reliance enkindles the issue. Does the individual conscience prevail, or the communitarian one? A resister chooses a war plant as a Plowshares target; the rest choose an air base. Or another insists on maximum damage at a hellhole; the remainder desires symbolic, real damage. Or while in the courtroom, another refuses to stand for the judge; others stand to concentrate on the trial. Or while jailed, one launches into jail reform, as others cling to the resistance that brought them there.

The tension between individual and collective consciences often becomes galling, intractable, even divisive. And never simple—always as complex as people themselves. On the one hand, an imperial culture mass produces subjects who are capitalistic, "democratic," and individualistic, infusing values like physical freedom, individual rights, personal autonomy and consumerist choice. On the other hand, and through rude awakenings, there happens exposure to the social and political emphasis of biblical theology and nonviolent philosophy. The culture stresses the "I," the Bible the "we." The culture consults the psychological industry and sociological chairs to maintain the public passivity. The Bible proposes community. The culture orchestrates the police, drugs, and jobs to keep social violence manageable. The Bible offers nonviolence. The polarities of cultural and biblical visions confront the disciple with an either/or—180 degrees distinct from one another.

What allows conscience to emerge, as it frees itself from the solipsism of ego, youth, or circumstance? Without engaging the question immediately, it might be useful to note that we are our consciences. Gandhi used to claim that we are what we think, but that seems superficial. Rather, we are where we are in the great clash between good and evil in our world. Most everyone applauds the performance of good. But where are they in this struggle against evil? It is in this rarefied arena that conscience and the person become defined. The Gospel lends clarity, spur, and nourishment to our consciences because it reveals the conscience of Christ—a conscience unvaryingly social, corporate, and political, a conscience aligned to the will of God and passionately devoted to our redemption and well-being.

If Jesus taught love of enemies, we would live and enact love of enemies— love of His executioners. His enemies numbered the Jewish and Roman hierarchies, the mob who held for His crucifixion, all the false Christians of history, ourselves before we knew better. His conscience was truly conscience—loving, communitarian, embracing all life, free. He went to his death freely, He prayed for his enemies freely, and He forgave the Disciples who abandoned him, freely.

The paradigm for the Christian is the conscience of Christ. And that conscience was for others. Everything He taught or did was for others—the way of God that He taught, the healings, His building of community, His resistance to the Jewish and Roman satraps—all for others.

To deny the self, shoulder our Cross, and follow Him is the way of abjection and humiliation. But it is also the way of liberation as we truly become daughters and sons of God.

The New Year One, Vol. 24, No. 1, February 1997, Jonah House, DP

Ash Wednesday Action

On Ash Wednesday, February 12, 1997, Phil, Susan Crane, Steve Kelly, Steve Baggarly, Mark Colville, and Tom Lewis-Borbely enacted the Prince of Peace Plowshares action and boarded the U.S.S. The Sullivans, a nuclear-capable destroyer at the Bath Iron Works in Maine. They hammered and poured blood on numerous parts of the battleship, read their action statement, and displayed a large banner. They were subsequently tried in federal court and convicted. Phil was sentenced to twenty-four months in prison. The following is a written statement Phil was not permitted to give in court.

My name is Philip Berrigan. I'm seventy-three years old—a married Catholic priest. Elizabeth and I have three children—two in their twenties—our youngest daughter is fifteen. As a World War II veteran, I served in northern Europe. As for education, I have two master's degrees. I have written and had published seven books. I have lectured on Scriptural themes, nonviolence and war/peace issues in most of the fifty states and abroad, mostly in western Europe.

My nonviolent resistance to the Vietnam War and, later, the nuclear arms race covers about thirty-two years. Of those years, I have been imprisoned about seven-and-a-half years. Of the twenty-eight years of our marriage, Elizabeth and I have been separated by over eleven years of incarceration, hers and mine. I agree with Gandhi that social betterment never comes from parliaments or pulpits, but rather from the streets, docks (courtrooms), and jails. That being said, what created my state of mind leading to disarmament at the BIW [Bath Iron Works in Maine] on Ash Wednesday, February 12? Here are the main influences.

I am a Depression brat, living my early years following the great crash in 1929. Our family of eight, six boys, was desperately poor. Our parents came from poor roots themselves and never forgot the poor, always sharing their few resources with the unemployed on the road and with the poor of our neighborhood. Consistent with that experience, I have always tried to share my bounty with the poor. At Jonah House in Baltimore (the community where I live), twice weekly for twenty-three years we shared a ton or more of fruits, vegetables, fish and packaged goods with poor neighbors. With such a history, how else could I look upon the *U.S.S. The Sullivans*, a billion-dollar monstrosity, as other than a theft from God and God's creation, as robbery from the poor (one of five American children goes to bed hungry every night), and as a blasphemous rejection of God's commandment "Thou shalt not kill!"?

Another factor contributing to my intent is the Catholic Church, which has given me the Word of God, the Sacraments, and the Cross of Jesus Christ. My ancestors were Catholic from Ireland and Germany, my roots are Catholic, and I am nourished by a 2,000-year-old tradition and ennobled by great women and men—prophets, scholars, nonviolent revolutionaries, martyrs. I carried my faith with me when I boarded the *U.S.S. The Sullivans*. My faith brought me there—my faith helped me control my fear, my faith sustained me through the consequences of disarmament.

My brothers remain Catholic—four of whom are alive, accepting as they do the premise that all of us are responsible for the Church—in fact, we are the Church. Moreover, my brother Dan, a Jesuit priest, is, in the opinion of many, the foremost radical theologian in the West. He has published over forty books on biblical thought, nonviolence and resistance, and I have devoured them all. He, more than any other source excepting the Gospel, confirmed my state of mind on Ash Wednesday.

Another spiritual contribution to my intent on Ash Wednesday at the BIW is community. For twenty-four years, I have lived in a nonviolent resistance community, holding all things in common as the early Christian communities did—working for our living and our work for justice/peace with our hands. Such communities take their inspiration and sustenance from God's Word, from the teachings and works of Jesus and His Apostolic community. A nonviolent resistance community has several benefits: First, it is a microcosm of the human family; second, it allows a style of life radically simple; third, it is the inspiration and support for resistance. Community allows both faith and sanity in a world increasingly deranged.

A final factor nourishing my intent at the BIW was my experience. My experience in one trying to be a Christian tells me that "Thou shalt not kill!" and "Love your enemies" are interpersonal laws, certainly, but global and cosmic ones as well. As a World War II soldier I saw northern Europe flattened and 70 million people dead. I learned later that Japan was suing for peace in 1945 and that President Truman had no need to use the Bomb at Hiroshima and Nagasaki. Instead, he used it to avenge Pearl Harbor and to intimidate the Soviets. My experience in New Orleans in 1962, during the Cuban Missile Crisis, indicated that President [John F.] Kennedy and Mr. [Nikita] Khrushchev risked [the lives of] millions of Americans and Soviets in an insane game of nuclear chicken. Khrushchev blinked, else you and I would not be here today.

My intent in boarding the *U.S.S. The Sullivans* was not vandalism, not sabotage, not destruction of government property but rather the conversion of war materials that in its perverted state, had no moral, legal or political right to exist. The prophecies of Isaiah and Micah require that we convert "swords into plowshares" and "spears into pruning hooks." And Christ's imperative to "love our enemies" implies that we disarm our weapons, become, in fact, weaponless.

The Beatitudes of Matthew include "Blessed are the peacemakers, they will be called children of God!" (Mt. 5). My friends are peacemakers, and I try to be [one]. Let God, this jury and the American people render a verdict.

The New Year One, Vol. 24, No. 2, July 1997, Jonah House. DP

Agenda for Renewal

"Woke up this morning with my mind set on freedom . . ."

Not usually. Not today, nor yesterday, nor any day in recent memory. That wonderful African American spiritual implies vigor and love of life. But in the half-life between sleep and wakefulness, the gift of another day nauseates and threatens me.

I have begun my daily wrestling with the culture—the siren song of an imperial society. The culture aims to conscript me, to enlist me in the slavery of its triviality and violence.

I've been doing civil resistance for nearly thirty-five years, challenging the empire's habitual orgy of lies, exploitation, and mass murder. I could be "set on freedom," but I haven't made it yet. The struggle is simply day by day.

The morning paper tells me that our bombers have escalated their savage pummeling of Iraq and Yugoslavia; the children of Iraq languish and die under our sanctions; a million refugees from Kosovo stagger into Macedonia and Albania; the Everglades burn for a week. The dogs of war rage and the ecology shutters. And few get the connection.

We Americans, Christians among us, are in deep crisis on so many fronts—nuclearism, interventionary war, the ecology, globalization of the economy, repression at home. The Domination Complex has enticed us into a Faustian bargain—short-term gain and false security for the price of our souls. Do we see the signs of the times? Can it be that already we are forced to pay up? To reap the whirlwind? Will we learn in time, before war and environmental corruption engulf us? Will we, an imperial people, trusting in omnicidal weapons, the greatest polluters in history, learn in time?

But as I usually do when the culture seeps into my guts and bones, rendering me suspicious of life and inert, I turn to the Word of Life, the Scripture. Let me share one passage: "You were once darkness, but now you are light in the Lord. Live as children of light, for light produces every kind of goodness, righteousness, and truth. Try to learn what is pleasing to the Lord. Take no part in the fruitless works of darkness, rather expose them, for it is shameful even to mention the things done by them in secret. But everything exposed by the light becomes visible, for everything that becomes visible is light. Therefore, it says: 'Awake, O, sleeper, rise from the dead, and Christ will give you light'" (Eph. 5:8–14).

These few verses in the Letter to the Ephesians expressed the same theme as John's Gospel (Jn. 3:19–21): "And this is the verdict, that the light came into the world, but people preferred darkness to light, because their works were evil. For everyone who does wicked things hates the light and does not come toward the light, so that his/her works might not be exposed. But whoever lives the truth comes to the light, so that her/his works may be clearly seen as done in God."

Here we have the authority of God's Word offering us an analysis of our interpersonal and political conduct—mainly, we face a verdict in God's court. The Bible often refers to the two-court reality—the human court a condensation of society, the heavenly court judging our testimony in human courts. Nonviolent resistance is implied—denial of Christ in human courts evoking Christ's denial of us in the heavenly court. "I tell you, everyone who acknowledges me before others, the Human One will acknowledge before the angels of God. But whoever denies me before others will be denied before the angels of God" (Lk. 12:8–9).

Exposure of the bureaucracies of oppression is a Gospel imperative. It is precisely what Christ did, and it is what those who "follow" him do. It is there that the Christian challenges the chokehold of the Principalities and Powers of the world, testifies to the sanctity of life, becomes a child of God, identifies with the human family, and becomes free. Nonviolent civil disobedience is above all an exposé of criminality in high places and dragging it out into the light, so that it may become light.

Moreover, civil resistance is a singular act of love for the functionaries of the empires, in the hope that they might turn from their complicity and economic terrorism and mass murder to truth and justice. True enemies of us, they hold us in contempt, lie to us, tax us outrageously, imprison us, and worse if we confront their greed and power lust. But they are creatures of God. And we must love them.

"It is shameful even to mention the things done by them in secret." Of course. Bureaucracies hide their crimes, even as we hide the sins that shame us. Hence, government classification of documents, security clearances, and official censorship of the press. Add to this the self-censorship of the press, self-censorship of the churches, synagogues, and education establishment, and the result is an institutional conspiracy of silence before the crimes of the high and mighty.

In the face of a world verging on self-destruction, where does one turn for truth, justice, and redress? Certainly not to the American empire, nor to the nations, nor to the institutions of the Domination Complex, so largely responsible for the tragic state of the human family. Rather, we turn to the God of life, to oneself and to sisters and brothers everywhere, to all those capable of faith, love, and justice. In contrast to trust in the coalition of oppression, mixed as it is, in its own violence, and captive to it.

But there's a rub: We are soft, unfamiliar with struggle, entangled with a seductive, deadly culture. We can extricate ourselves only with God's help, renewing our faith and renewing trust in one another. In broad strokes, this would mean educating ourselves in the nonviolence of Jesus as a way of living, building communities of dissent and resistance, reducing our consumerism of seven to eight times our share of the world's resources, husbanding the Earth and its life.

As the Psalmist says, we move from grace to grace. That is to say, an action befitting life and justice prepares us for a more serious one. One day, out of our championship of life, we will nonviolently rebel against the institutions of death. Our mutiny will take us to the streets, military bases, war factories, warrens of decisions, our "No!" to death, which is simply our protection of life, that will lead us to court and prison.

There is no such thing as cheap freedom, any more than there is cheap grace: "Awake, O, sleeper, rise from the dead and Christ will give you light."

DP

No Freedom without Love

The early Christian Church could not bear the purity and weight of the true meaning of Jesus's execution. It could not grasp the sheer voluntariness of the Cross, the voluntary love of His choice. And so the belief grew that God sent Jesus to die, that from His conception He was doomed to die, the divine scapegoat. Theology acquired a determinism, even tinges of fatalism. The divine/human mission to restore God's kingdom began to fade; the Church's unequivocal condemnation of violence and war began to fade. The empire began to absorb Christians, exacting taxes and military service from them. In contrast to this view, a point made clear in John's Gospel—Jesus freely chose Calvary out of love for us, giving us the means of salvation yet preserving our power of choice. By choosing the Cross and a criminal's death, He exemplified for us love and freedom. For there is no freedom without love.

Our scapegoating and victimizing of one another killed Him, our hatred and violence. But in turn, by the power of God He killed sin and death; all violence stopped in him and died. So Paul would reflect in wonderment: "Death is swallowed up in victory. O death where is your sting? O death where is your victory?" (1 Cor. 15:55).

An old axiom of nonviolence is this: We become what we hate. If we hate an enemy, we become an enemy. Violence begets itself; it becomes contagious. When we react violently to violence done to us, we mimic the enemy. We become them, a law applicable to individuals, groups, nations, empires.

When we devastated the Nazis and Japanese with weapons more terrible than theirs, we became fascist.

When we threatened the Soviets at Hiroshima and Nagasaki, and in every subsequent stage of the nuclear arms race, we became totalitarian.

When we created agency upon agency of spies, under the euphemisms of intelligence and security, we began to spy upon and harass our own citizens. And civil liberties evaporated.

When we scapegoat and victimize and terrorize, we lapse into an interchange of characteristics. The devastation we wreaked on Indochina, Central America and Iraq now plagues us with the death of the trees, global warming, depleted ozone layer, acid rain, erratic weather patterns, widespread radioactive poisoning. Indeed, the violence we do to others, we do first to ourselves.

Conversely, when we go to the hellholes of imperial policy and war, there to break laws legalizing nuclear scapegoating, accepting the consequences of judicial charade, of separation and prison, we accept mimetic violence into ourselves, and there it stops and dies. In our small, modest way, we repeat what Jesus accomplished on the Cross.

Among the world's great texts, only the Gospel was written from the standpoint of the victims. Victims have a far more radical grasp of reality than oppressors. Theirs is the epistemological privilege—they see reality from below, they stand under repression because they suffer it. "Let the groaning of the prisoners come before you. According to the greatness of your power, save those who are doomed to die" (Ps 79:11).

With all my heart, I agree that the Gospel alone will destroy scapegoating and needless killing. The Gospel alone offers the truth and strength necessary to disarm and eliminate nuclear terror. But the unknown quantity are Christians and our disbelief. Luke's Gospel (11:29) speaks of an "evil generation," and ours is certainly that. No sign is allowed this generation except the sign of Jonah the Prophet. And that sign is the Cross—the execution, burial, and resurrection of Jesus. Fidelity to that sign will not be easy, but it will not be hard. "His yoke is easy, and his burden light" (Matt. 11:30). "We are not to be afraid. Just believe" (Mk. 5:36).

The New Year One, Vol. 25, No. 3, Jonah House, November 1998, DP

Loving Our Enemies

"You have heard that it was said: 'You shall love your neighbor and hate your enemy.' But I say to you: "Love your enemies, and pray for those who persecute you" (Matt. 5:43).

It must be said, Americans obey the first part of this Christian teaching and reject the second. We don't love our enemies, and we take great pride in believing that no one would dare attack or persecute us.

Nonetheless, we must try to understand the profound significance of "love of enemies," and to link the survival of humankind and the planet to embracing and acting on these words. God's love, which alone makes love of enemies possible, is present in all human beings; indeed, that love is not a philosophical abstraction or a biblical anachronism but a vital possibility, the measure of hope that guides us in the emperor's apocalyptic world. What, then, is our choice? Either we enact love of enemies, or we die by global poison and/or nuclear firestorm. We must clearly acknowledge the spirit behind weapons which technologize our ancient hatreds, violence, bloodlust, and wars.

It occurs to me that love of enemies and Jesus's new commandment—"Love one another as I have loved you" (Jn. 15:12)—paraphrase one another, because Christ died for us while we were enemies (Rom. 5:8). We might also regard them as compliments, the inexhaustible love of God bolstering our weakness, so that we love our enemies. Together, these teachings encapsulate and summarize the Word of God, containing faith, justice, life itself.

One should mention that our enemies are not the ones we commonly identify, nor the ones the empire encourages us to fear and hate. We can list them, beginning with our false self as our number one enemy, even as the Gospel does: "Whoever wishes to come after me must deny herself, take up your cross and follow me" (Mk. 8:34). The false self exposes itself by anything not compassionate and just—egotism, greed, arrogance, bellicosity, racism, sexism—preventing any acceptance of the Cross, and hence any struggle for liberation.

High officials of the empire—the president, vice president, secretary of state, secretary of war, Joint Chiefs of Staff, the nuclear war-fighting party—all those who, under the figments of deterrence and national security, threaten humankind and the planet with the Bomb. These blind leading the blind have done more than threaten us with doomsday scenarios. They have, with a devilish ingenuity, convinced us that we ought to pay, through taxes, for our own destruction.

Next on a listing of enemies—the CEOs and executives of the war-making corporations like Lockheed Martin, Boeing, McDonnell Douglas, Raytheon, General Dynamics. The politicians, generals and arms dealers who strew the planet with terror, destruction and death are the enemies of humanity. Not, as the emperor insists, the North Koreans, Iraqis, Iranians, Libyans, Cubans. And Christians are enjoined to love all of them, even as God does. "Be perfect even as your heavenly parent is perfect" (Matt. 5:48).

Twice, during demonstrations at the White House—we were planning to pour blood on the pillars of the emperor's residence—I was interrogated by Secret Service agents. "Did you intend to harm the president?" they asked. "Of course not," I answered. "Christ requires that I love everyone!" I didn't try to explain that while I view the emperor as the enemy of peace and social justice, here and abroad, that doesn't mean that I wish to harm him, nor would I do anything to injure the men and women who devote their lives to protecting the emperor.

I recall A. J. Muste's remark: "If I can't love Hitler, I am no Christian!" But how can we bring ourselves to love a mass murderer like Adolf Hitler or, closer to home, an emperor who lives in regal splendor while just down the street children live in rat-infested tenements, attend segregated schools, go to bed hungry every night? How might we go about loving an emperor who professes his love for children while condemning millions of young people, again here and abroad, to a lifetime of hunger and misery? How can we love an emperor who talks endlessly about peace and social justice while supporting a new round of designing, building, and testing nuclear weapons?

My answer, and that of other Plowshares folks, is that we must love the emperor by exposing him through nonviolent civil resistance—not only him, but all of the nuclear priesthood. We must cry out, loud and clear, that the emperor and his mighty army are preparing, every single day, for wars of mass destruction. We must tell the world that more than 700,000 Iraqi children have died as a result of the emperor's Iraqi massacre; that high in the mountains of Guatemala the Mayan people are digging up the remains of loved ones killed by U.S.-trained and U.S.-funded soldiers; that the children of Nicaragua, hungry and ragged, are rummaging in garbage dumps because the emperor waged war against the people of that nation.

Through civil disobedience, we repent the emperor's sins, take them as our own, take stock in our commitment to justice, and resolve to continue the struggle to love our enemies, now, and for as long as we live. Through civil disobedience, we enact our love for those who would tap our phones, intercept our mail, try us in kangaroo courts, and sentence us to prison. We demonstrate, in this way, that Jesus did not offer us pleasant slogans but challenges that are sometimes painful, difficult, and even frightening to accept. We are human beings, not saints.

We know how easy it would be to succumb to bitterness and anger, to hate our enemies, and curse those who persecute us. We are trying to live, to practice, our belief that social justice begins in our own hearts, that love is the measure of our own strengths and weaknesses, that while we are not perfect, we can and must live what we contend is true—that love is more powerful, more lasting, more healing, than hate.

DP

We Aren't Doing OK by Ourselves

From a keynote address given at the 1999 "Working for Global Justice" conference at American University.

At your convenience, please read a great American author, Flannery O'Connor. In one of her short stories, "A Good Man Is Hard to Find," a psychopathic killer, recently escaped from prison, encounters a family on vacation—a grandmother, her son and his wife, and their two children. The son, who was driving, had taken a wrong turn, and the family becomes lost in a rural wooded area and there they run into this guy and his brothers—four of them—recently escaped from prison. The grandmother recognizes the psychopath, and so the killers, just to protect themselves, take the young family into the woods and shoots them one by one. The grandmother is the last and she begins to bargain for her life. "Don't you ever pray?" she says. "Don't you ever ask for God's help?" And the answer is "I used to but I don't anymore." And the grandmother persists: "We all need God's help. Why don't you start praying again?" And the killer answers, "Why should I? I'm doing OK by my own self." And a few moments later he takes her into the woods and kills her also.

Most of us, me included, have had the attitude of that psychopath: Why should I pray? I'm doing OK by my own self. But are we? Are we doing OK by ourselves?

In this, the bloodiest of centuries, war has killed over 200 million people. And of those 200 million, Americans have killed more than any other people in the world, including Stalin and Hitler. I read some statistics here recently that deal with our interventions in the affairs of other nations, and since 1946 there have been, on the average, one a year. So clearly, we aren't doing OK by ourselves.

We aren't doing OK by ourselves when we allow war to become our number one business, requiring more money, more scientific and technical genius, more research, more laboratory space, than any other national endeavor. In fact, a Brookings Institution study maintains that since 1940, the United States has spent nearly $19 trillion on past, present, and future wars—more than the rest of the world combined. And we are 5 to 6 percent of the world's people.

We aren't doing OK by ourselves when we permit politicians, generals and arms makers to threaten the world with the Bomb, and to infest the planet with radioactive garbage. Of all the nuclear tests, we Americans have done over half of them, and we've gotten away with nothing in testing the Bomb, because the stratosphere has been choked with radioactive debris, and eventually it comes down. You and I carry portions of it in our bodies right now. It is the reason for the cancer epidemic that is now raging in the world.

We aren't doing OK by ourselves when a vast conspiracy of silence insulates the Bomb and war-making from national attention and debate. A conspiracy embraced by politicians, pulpits, campuses, including this one, and the media. Are the American people ever warned of the danger that we're all in? I heard an expert on disarmament here recently and he claimed on good authority that of all the people in the world, we are most threatened by our weapons.

We aren't doing OK by ourselves when Americans corner 60 percent of the world's arms market and sell guns like toothbrushes to the Third and Fourth worlds, sometimes to one or both sides in each of the thirty-five wars now raging on the planet.

We aren't doing OK by ourselves when we crush Iraq with our sanctions and bombs, killing nearly 2 million through war and economic terrorism. Those are the totals of fatalities as we meet tonight.

We aren't doing OK by ourselves because of the big guns–little guns connection, the blood flowing in our homes and on our streets. I remember a Supreme Court justice's commenting on that. He said when the leadership of a nation goes berserk and to violence, then the people are going to start killing one another, and so it's come to pass.

The 115th Psalm reminds us that our idols or false gods are dead, with no sight, no hearing, no taste, no touch. They do, nevertheless, have the power to turn us into themselves. So, a lot of the billionaires around get turned into their money. That's all they think of. Money becomes obsessive to them. They can't spend it all, but they can't stop making it. So idols have the power to turn us into themselves. We become what we idolize. We become walking guns because guns, little or big, are national business and they are our national priority. Another way of saying it is that when we cease to love God and our neighbors, including our enemies, we destroy ourselves and one another.

So, let me refer briefly to nearly twenty years of disarmament. The Plowshares people believe in that with all their hearts, and they risk their lives since the government won't disarm. Beginning in 1980 with the first Plowshares witness in Pennsylvania, militants have enacted over sixty Plowshares actions in the United States mainly, but also in Australia, England, Scotland, Sweden, the Netherlands, and Germany. The majority of these witnesses have addressed first-strike nuclear weaponry at severe risk to the people involved since these hellish weapons are guarded by deadly force. In brief, one can be shot, or one can be injured or killed.

Each Plowshares person carries two symbols: a half-pint of blood and an ordinary carpenter's or mason's hammer. Blood because the weapon is a bloody business, obviously, and because Christ's covenant of disarmament must be renewed. The night before he died, Christ said, "This is the new covenant in my blood," so it has to be renewed. The people who know blood and these indescribable weapons are saying they won't shed blood, and this weapon must be dismantled. Hammers because they are a universal tool suggesting a universal responsibility to disarm. We try to say to folks, "Look, we're all in this together, we're all threatened by it, and you have a responsibility as well as us."

So too, these weapons have no right to exist. We made them, and we must unmake them. Everyone must. We must do something to unmake them. Now, going deeper into the question of disarmament, God's commandment "Thou shalt not kill" is pivotal, implying no permission to take the materiality of this world, apply to it the genius of mind and training, and make a legal instrument to kill another person. Nobody has the right to do that. No permission indeed, and no right whatsoever. Both matter and mind belong exclusively to God, and when we presume to fashion a gun or a tank or a bomb, we rob God and we rob our neighbor. We do more than that; we go to war against God and our pride and arrogance. That's a risky proposition.

God made us, we belong to God, we return to God. That's the human cycle. And as the nations struggle up the mountain, they entreat God to instruct them in Her ways so that they may walk in Her paths. What are God's ways and paths? Disarmament. Beating swords into plowshares and spears into pruning hooks and learning war no more. We have to abolish war if we are to survive on this planet. No question about it. We've come to that turning of the corner in our history where we fashion weapons of indiscriminate destruction, and we must disarm them if we're going to survive, because eventually they're going to be used. Now, are the nations, especially the United States, about to disarm? Of course not.

Therefore, where does it begin? With you and me. That's where it begins. When the Berlin Wall fell, it was because millions of East Germans, Czechs, Hungarians, and Romanians took to the streets with nonviolent resistance, and when that happened the nations conformed. They couldn't do anything else. And the nations became the people. Eventually the people of this world will choose God and one another as sisters and brothers.

It's a personal and public stance assisted by the Word of God and by nonviolent philosophy. And so, faith and trust in a nonviolent, loving God and hope for the human family against the despair over the nihilism of politicians, generals, and arms merchants. And so, nonviolence against the colossal violence of the empire. And so, a civil resistance against the stagnation and cowardliness of the establishment.

We Americans in our relationship with other folk are very often bullies, and the other side of being a bully is a coward. And so, community against the alienation and hyper-individualism of our society. And so, mercy and forgiveness against the rancor and hatred so often common among our people. And so, peacemaking built on justice and against war-making as our number one business.

My dear friends, sisters and brothers, there is a powerful case for building peace on a foundation of justice. I hope that some of you will give it serious thought.

DP

A Harvest of Death

On December 19, 1999, Phil, Fr. Steve Kelly, Susan Crane, and Elizabeth Walz entered the Warfield Air National Guard Base in Middle River, Maryland, and hammered and poured blood on two A-10 Warthog aircraft. The A-10s fired enormous amounts of depleted uranium in Iraq, poisoning the people and the environment. Phil wrote the following while in prison and facing up to five years for the action. Sentenced to thirty months' imprisonment, he was eventually released on December 14, 2001. This was Phil's last action and incarceration.

"If they do these things in the green wood, what will they do in the dry?" (Luke 23:21).

Recall that Jesus spoke these words to the "daughters of Jerusalem" as he carried the cross. Then, he went on to his execution.

It's December 31, 1999, as I write from my jail cell in Towson, Maryland. One looks to tomorrow, the new century and the new millennium with gratitude and hope. But what prepares us for this new time? Who will remake tomorrow's world, and with what? Have we learned from the crimes of the past, pledging not to repeat them?

The twentieth century has been dubbed "the bloodiest of centuries," with over 200 million dead from war. How many more are crippled physically, psychologically, spiritually by war? Four hundred million? How many more victimized and destroyed by the spirit of war, genocides, tortures, disappearances, Gulags, pogroms, economic sanctions? Incalculable! How many are alive today who have not been scarred in some way by war? The harvest of death and destruction from wars is appalling, stupefying.

If we executed the Lord of Life in the green wood, what would we do in the dry wood? The twentieth century's wars reveal a dramatic shift from the number of soldiers killed in war to a huge increase in the number of civilians killed in war, as well as the introduction of nuclear weapons, more efficient weaponry and the development of entire economies, such as that of the United States, based on war. Unless these trends are checked in reverse, the bloody twentieth century will become a template for the twenty-first.

What does the general silence over war from pulpits, Congress, the media, campuses, and business communities indicate except a sullen insistence on the right to kill one another?

As I have asked these questions during this past year, I watched as the United States used "depleted uranium" with its special bomber, the A-10 Warthog, not only in Iraq but on Yugoslavia.

As my friends brought back reports of fatalities from the scourge of economic sanctions on Iraq, they also spoke of witnessing hideously deformed "jellyfish babies," Iraqi children reminiscent of children born out of nuclear testing in the South Pacific. These cruelly deformed children are the children of fathers who were exposed to depleted uranium during the [first] Gulf War and recent bombings.

Just before the war ended in Yugoslavia, NATO admitted firing depleted uranium again, using the A-10 Warthog in the Balkans. "My God," I thought, "the nuclear alchemists have succeeded in doing something that they've tried to do for decades, compress the gap between nuclear and conventional weapons." It hit me with crushing force that our warriors were fighting with nuclear weapons again. Whatever faint illusion I had about American goodwill toward disarmament fled abruptly.

I found my anti-war friends, staunchly biblical and committed to nonviolence, slow to comprehend the ominous nature of depleted uranium. This mystified me. Was this another instance of the Bomb covering its tracks, creating a demonic aura around itself that befuddled and obscured its sensitive consciences? Whatever the case, it helped to explain the virtual absence of resistance to our nuclear warring in Iraq and Yugoslavia.

The New Testament sums up "the Law and the Prophets" with the simple commandment "Love your neighbor as yourself." If that's how we are to worship God, if that's how we build justice and peace in the world, then how do we regard depleted uranium except with horror?

A depleted uranium shell, fired from an A-10, strikes a tank or personnel carrier, quickly penetrates the armor, and burns the crew alive. Meanwhile, its impact aerosolizes radioactive heavy metal particles, scattering them up to twenty-five miles, to be breathed or ingested. These dust-like particles are not only carcinogenic, but they are also genetically destructive. Hence the chronically ill or deformed children of Desert Storm veterans.

Susan Crane, Liz Walz, Steve Kelly and I decided to engage in a Plowshares action aimed at depleted uranium. We chose December 19, the last Sunday of Advent, as an appropriate time to enact the conversion and atonement needed to welcome Jesus into this deranged world. We saw our act as public worship and reparation for our sins and those of our country.

At 4:00 A.M., we cut the chain locking an antiquated gate (the security around our nation's weaponry is often a joke) at the Warfield Air National Guard Base in Essex, Maryland, and discovered two rows of A-10 Warthogs parked on the tarmac, some 100 yards from the gate.

We picked two Warthogs and hammered on them to remind Americans that these perverted aircraft fired 95 percent of all depleted uranium munitions during the Iraqi and Yugoslavian wars and that they must be disarmed. The World Court maintains that the use of the A-10 and its depleted uranium is illegal. We maintain that they have no right to exist.

Liz Walz and I hammered first on the Gatling gun protruding like a shark snout from the nose of the A-10. Then, we struck the bomb and missile pylons beneath the wings, and then the undercarriage. Finally, we poured our blood onto the fuselage. Susan and Steve did similar disarmament on the other Warthog. In fact, Steve discovered a ladder, climbed on a wing, removed the vinyl cover from an engine and poured his blood directly on it.

Our disarmament of the A-10 and depleted uranium munitions was certainly symbolic, but no less real. We kept our actions symbolic by refusing to do the maximum damage possible, to show the universal need for and possibility of disarmament. We represented everyone in disarming these deadly planes. In turn, everyone has a responsibility to disarm nuclear weapons and all weapons of war.

Where does one look for hope as the world sinks deeper into social psychosis? To the people alone, particularly to people of faith. In the past, the people alone checked the mad ambitions of the pharaohs. Today, those who try to follow Jesus throughout their lives and through their actions can do the same.

If we wake up and live out the nonviolent resistance exemplified by Jesus, we can discard the biblical metaphors of the green and dry wood. Jesus Christ will live, now and forever. And so will we.

National Catholic Reporter, February 2000

The Trial of Depleted Uranium

Lest the reader be misled by this article's title, let it be said: There was no trial of depleted uranium. The four of us who took action last December to protest this horrific evil were indicted, charged, convicted, and imprisoned. As for depleted uranium itself: no indictment, no trial. Nor is there likely to be.

No trial, despite a staggering total of dead in Iraq, as high as 2 million since 1991, the harvest of U.S.-led international sanctions and depleted uranium.

No trial, despite the deaths of over 400 U.S. veterans of Desert Storm, victims of cancer or respiratory, liver, or kidney failure.

No trial, despite the chronic illnesses of 110,000 veterans, none of them told about the deadliness of depleted uranium.

No trial, despite the pitiable appearance of grossly deformed babies, born to Iraqi, British, and American soldiers exposed to depleted uranium.

No trial, despite the Pentagon's refusal to clean up an estimated 300 to 800 tons of depleted uranium in Kuwait and Iraq.

No trial, despite U.S. giveaways of depleted uranium to a score of "friendly" nations, a blank check to build their own nuclear weapons, fight their own nuclear wars, and further contaminate the planet with radioactivity.

No trial by the media, no trial in pulpits, no trial on campuses, no trial by politicians, no trial by public opinion. A little noise over depleted uranium from veterans' groups and the peace movement, but overall, no trial. And especially, no trial by widespread nonviolent civil resistance.

The volume of silence over these hellish weapons is surreal, numbing, stupefying. How to explain it?

Certainly, in their fifty-five-year love affair with the Bomb, Americans have not measured the cost of this idolatry: spiritual numbing, social denial, moral paralysis. A $19 trillion price tag since 1940 for past, present, and future wars reveals our addiction to war and bloodshed. "Where your treasure is, there will your heart be also."

The War Department has become a master, as far back as the [1983] invasion of Grenada, at suppressing media. "Control the media and win the war." We continue to bomb Iraq—monasteries, grain fields, shepherds and their flocks—but few of us know about it. The war-makers understand that suppression of key facts, along with dissemination of lies and disinformation, leaves the public uncertain and confused, especially about what to do.

What to do? There's the rub. Something that will witness to Christ's victory over death and God's sovereignty over life. How about enacting the "swords into plowshares" prophecy of Isaiah 2:4, which states that only the weaponless can climb God's mountain and achieve union with God? How about loving enemies as Christ did, even as we realize that we must protect our enemies in order to love them? How about reminding sick and dying Gulf War veterans, in fact all GIs, that the Pentagon judges them expendable? How about allowing our actions to speak our conviction of the absolute necessity of disarmament? How about a public expression of faith and sanity in a society that appears to have lost both?

Do we desire a taproot for peace? Then we must stop the killing—killing in war, killing on Death Row, killing the weak and the powerless. The commandment "Thou shall not kill!" is absolutely elementary and pivotal. Until we honor the image of God in the neighbor, until we eliminate our sins of omission (our failure to protect others), until we understand that we can't believe or love unless we stop the killing, then the pursuit of disarmament, justice, and peace is a melodrama of contradiction and futility.

Perhaps depleted uranium requires no trial. God's Law has already found it guilty. International law has already found it a war crime. When Americans find the faith to stop the killing, the prophecy of Isaiah and the Sermon on the Mount will become the ultimate political statement. Only then will we outlaw depleted uranium, dumping it, along with other nuclear weapons, into the dustbin of history.

The Other Side magazine

God Becomes Light to Us

"Through him was life and this life was the light of the human family" (John 1:4).

John begins his Gospel with a synopsis of what is to follow, and he boldly asserts that God is life. God created life and its stunning diversity and beauty. God continues Creation, a miracle we have come to understand as 100 billion galaxies across 300 billion light years of expanding space. God sustains Creation by concurring with all life and by sharing life with us. Grace is what we call God's sharing.

When we consider the book of Genesis, we find that God created us in His divine image and likeness. God is truth and love in Genesis—that is to say, God is thought and volition. Genesis proposes that we're in a fallen state, with an attraction to evil nearly as intense as our attraction to good, and gaps in our human makeup manifest themselves to put us at odds with light or truth. Our minds do not comprehend reality as it is.

Enter the life of God. How does the life of God become light to us? There is an example in Mark's Gospel. Scholars say that the middle section of Mark's Gospel is a "discipleship catechism," opening and closing with cures of the blind—the blind man of Bethsaida and the blind Bartimaeus. Mark shows that literal blindness can be healed and its metaphorical meaning shine through: If they can be healed of their blindness, we can be healed of ours. We can see the light. We can experience God's grace. We can oppose the expectations of Genesis. We can make twisted action straight and violent action nonviolent. We can take action instead of remaining inactive.

The healing of God remedies the spirit first, requiring faith and repentance. Then the body is healed: "It is the spirit that gives life; the flesh profits nothing" (John 6:63).

God grants forgiveness in every healing, and it works two ways—restoring one to God as a daughter or son and restoring one to humanity as a sister or brother. Furthermore, when God's grace heals our dead sight, we see by degree, usually, like the blind man of Bethsaida. Slowly, little by little, life takes on a new perspective as we begin to see reality as it is: God, neighbor, ourselves, Creation. Slowly, ever so slowly, we discard infancy and adolescence to assume the duties of adulthood. Duties broaden in concentric circles until they include the world—the bombed, starved, tortured, homeless refugees, victimized. In a word, we become "keepers" of the "least of these," attempting to do justice and good for them where we can, but, more important, engaging the evil that persecutes, crushes, and kills them. Confronting evil is the ultimate test of God's life, which should become light for us. Life is there, and light depends on us. We must want our blindness healed in order to be given light.

It is like arising from sleep, like waking up, and other frequent metaphors in Christian Scripture. The Word of God tells us that life is too precious to live any other way but awake. The truth or light keeps us awake. We need the light to shine on ourselves certainly—on our fears, illusions, and denials. But, just as urgently, we need light to shine on our government and its darkness of lies, secrecy, covert operations, and mass murders.

"Through him was life and this life was the light of the human family" (John 1:4).

DD

The Healing Act of Forgiveness

I am beginning to understand that Jesus's forgiveness of sins was the ultimate revolutionary act, because it took from the state the power of death, restoring it to God. In the same fashion, when we extend mercy and forgiveness to another, the violence of sin stops in us. We take it into ourselves, where grace, the life of God, destroys it. It stems from Calvary—Jesus killed sin, law, and death on the Cross to rise victor over them in the Resurrection. When we forgive, Jesus's risen life in us kills the offenses of others against us. Furthermore, our forgiveness allows us to join the nonviolent revolution of Jesus.

Forgiveness has political aspects. Jesus's healings were essentially acts of mercy and forgiveness that resulted in the restoration of physical and spiritual health. Disease and disability were not God's will for humanity; humanity chose disease and disability in Eden. Human beings then chose to ostracize the blind, diseased, and paralyzed. When Jesus restored a victim to social status by physical healing, He restored the order preferred by God. Through each healing act, He caused a political outcome. Further, human societies achieve cohesion and survivability by violence. They are born in violence. They reject God, wage war, or undertake violent revolution.

Sometimes, societal violence enacts the death penalty and centers on a victim upon whom the social order heaps its sins. Such scapegoating echoes the ancient Hebrew practice of symbolically loading a goat with the community's sins and driving the goat into the wilderness. The act rids the society of sin and thus saves the social fabric from being torn apart.

When we take upon ourselves the social burdens of the victim by becoming the victim, as Christ did, lending our voice, our hands, and our freedom in civil resistance, we break the scapegoating mechanism because we take violence upon ourselves, absorb it, stop it, terminate it. Nonviolence provides a voluntary scapegoat as victim.

Furthermore, it is the will of God for people to live in community as Jesus did. It is the will of God to live in communities that embody the eventual unity of the human family, communities whose truth of nonviolence withstands the age-old reliance on lies and bribes, communities whose resistance defends and rescues the whole body, communities that guarantee the needs of the human family by voluntary poverty.

Finally, it is the will of God that we become people of the Word—eager to know God, determined to live the divine will.

DD

Doing Good and Resisting Evil

"Whoever is ashamed of me and my words, of them the Human One will be ashamed when he comes in his glory and the glory of Abba God and the holy angels" (Luke 9:26).

What is the Word of God telling us here? That the world is a vast courtroom and that we are on trial? That trial before the powers for fidelity to Jesus is the pinnacle of one's life? Probably both. Jesus certainly speaks of fidelity, allegiance, and perseverance in doing good, confronting evil and even overcoming it. Jesus certainly speaks of a failing common to Christians, being ashamed of him and his teaching. Jesus certainly speaks of a reaction in the heavenly court, shame for shame. He will do no less, respecting our choices as he does.

As long as humans make laws, they will set up courts. Courts are condensations of society, they package these condensations for viewing, if we would look. They are social yardsticks or barometers; as the society goes, so go the courts. It should be no cause for wonderment that American courts sidestep positive law, divine, international and constitutional—to railroad nonviolent war resisters into prison. War is, after all, our number one business, and the courts will scrupulously reflect that.

But to return to the two courts. Apocalyptic books like Daniel, Ezekiel and the Book of Revelation refer frequently to the heavenly court, as do the apocalypse sections of the Gospel. In fact, the context in Luke for shame in the two courts is the First Prediction of the Passion. "If anyone wishes to come after me, he must deny self, take up the cross daily and follow me" (Luke 9: 23). The cross then is symbol and judgment in the earthly court, since our allegiance to Jesus and to the cross are inseparable.

The Christian life includes two aspects: doing good and resisting evil. Obviously, we must resist both personal and interpersonal evil. But above all, we must resist bureaucratic evil—the evil of massive institutions, like government, corporations, the military, churches and synagogues, media and educational establishments. The Word of God exposes them as demonically possessed, as betraying their vocations, as lying, oppressing, and murdering.

These massive institutions form the Domination Coalition. They form and project the culture; they are the economic, political, and ethical reasons why we are ashamed of Jesus Christ during His life. Their vocation is social justice, human equality, welfare, and betterment—a vocation they betray by seeking themselves (power, privilege, survival) through controlling us. Because seductively, they all have the same goal (themselves).

They have a concision of interest: bail one another out in emergency, scratch one another's back, and practice an ethic of the "Old Boys Club."

Only slowly, through thirty-five years of nonviolent resistance to the empire's wars and nearly eleven years of imprisonment, have I moved painfully from outrage to faith. That is to say, my motivation for resistance was initially fury over my country's sellout—it's nuclear diplomacy, it's manipulation of the truth, it's greed and cruelty. So I developed a dread of going belly-up, of being conscripted, of quitting, of becoming a tool of The System. Imperceptibly, I learned a better basis for perseverance, which is the stamina of the faithful. I learned a terrible dread of being ashamed of Jesus Christ and His Cross.

The Word of God has taught me perseverance, and so has my community at Jonah House with its dedication to nuclear disarmament and the abolition of war. Strangely enough, it is a dedication widely misunderstood and unpopular. Jonah House clings to the "swords into plowshares" prophecy of Isaiah and the "love of enemies" admonition in the Sermon on the Mount because both require a revolution of spirit necessary for reconciliation with God and neighbor. Put bluntly, until we stop killing one another—in war, from Death Row, and killing the unborn and the elderly—the world will plunge deeper into madness and destruction.

Everything, then, in the physical and moral, and, indeed, the cosmic universe depends on our refusal to kill. Until we make that momentous "No!" we risk killing on an unimaginable scale, one which extinguishes ourselves and all life and reduces the planet to cinder. One is not crying wolf to offer that reminder. In fact, the absence of that reminder from political circles, from the business community, from pulpits, classrooms and broadcasts, is precisely what is lacking.

For their part, the high and the mighty censor from public discourse anything controversial or wrenching, anything threatening the flow of profit, while the service bureaucracies, with a craven concentration on their own survival, betray truth, vocation and trust. Perseverance and justice and peace-making remain rare. In such a noxious climate, we even tire of doing good, performing it in an indifferent and desultory fashion. Worse still, we fail miserably in the prophetic side of our rebirth in Jesus—speaking truth to power, exposing the crimes of Caesar, saying "No!" to the Coalition's lying and mass murder. The sweet life, with its overflowing goodies, confuses and deters us—and in many cases paralyzes us.

Two main measures ought to inspire and strengthen our resolve for nonviolent resistance. The first is the Word of God that fiercely shouts at us with its imperatives of compassion and justice for the poor and for victims. What we do when "following" Jesus and accepting the Cross fashions us into co-creators, co-redeemers and co-advocates of The Word made flesh. The second is the quick death and slow death of nuclearism, as it cripples and kills people and the environment.

I'm sure the reader gets the point, not to be ashamed of Jesus Christ and the Cross. To believe is to love, and to love is to believe. If we pray steadfastly to God for faith, love and justice, we will know what to do against the looming darkness and death.

Radical Grace Newspaper (the newsletter published by Fr. Richard Rohr and The Center for Action and Contemplation), Volume 14, No. 3

Time for a National Strike

I've been reading *A Force More Powerful* (by Peter Ackerman and Jack DuVall), the new study of modern nonviolent resistance. I was particularly struck by the Russian Revolution of 1905 and its tactic of the general strike, supported by peasants, workers, and intellectuals against the autocracy of the czar. Gandhi used roughly the same tactic against the British. He had been in lengthy correspondence with Tolstoy, a veteran of the 1905 events.

A third example struck me. Poland was under the heel of the Soviets when Solidarity began insisting on the right to unionize, later expanding its program to challenge nonviolently the legitimacy of the regime itself.

In all these crises, the tactic was the same: a general strike, nonviolent non-cooperation. In effect, the people refused any longer to run the country for the benefit of the bosses. The people held marches and demonstrations, signed petitions and practiced civil disobedience. Underlying these measures was the refusal of work and money, sending the strong message "No More Oppression."

I wonder if these stories could serve as blueprints for a response to our situation in the United States. I wonder if we have reached the historical point of saying enough is enough and seeking together our nonviolent options. I wonder whether it is time to decide that living with the Bomb for half a century is enough, enduring a war every year is enough, the bloated Pentagon system is enough, an environment poisoned by nuclearism is enough, a government run by the rich and their corporate lobbyists is enough.

In the lunatic lunge for world domination, the bosses have threatened nuclear war repeatedly. Meantime they sow the planet with nuclear rubbish. All of us have relatives or friends victimized by cancer. All of us carry radioactive elements in our bodies.

There has been no halt to this race toward oblivion, no accounting, for fifty-five years now. And the dead, the maimed, and dying together make for a holocaust that dwarfs the crimes of the Nazis. Are presidents alone accountable, from Truman to Bush? Are the politicians and generals to be included, the scientific community, the CEOs of the war-making corporations, the American taxpayers? All of these? I raise the question not to condemn, but because (if we ourselves survive) there must one day be a reckoning, a summons to a truth commission or a war crimes tribunal.

A question: How are we to halt this harvest of death? Nuclear deaths are global, constantly accelerating in momentum, out of all rational control.

I do suggest that we take seriously the possibility of a nationwide strike through nonviolent non-cooperation.

Let's speculate briefly. What might a general strike accomplish?

It would shut down the overbearing Domination System, whose hallmarks are human misery, despair, and degradation of the cosmos.

The strike would underscore the great issues of our time (presently obscured and ignored by the bosses and their subverted media)— issues like war and nukes, high offices prostituted, disgraceful stewardship, international arms huckstering, globalization—issues that are off the radar of the present incumbents and their politics of frivolity, greed, and contempt.

The strike would challenge people of faith, injecting a transfusion of life into moribund congregations.

In forging a history, an exodus from spiritual enslavement, politically inert people would discover that they too count for something, and greatly so.

Where do we start? We start with the common agreement that nonviolence, whether religious or secular in understanding, is the essence of our effort. If the proposal has merit, who is invited for dialogue? And supposing a core group emerges, what of funds, office, staff? All of this will emerge step by step. Perhaps the time has come to dream, to discuss, to pray for and even to organize such a strike for peace.

Fall 2002, *The Servant Song Newspaper*,
Agape Community, Volume 12, No. 2

Notes from Prison on 9/11

The following are handwritten notes from Phil while still in prison during the fall of 2001.

Tuesday, September 11, 2001—A tragedy of immeasurable dimensions unfolds, one commercial airliner crashes into one tower of the World Trade Center, another plane hits the other tower, then reports arrive that another commercial jet has crashed into the Pentagon, now a fourth plane has crashed outside of Pittsburgh. One tower of the World Trade Center has collapsed, and I watch horrified as the other comes down. Thousands die, more than at Pearl Harbor.

A guard beckons. Earlier that morning, I had thought, this is big enough for the bosses, warriors and gumshoes to be rounding us up, recall the Japanese routed out in early 1942? But not this fast. Two guards take me to the lieutenant's office, where chains and shackles await me. They tell me SIS investigation. I ask what that means. One guard mumbles something about security. I should have insisted on getting my glasses. The turnkeys lock me up. I start to agitate for my glasses, receiving promises, promises. The Fed aptitude for lying is phenomenal.

Wednesday, September 12, 2001—Still agitating for my glasses. No dice. The turnkeys do bring me a King James New Testament (ugh!) and a couple of novels. Reading is slow and painful.

Thursday, September 13, 2001—Everything stands still in the Special Housing Unit. Guards, medics, chaplains listen, nod, promise, nothing happens. I do lots of praying for the resistance, and victimizers.

Friday, September 14, 2001—Same as above. I won't risk on papers the American karma in this tragedy.

Saturday, September 15, 2001—A light shines in the darkness. Just barely. A lieutenant comes by to announce, "No visitors, no phone calls!" I ask him why I'm here: "What are the charges?" He says, "Security!" "Security for what? Are they trying to hook me up with the World Trade Center disaster?" "Look," he said, "I don't know nothing." Now, I hope to buy stamps tomorrow and get a few letters out, the only way to alert Carol and Jerry and, perhaps, save them a fruitless trip. No glasses forthcoming. I can read, but only with some effort. Doing a lot of praying, especially for the victims and victimizers.

Monday, September 17, 2001—No change here. Nobody knows nothing. I'm reading and praying the Gospel with great satisfaction. And continuing to pray for my poor country, wondering too about the temper of the country, what is the national reaction? Has anyone claimed responsibility? Are the spin doctors fabricating some responsible group or country so as to retaliate? Divert attention from their own complicity?

Tuesday, September 18, 2001—No change. The last two days, I've been bleeding from the rectum. Strange oversight, I neglected to drink water. Doing that again rectified everything. "How about you, who do you say I am?" He asks me that, he asks every Christian that. I try to answer: You are Son of the Father who became human (us) so that we might become your sisters and brothers. And the means to become that are your Word, your Sacrament and your Cross.

Friday, September 21, 2001—Yesterday I signed a release of information as to reasons why I'm here. Liz had gotten to Barbara Mikulski, who contacted this prison. Barbara is a U.S. senator from Maryland and a good friend. But as of now, no change. The turnkeys did, however, bring my glasses. It would surprise me if I weren't kept in segregation for the duration (three months).

Friday, September 21, 2001—Continued: Things move very fast. I am to speak with the warden. He arrives with an entourage, spick and span, mostly interested in my "philosophy." I answer that it's simple, stop the killing, that I mourned and prayed for the 3,000-plus dead at the World Trade Center, and the 200 dead at the Pentagon. I didn't mention the Gospel view that those who take the sword will perish by it, that the karma of war killing asserted itself in those two horrific tragedies, that retaliation is insane, fueling more killing of those abroad and more Americans. It is Liz's intercession with Senator Barbara Mikulski and another, unnamed, U.S. senator that sparked my release.

Thursday, September 27, 2001—I neglected this, getting out letters to George Soros and Ben Cohen. Still to go, Joan B. Kroc and Ted Turner.

Their response will indicate whether to advance with that proposal. I called Liz last night and she insists on coming tomorrow. She is such a paragon of self-sacrifice, loyalty, love.

Friday, September 28, 2001—"God is not the God of the dead but of the living. You are greatly misled" (Mk. 12:27). Jesus discusses the resurrection of the dead with the Sadducees. And I recall the life of Mother Jones.

DP

Final Journal Entries 2002

The following are handwritten notes by Phil from the fall of 2002.

September 11, 2002 — The U.S. is everywhere with demonstrations calling for peace, or the hand-wringing commemorations of a year ago. But what is notably lacking in the sorrow and grief is reality — a grasp of what we inevitably brought on ourselves by our terrorism around the world. So paranoia reigns in every quarter — [Vice President Dick] Cheney goes into hiding; fighter bombers patrol cities, notably New York City and Washington — cops double, troops on alert, and politicians and newscasters talk, talk, talk. They don't talk of truth and justice, they don't talk of the madness of war, they don't talk about why economics and culture require violence and war. In several instances, the Scripture calls for refusal by people, to renounce their idolatries, exploit actions and injustices. They ridicule the prophets who demand this.

September 23, 2002 — I am pathetic and feeling pathetically lousy, weak, bad stomach, fuzzy in my head, and no progress with the new hit. Worse still, I have no idea what's wrong. I've quit smoking again, and eating only soup and vegetables, no noticeable difference. Our therapist friend, David Rust, comes in on Thursday, and we'll see what he says. With commitments in Los Angeles and Massachusetts next month, I had better see some improvement.

October 1, 2002 — Back from another test. Our friend, Dr. DuBois, is energetically trying to discuss the reason for my lassitude, weakness, upset stomach, and continually weak right leg. I'm nearly three months from surgery and can't walk without a walker. So far, since the tests are positive (no problems), the big discoveries are anemia and weight loss of at least twenty pounds. Today's test was a scan of the abdomen, liver and pelvic area. Test results on Thursday.

October 8, 2002 — Well, the manure has hit the fan. Our medical doctor friend, DuBois, reported on the biopsy of my liver this afternoon. She [confirmed] that the tumors on my liver were cancerous, but the source of the cancer is unknown. It has metastasized to the liver from elsewhere. She will consult with a cancer specialist from Johns Hopkins. He in turn will search out a reputable oncologist to pursue options. Needless to say, we're not jumping into chemotherapy or surgery. I haven't lost my distrust of the medical industry.

October 14, 2002 — Liz and I returned from Los Angeles last night after a Friday, Saturday, retreat with Catholic Workers from Los Angeles and Mexico. A stunning lunch, loving, biblical and well informed. Martha and Jesse, two Catholic Workers from the Los Angeles house, were to be married on Sunday morning, right after our leavetaking. This tiny knot of Catholic Workers stands as a shining exception to this hedonistic, myopic culture.

October 24, 2002 — In the interim, I go to Johns Hopkins to meet with two oncologists. They tell me that in my case, surgery on the liver is out, leaving chemotherapy. I wince at this, having no desire to cope with chemo and its byproducts. Now, it develops, the oncologists want more blood work done, to have some clarity regarding the type of chemotherapy. So, we're in the business of settling that now.

On Wednesday, Liz and I sit with Frida and Jerry to gauge their reaction to the cancer, which admittedly is serious, perhaps life-threatening. They both were admirable, though Frida took it hard with many tears. We'll meet this as a family, they vowed, and be available for any crisis. I told them my dearest wish — that they both get married. This they intend to do, probably within a year. More later.

November 3, 2002 — Just returned from a visit to Carol and Jerry in Syracuse, my sister-in-law and brother. Dan appeared on Saturday and we had lavish group palaver, mostly catching up, centered on my liver cancer. At every turn, they were there to feed me and guide me. I found the stairs very difficult. Marvelous to see Philip and Jay-Jay, Carol and Mark, Kathleen Rumpf, an extraordinary champion of prisoners and poor women. Friday's trip to Syracuse, we encountered snow flurries, yet on the return South, the roads were dry and clear.

November 2002 — [No entry for this, only the month and year written. No subsequent diary entries found. Phil passed on December 6, 2002, at Jonah House, surrounded by family and friends. He was seventy-nine years old.]

DP

Phil's Last Statement, Unfinished, November 2002

While gravely ill, Phil dictated the following statement the weekend before Thanksgiving, 2002, at his home at Jonah House. His beloved wife, Liz, wrote it down word for word. Phil would pass from cancer on December 6, 2002.

I die in my community, with my family, my beloved wife, Elizabeth, Susan Crane, and three great Dominican nuns—Ardeth Platte, Carol Gilbert, and Jackie Hudson, in jail in western Colorado, as well as other local friends and some from across the country. They have always been a lifeline to me. I die with the conviction, held since 1968 and Catonsville, that nuclear weapons are the scourge of the Earth; to mine for them, manufacture them, deploy them, use them, is a curse against God, the human family, and the Earth itself. We have already exploded such weapons in Japan in 1945 and the equivalent of them in Iraq in 1991, in Yugoslavia in 1999, and in Afghanistan in 2001. We left a legacy for other people of deadly radioactive isotopes—a prime counter-insurgency measure. For example, the people of Iraq, Yugoslavia, Afghanistan and Pakistan will be battling cancer, mostly from depleted uranium, for decades. In addition, our nuclear adventurism over fifty-seven years has saturated the planet with nuclear garbage from testing, from explosions in high altitudes, from 103 nuclear power plants, from nuclear weapons factories that can't be cleaned up—and so on. Because of the myopic leadership, of greed for possessions, a public chained to corporate media, there has been virtually no response to these realities . . . .

The following was written by Liz McAlister after Phil passed and picks up right where Phil left off in his statement above. Both statements were later published in the Jonah House newspaper, Year One.

At this point in dictation, Phil's lungs filled. He began to cough uncontrollably. He was tired. We had to stop, with promises to finish later. But later never came, another moment in an illness that depleted Phil so rapidly that it was all we could do to keep pace with it . . . and then he couldn't talk at all. And then—gradually, he left us.

What did Phil intend to say? What is the message of his life? What message was he leaving us in his dying? Is it different for each of us now, now that we are left to imagine how he would frame it?

During one of our prayers in Phil's room, Brendan Walsh remembered a banner Phil had asked Willa Bickham to make years ago for St. Peter Claver. It read: "The sting of death is all around us. O Christ, where is your victory?"

The sting of death is all around us. The death Phil was asking us to attend to is not his death (though the sting of that is on us and will not be denied). The sting Phil would have us know is the sting of institutionalized death and killing. He never wearied of articulating it. He never ceased being astonished by the length and breadth and depth of it. And he never accepted it. O Christ, where is your victory? It was back in the mid-1960s that Phil was asking that question of God and Her Christ. He kept asking it. And, over the years, he learned:

> that it is right and good to question our God, to plead for justice for all that inhabit the Earth.
> that it is urgent to feel this: Injustice done to any is injustice done to all.
> that we must never weary of exposing and resisting such injustice.
> that what victories we see are smaller than the mustard seeds Jesus praised, and they need such tender nurture.
> that it is vital to celebrate each victory—especially the victory of sisterhood and brotherhood embodied in loving, nonviolent community.

Over the months of Phil's illness, we have been blessed a hundred-fold by small and large victories over anti-human, anti-life, anti-love culture, by friendships—in and out of prison—and by the love that has permeated Phil's life. Living these years and months with Phil, freed us to revert to the original liturgical question: "O death, where is your sting?"

Published in *Year One,* 2003

Afterword

John Dear

Reading these writings by my friend Philip Berrigan written over the course of his extraordinary life takes me back to another time and place yet also pushes me forward into the future to carry on his holy mission of disarmament, justice, and peacemaking. Daniel and Philip Berrigan were legendary figures in the 1960s, '70s, and '80s, household names for their Catonsville Nine action against the Vietnam War and their imprisonment, and then later for their Plowshares disarmament actions, prison time, and countless other civil disobedience actions. For me, they were mentors, jailmates, and friends.

I met Phil in 1982, when I was twenty-two years old, during a Christmas retreat in a church basement in Washington, D.C., that ended with nonviolent civil disobedience at the Pentagon to mark the Feast of the Holy Innocents. Meeting Phil was like meeting Ezekiel, Jonah, or Jeremiah themselves. I'd never met anyone like him. He was like the great abolitionists of the nineteenth century, like William Lloyd Garrison, Frederick Douglass, or even John Brown. He spoke the truth fiercely, talked about nuclear disarmament passionately, and urged everyone he met to engage in nonviolent civil disobedience and resistance to the culture of war. He had the greatest sense of urgency of anyone I've ever met. During the twenty years I knew him, he was always in jail, in court, awaiting sentence, or planning his next action.

If you were with him, you had to get involved in the peace movement. You could not remain neutral in his presence. He told everyone he met to get involved, come to the next protest, speak out, and risk arrest in resistance to the culture of war. It was just a matter of months after meeting him that I was first arrested for a protest at the Pentagon.

Through his and Dan's "ministry of risk," I learned to make nonviolent resistance to the culture of violence, injustice, and war a way of life, a regular part of my faith in action. I can't remember all the talks, protests, and arrests with them in the 1980s because there were so many. As of this writing, I've been arrested some eighty-five times, but each of them was arrested hundreds of times for their public stand against war and injustice. It was indeed a way of life, but also, more important, it was a way of discipleship to the nonviolent, peacemaking, risen Jesus. It was an expression of faith, enacted in love, compassion, truth, and nonviolence that targeted the structures and insanity of death as a social method.

I corresponded with or saw Phil regularly until the night of his death. I heard him speak many times and had begun to speak out for justice and peace myself when I finally felt the call to join him and the others in a Plowshares disarmament action. Dan and I started our own Plowshares group in the late 1980s, but both of us were unable to do it. Then in 1993, I met with Phil, and we planned what became the "Pax Christi–Spirit of Life Plowshares action." With our dear friends Bruce Friedrich and Lynn Fredriksson, Phil and I walked onto the Seymour Johnson Air Force Base in Goldsboro, North Carolina, right through national war games, came upon an F-15e nuclear-capable fighter-bomber on alert to bomb the former Yugoslavia, and hammered on it several times to fulfill Isaiah's mandate "to beat swords into plowshares." Together we each faced twenty years in prison. Phil and I landed in a tiny jail cell for eight months in rural North Carolina, with young Bruce in the next cell over, and we never left our cells except once or twice for the entire time. It was the most intense, difficult, and blessed experience of my life. Phil was in the bottom bunk, I was in the top bunk, there was an open toilet and the space was about ten feet by ten feet. Bruce was allowed to come into our cell, courtesy of the warden whom we'd befriended, and together we embarked on a sort of modern day "monastic routine." Lights came on at 6:00 A.M., they gave us black water (which they called "coffee") and usually a slice of "wonder" bread and something that resembled beans, then we held a quick check-in to see how we were each feeling. Then we embarked on a two-hour Gospel study. As we read through Mark and John, I learned more about Jesus in that jail cell than I had in four years of graduate theology school. This was followed by the breaking of the bread and the passing of the cup (in this case, stale grape juice, which we received once a week in a little container). Then we tackled the mail. Phil and I each received fifty letters each day. After a quick lunch, we spent twenty minutes together in prayer, mainly petitioning the God of peace for the gifts of peace. Then, we began a one-hour period of timed, disciplined writing.

Over many months, we churned out dozens of articles and essays for journals around the world. Some of Phil's pieces are in this book. As I read them all these years later, I recalled watching him as he wrote them, and listening as he read them back to me. The statement on Dr. King to be read at the peace vigil on the King holiday and his article about our action "Isaiah in North Carolina" both shook me to the core as he read them aloud to me. They still stir me to action today.

So many moments stand out (and you can read them all in my book, *Peace Behind Bars: A Peacemaking Priest's Diary from Jail*, which is still in print). It was Christmas 1993, and we had nothing to do, so I asked Phil to tell us the story of his life. He talked for a week, with Bruce and me literally sitting at his feet, taking in all the details. I'm not sure he had ever told anyone his life story like that—who gets to experience that?—but we were overwhelmed and inspired. It was like sitting at the feet of St. Peter or St. Paul. Afterward, I suggested he put it all on paper, and a year after he was released, he published his autobiography, *Fighting the Lamb's War*.

We endured many arraignments, being led around in chains, meeting all kinds of visitors, being interviewed by the press, dealing with the guards, wardens, prosecutors, FBI agents, judges, and marshals. Eventually we were released, and as I recall, about a year later he was back in prison and I was visiting him. I shared one year of his lifelong resistance, and I'm still trying to process it. I cannot imagine what it felt like to actually live his life, to be Philip Berrigan.

Altogether Phil spent more than eleven years of his life in prison for taking public nonviolent action in Jesus's name against war and nuclear weapons. Resistance to the culture of war was his ordinary, day-to-day way of living. I attended many of his trials but was usually not allowed in to visit him because of my own criminal record. So we continued to write and I typed up many articles he wrote from prison. I remember great parties with him hosted by Dan at our community in New York City between prison stints.

In the spring of 2002, Phil was released from prison after several years for his last Plowshares action. I met him that May at a massive anti-war demonstration at the Washington Monument. He was frail, using a cane, suffering from hip pain but as feisty as ever. He then underwent hip surgery and never recovered from it. On the morning of October 5, I called him for his birthday, and he told me that he'd just walked in the door after getting the bad news from the doctor that cancer had spread all through him, and he had only a short time to live.

In early December, several of us journeyed to Jonah House in Baltimore to join Liz, Frida, Jerry, and Katie and Dan and Jerry [Phil's brother] in the vigil. He died on Friday night, December 6, 2002, with dozens of family and friends with him. It was one of the most powerful experiences of community and care for the dying that any of us, including Liz and Dan, had ever experienced. I presided at his funeral a few days later in a packed inner-city church. A small circle of family and friends buried him later that night at the nearby cemetery. We stood under massive, fiery torches, lowered him into the ground, poured holy water on the coffin, and offered prayers, blessings, and gratitude. One friend said it felt like a scene out of *Lord of the Rings*, like the burial of King Arthur or one of the Knights of the Round Table. We were burying one of the greatest prophets of peace in modern history, and we knew it. Really, we were celebrating his resurrection into the eternal life of peace and pledging to carry on his steadfast determination to do what we could to end war, nuclear weapons, and injustice, and welcome God's reign of justice and nonviolence here on Earth.

During the march to the church for Phil's funeral, I overheard Martin Sheen telling Amy Goodman of "Democracy Now" what he'd learned from Phil. "Phil took the Gospel personally," Martin said. I was stunned by that insight. Phil acted upon every word of Jesus as if it were directed to him personally. That is what every Christian is supposed to do!

Now, thanks to my friend Brad Wolf, with this collection of writings Phil comes alive once more, speaking to us from churches and the margins, from protest lines, Catonsville, Danbury Prison, Jonah House, and a long list of jails and prisons around the country. With this book, we recognize the gift of his great life, his lifelong resistance to the culture of war and death, and his profound faith in the God of peace and love. Thanks to Brad Wolf, we now have access to Phil's truth-telling legacy to inspire us, strengthen and encourage us, on our own peacemaking journeys.

Reading these pages takes me back to a memorable moment long ago in that dungeon-like North Carolina jail cell. It was late morning, and we were reading the pile of letters that had just been delivered. Thousands were writing to support us and encourage us, and many of them said the same thing: "I wish I had your courage."

Phil, after reading one such letter, put it down and said to me with a bit of frustration, "Can you believe these people? Saying they wish they had our courage?"

I was a young, clueless whipper-snapper—so of course, I had no idea what he was talking about. I was sitting in jail with Phil Berrigan, facing twenty years in prison, and I wished *I* had his courage! To hide my own ignorance, I said, "No, I can't believe they would say that! Say a little more."

With that he said, "They don't seem to realize—it's not about courage. It's about faith."

That was one of the greatest teaching moments in my life. Suddenly, I understood Phil and Dan in a deeper way. Everything they did flowed from their profound faith in the God of peace and love. They were not so much courageous activists as faith-filled disciples of the nonviolent Jesus and keepers and doers of the Word of God. I see that great faith shining between the lines throughout this collection, and I hope readers won't miss it. While millions claim to be fundamentalist Christians who study the Word of God, Phil let the Word of God form and change him.

Phil took the fundamental bottom-line teachings of the Gospels as matters of life or death, as they are, and so he put those commandments first and foremost in everything he did: "Love your enemies, hunger and thirst for justice, be as compassionate as God, put down the sword, offer no violent resistance to one who does evil, and seek first God's reign and God's justice." He lived according to these hard Gospel teachings, and he became a true disciple of the nonviolent Jesus and thus a prophet of peace to the world of war, which is the mark of authentic biblical faith and witness.

As we close this book, let me point out a few key themes and lessons that I will take with me, and let me invite you to ponder Phil's message, witness, and writings and what lessons you might take to heart as you go forward to be a better peacemaker, a doer of the Word, a faith-filled, faithful disciple of the nonviolent Jesus, come what may.

First, Phil spent every day of his life naming and condemning the culture of violence, injustice, and war. From the first day I met him, he was talking about a world of "perpetual war" and the "plague of violence" that is destroying us. Phil was trying to wake us up to the reality of the world—its addiction to death and destruction—which meant that's what he talked about morning, noon, and night, whether you wanted to hear about it or not. Wars are constantly being fought, but more, our nation, he repeated, is the greatest force of war and death not only in the world but in the history of the world. We build, maintain, and sell weapons to every nation and on all sides in every war, and we continue to prepare for nuclear war and upgrade our nuclear weapons as if doing so were a reasonable, even spiritual, necessity, and it has got to stop, he would insist.

He always pointed out, too, that preparations for the destruction of the planet are perfectly legal. Phil wanted us to name the idolatry, blasphemy, and heresy of war as the ultimate sin in which we all participate to varying degrees. He thought the God of peace was calling us to non-cooperate with the culture of war and the insanity of nationalism, corporate greed, racism, and violence in all its forms, which meant he had to talk about it incessantly. His whole life was like one long intervention in the culture of addiction to violence and war.

Second, notice how Phil does not speak the language of piety but refers consistently to Jesus as a nonviolent revolutionary who comes to overturn the tables of the culture and invite us into God's reign of peace and nonviolence. Because Jesus was not passive, but an active, nonviolent revolutionary, he was one too, and so were Dan, Dorothy Day, and Dr. King, and, Phil taught, that's what every Christian is called to do. "A person cannot be a Christian without being a revolutionary," he writes. Then later, again, "The Christian who follows Jesus must be a nonviolent resister and revolutionary."

Third, Phil insists that resistance must become the new normal, our ordinary way of life in this culture of war and death. From now on, we live, as Phil and Dan did, in permanent nonviolent resistance to war-making and every form of violence and injustice. Perhaps we do not have to spend eleven years of our lives in prison as Phil did, but we have to do something to contribute to the bottom-up, people-power grassroots movement of nonviolent resistance and positive social change. "Common sense tells me that the profession of life is an unalterable resistance to the high and mighty, who pose as patrons of humanity while they destroy humanity. Resistance is essential. Without it, one cannot realize humanity in oneself or in others, only illusion, euphoria, comfort, and escape."

Fourth, Phil teaches us the importance of speaking out publicly. That is the duty of the prophet: to proclaim the truth one hears from the God of peace, and so to publicly denounce war and systemic violence and publicly promote disarmament, nonviolence, and peace. The point here is not so much political work as *public* work—we take what we hear from the God of peace and share it with humanity. "The virtuous person is a public servant," he writes. That is a beautiful calling, and certainly the calling of everyone who dares to follow the nonviolent Jesus. Like Phil, we have to get over our fears, ego, complacency and self-centeredness and speak out for the coming of God's reign of peace.

We hear this teaching and witness him enacting it in his essay from jail, "Isaiah in North Carolina": "'Stop the killing!' is now the most urgent cry in history. 'Stop the killing!' Becoming human begins with that. There's been enough killing in the twentieth century, the bloodiest of all centuries. The killing is killing us. 'Stop the killing!' is the sane choice. Let's stop the killing, beat our swords into plowshares, and study war no more." With this clarion call, he sums up the message and truth he hears, names it as the most urgent cry in history, and urges us to take the only path to sanity and becoming human. One immediate response to Phil's life and witness is to take up the baton and carry forth his message to the world: "Stop the killing!"

Fifth, Phil spoke regularly about taking up the Cross. Who talks about that anymore? Rarely, even in church, do we hear sermons encouraging us to take up the Cross and follow the nonviolent Jesus. The Cross has been watered down into any personal, private difficulty. You get a flat tire, and you think you're carrying your Cross. "War, racism, and poverty can be traced to our desire to avoid the Cross," he writes with brilliant insight. Phil understood that the Cross was capital punishment for the capital crime of nonviolent resistance against systemic injustice and empire. When the Gospel of Jesus calls us to take up the Cross, it summons us to carry on Jesus's grassroots campaign of permanent nonviolent resistance to the culture of violence and war, even unto suffering and death—and to accept the political consequences.

For Phil, the work of peace and disarmament was costly, and a requirement of our faith. If we are not causing "good trouble," if the war-making government is not threatened by our efforts to make peace, then we are not following Jesus and taking up the Cross. Phil learned from Jesus that we have to speak out and take action against war, weapons, injustices, and preparations for nuclear war and know that there will be hard, inevitable consequences for our stand. They may not nail us to a tree as they did to the nonviolent Jesus, but they will harass us, persecute us, arrest us, condemn us, imprison us, and try to crush us, as the system tried to crush Phil. As we undergo arrest and imprisonment, we do so in a spirit of love and peace, trusting that we are serving Jesus in His ongoing effort to bring down the culture of war and welcome God's reign of peace on Earth.

That is why Brad Wolf named this book after Phil's unusual phrase "a ministry of risk." With this title, he sums up Phil's lifetime of nonviolent resistance. If we want to work for peace, if we dare try to follow the nonviolent Jesus, we have to take risks. These risks will upset our lives, affect our families and jobs and even our freedoms and reputations, but if we surrender ourselves to the God of peace and keep our eyes on the nonviolent Jesus, we will gladly undertake risks because they are in service to the God of peace. The focus of our peacework is not ourselves, not even the results of our actions; the focus is the God of peace, and so this work of peace is a *ministry*.

"There will be no peace unless Christians accept the Cross," Phil writes. "It summons us to a revolution of values, to a resurrected life, to peacemaking after war-making. It summons us to banish the war in our hearts and to resist the war-making of our government. It summons us to search for Him in silence, in action and in peace. . . . A Christian must take risks for the Kingdom of God, the New Jerusalem, the new sisterhood and brotherhood. Christians are obligated to resist collusion between church and state, and to fight nonviolently against tyranny, injustice, and oppression."

Finally, in the end, Phil Berrigan's life, writings, and witness from prison for his anti-war actions pose a radical question to every one of us. In this world of perpetual war, nuclear weapons, systemic injustice, racism, poverty, and environmental destruction, he asks: What are we going to do? Are we going to stand on the sidelines and do nothing? Are we going to enjoy the benefits of the culture of violence and war and live comfortably while billions suffer and die? Or dare we join Jesus's grassroots campaign of revolutionary nonviolence, resist the war machine, and speak out for the coming of God's reign of peace on Earth?

In his Introduction, Brad Wolf highlights Phil's 1958 talk to a youth group, and so we return to that question he posed then to young people. "What's it going to be with you?" Later on, from jail, he put it this way: "A simple choice beckons: Are we going to be people of perpetual war with darkened souls and bloody hands? Or are we going to be people who dare to be the sons and daughters of our nonviolent, just, and compassionate God, who face the world's lunacy disarmed?"

We know how Phil went on after 1958 to live out that question by joining the civil rights movement, going to prison in opposition to the Vietnam War, and spending the last decades of his life resisting nuclear weapons morning, noon, and night. He died surrounded by family and friends, content that he had done everything in his power to wake humanity up to the dangers of war, nuclear weapons, and global violence. He challenges us to give our lives to the same urgent cry that more and more of us might stand up, take his place, and build a global grassroots movement of nonviolence, disarmament, and justice the likes of which the world has never seen that will lead to a global transformation: the abolition of war, poverty, racism, nuclear weapons and environmental destruction, and the creation of a new culture of nonviolence, justice, and environmental sustainability.

His message from jail to supporters: "Let's build a real movement by building real people. Let's give one another hope and love. That's all people need—hope and love. Let's push back the darkness! That's what they said about Christ, you know, he pushed back the darkness—once and for all!"

Thank you, Phil! Thank you, Brad Wolf! May we all do our part to help humanity beat swords into plowshares, study war no more, push back the darkness, and walk in the light of the God of peace and the risen, nonviolent Jesus in God's reign of peace and love forevermore. Amen. Onward!

Pentecost, 2023

Acknowledgments

My deepest thanks:

To Philip Francis Berrigan, who by his extensive writings allowed me to enter the life and mind of an individual who so thoroughly combined Christian word and deed into one. May we all "have trouble with surrender" and choose to affirm life through constant resistance and peacemaking;

To Elizabeth McAlister, Frida Berrigan, Jerry Berrigan, and Kate Berrigan for supporting this project with encouragement, guidance, and grace;

To John Garza, Eric Newman, and the other editors at Fordham University Press who received this manuscript with excitement, gratitude, and a clear understanding of the importance of Phil's writings;

To the Rev. John Dear, who provided tremendous advice, editorial assistance, and continuing friendship, and without whom this book would not have made it to publication;

To Kathy Kelly and Bill Wylie-Kellermann for serving as peer reviewers and giving enormously of their time to provide comments on the manuscript;

To Fred Wilcox, who gave his time and editorial skills, shared his memories of Phil, and provided constant encouragement;

To Mary Anne Grady, Ellen Grady, John Grady, and Clare Grady for sharing their wonderful memories of Phil;

To Nick Mottern, John Stoner, H. A. Penner, Bob Smith, and so many others whom I am blessed to call colleagues, friends, and partners in peace;

To the staff at Cornell University Library, Division of Rare and Manuscript Collections, and the staff at DePaul University, Special Collections and Archives, for their assistance in providing the necessary research materials needed for completion of this book; and

To Lisa, Dylan, and Emma, my incredible wife and children, for traveling with me through life and listening to my ideas with thoughtfulness, insight, support, and love.

In editing this collection of writings, I shortened several of Phil's passages, changed outdated terms, and made grammatical adjustments where necessary for clarity. Many of the titles of the passages were taken from the body of the passage itself or were of my creation in an effort to reflect the contents of the particular writings. Throughout, I attempted to maintain Phil's unique voice, vernacular, and emphasis.

The efforts of many people are necessary for a book to come to fruition. Some are listed above, but I also have deep gratitude for those who have put in the long hours to write the countless other books that have nurtured me, deepened my faith, expanded my compassion, and given me hope. I now know some of the difficulties and anxieties an author endures when researching and compiling the writings of a person they believe to be of exceptional importance and influence.

Upon reading this collection, may we hear Phil ask us the same challenging question he asked his young listeners at Father Higgin's Youth Retreat in 1958: "What's it going to be with you? Are you going to recognize God's goodness on your behalf and submit to His desires for your salvation? Or are you going to go through life playing both ends against the middle, playing cozy, not committing yourself, sitting on the fence?"

Contributors

Frida Berrigan lives in New London, CT, with her husband and three children. She is an urban farmer and community activist, organizing around affordable home ownership with the Southeastern Connecticut Community Land Trust, and against the ever-stretching shadow of militarism with the Connecticut Committee on Nuclear Prohibition. She writes periodically for WagingNonviolence.org, TomDispatch.com and In These Times, and is the author of the 2015 book *It Runs In The Family: On Being Raised By Radicals And Growing Into Rebellious Motherhood.*

Philip Berrigan, an American peace activist and Catholic priest, spent 11 years in prison for advocating nonviolent resistance to war. Notably part of the Baltimore Four and Catonsville Nine, he protested wars from Vietnam to Iraq. The author of numerous books, he was a Nobel Peace Prize nominee.

John Dear is a long-time peace activist, priest, and author of 40 books on peace and nonviolence. He is the director of BeatitudesCenter.org and was a close friend of Philip Berrigan. He is the executor of the Daniel Berrigan Literary Trust and lives in California. For more information about John and his work, visit www.johndear.org.

Brad Wolf, former prosecutor and professor, co-founded Peace Action Network of Lancaster, PA. He coordinated the Merchants of Death War Crimes Tribunal and writes for numerous publications.

Bill Wylie-Kellermann is a retired Methodist pastor, nonviolent community activist, teacher, and author. His books include *Celebrant's Flame: Daniel Berrigan in Memory and Reflection* (2021); *A Keeper of the Word: Selected Writings of William Stringfellow* (1996), *Principalities in Particular: A Practical Theology of the Powers that Be* (2017), and *Seasons of Faith and Conscience* (1991). He was also a contributing editor of *Sojourners.*

Printed in the USA
CPSIA information can be obtained
at www.ICGtesting.com
JSHW071045300524
64063JS00008B/71